Lucy Cavendish

The LOST LANDS

A Magickal History of Lemuria, Atlantis & Avalon

BLUE ANGEL®
PUBLISHING

The Lost Lands

A Magickal History of Lemuria, Atlantis & Avalon

Second edition
Copyright © 2013 Lucy Cavendish
First edition published in 2009

Published by Blue Angel Publishing®
80 Glen Tower Drive, Glen Waverley,
Victoria, Australia 3150
Email: info@blueangelonline.com.au
Website: www.blueangelonline.com

Cover illustration by Selina Fenech®
Designed in Paris for Blue Angel Publishing

Blue Angel is a registered trademark of Blue Angel Gallery Pty. Ltd.

ISBN: 978-0-9805550-6-6

Contents

An Invitation   5

Introduction   7

Immrama One: Discovering Lemuria   35
Immrama Two: Voyage to Atlantis   101
Immrama Three: Return to Avalon   173

Afterword: Travelling well when on your Immrama   257

Bonus Chapter - 2013 Edition: The Priestesses of Atlantis   263

Recommended Reading, Listening and well, Anything List   271

About the Author   275

An Invitation

From: The Lost Lands

To: Your soul

For: A mystic adventure, a spiritual journey, a voyage to your home beyond space and time

When: Divine right timing

I invite you to take a journey with me. A sacred pilgrimage, if you will. Only we will need no passports. No tickets. No currencies.

But you *will* need to pack a few simple items. I'm sure you'll find you already have these, even if they have been stashed away, way up the back of an ancient wardrobe in a forgotten room, or in your grandmother's chest in the attic. Go and look. Before too long, you will find what you need...

*An open heart
*Curiosity
*Courage
*Creativity
*Imagination
*Faith

Have you found them? Ah. Good. You see, you will need all of these qualities in order to become your true self: which is, of course, a Mystic Explorer. Because where we are going will be, in some very real ways, beyond belief.

Although you may have visited these places before, your mind may have shut out the memories. But I know that with some courage and love, we can bring back the memories, and reawaken you to who you truly are, via acknowledging all that you have been. A galactic being...a Lemurian...an Atlantean...a wise one of Avalon...

Yes, you have danced the dance of power around a fire you lit with your mind...you have swum beneath the surface of the waves with your soul-kin, the dolphins... You have seen the injustice that led the sea to surge forth and lay claim to the land, and you have climbed the winding path to the top of the Tor to send your messages to the other sacred points both of, and beyond, this planet called Gaia.

You are an old soul, who has stayed alive, for thousands upon thousands upon thousands of earth years...and now it is time to learn of your story, so we can go forward in truth, and love.

Like you, I am an open-hearted wanderer – and I've found so many wonders in these Lost Lands. So much wisdom, which leads to an understanding of some of the greatest of Time's Mysteries.

So. You seem ready to me. Your light is shining brightly. You seem excited, and strong. Let's go forth and embark on this journey of discovery together, with eyes and hearts and minds wide open. For we are spirit explorers – and together, we can go to places where you have been told no person has ever been. Could ever have been.

Are you ready?

Come. Take up your compass and your staff. And let us explore these lands...these Lost Lands, together.

INTRODUCTION

The Lost Lands

The Lost Lands

It always seems to start with the same words... those same words by Plato, quoted by so many...and yet, I want to begin somewhere very different, and really, a whole lot more everyday. After all, that's where Atlantis, Lemuria and Avalon are...always with us, disguised so often in the cloak of familiarity – so often so that we dismiss their presence.

My exploration into the Lost Lands began at the pebbled edge of a backyard swimming pool in a very everyday sunny seaside town in Australia. I am very young, I have yet to reach puberty, I am somehow a woman and somehow a girl. I worry about my skin, my body; I love my friends and find life a curious adventure. At the same time, I have a deep yearning for magick, have already encountered spirits and ones who've passed beyond the veils, and feel sometimes like Alice on the other side of the Looking Glass.

So there I am. Young, sunburnt, and convinced I am a mermaid. And it's not a fantasy. It's something I feel utterly sure about. And I am about to embark on an experiment to discover whether I can get some of my abilities back…

I have never seen the Little Mermaid. I just know I should be able to breathe underwater, and that in place of legs I should have a tail. Curiously between my eyes is a peculiar breathing device, an opening that enables me to see into the distance clearly, and to breathe. I am determined to investigate this further.

So that is where my journey begins. I am standing at the roughened edge of the turquoise pool, clustered as it is with pebbles. I dive…and swim to the bottom…and am sitting at the bottom of the pool, staring upwards… The sun is hitting the azure surface of the water randomly, I can see a gentle breeze moving its surface, and I can see the prism of rainbows within every single reflection of light. I can stare at this for hours it seems. But I can only stay a minute or two, because as natural as it seems to be and to breathe underwater, this time, I am human.

It just never felt right to me that I could not stay underwater for much, much longer. So, I began to challenge myself, to dare myself to stay underwater for as long as I could. Not only must I stay underwater, I must swim underwater as I somehow knew I had in the past, for hours and hours, and slept underwater in my scallop shell bed, too. No breathing, not of the air, not in the way I do now. None allowed. So I began to train myself. I started by pushing off the side of the pool, and keeping my legs tightly together, I moved them in the sinuous movement of a mermaid. I completed one, nearly two laps underwater…and pushed up… I loved the feeling of oxygen, air, fragrant with eucalypt and willow and mulberry, entering my lungs in a rush.

I know though, that once there was a time when I could stay, and stay underwater… and the young woman I was then was so determined to capture that feeling again. So, I spent a lot of time with the water. In the bath. At the beach. In the pool. Puddles, streams, rain showers. I loved being under water. Surrounded by her, moving within her. I loved the weightlessness of my limbs, the way my hair floated up, reaching out, searching through the water, I loved the mystery and the wonder of this life beneath and within an element… Even within this pool, in my suburban backyard, I knew I was transported so far away when I was beneath the surface. To a place where I once lived, long, long ago.

In time, I began to be able to move with lightness and freedom underwater. Soon, I took to tying my legs together with strips of cloth I'd smuggled from my mother's fabric closet. I bound my legs together, and started again, diving in and moving up and down the pool, beneath the water. After a while I felt that I'd got the right rhythm and my legs stayed together easily...I moved from below the waist as though I had a tail, and I twisted and turned and flipped in the water. I loved it there. And so I swam and dived and tumbled, up and down my backyard underwater paradise, till soon, after each day's adventures, I could complete two laps underwater.

When I was not in the pool, under the water, wanting to swim in exactly the right mermaid way, I was at the beach. For hours on Saturday morning my family would go to swimming training, where we competed in races in a fifty metre saltwater pool, which waves crashed over in strong seas. My father, a seamless, athletic swimmer, a Bondi lifeguard of the 1950s, taught my brother and I to swim. I cannot remember NOT being able to swim.

I truly pushed my physical self in this quest to re-become the merbeing I know I once was. I knew I could breathe through a hole positioned around what I would now call my third eye area. It was open, and through it I breathed. At the beach I ran over rocks, again and again, with my bare feet, knowing I had to be able to do this – to dash to the end, whether my feet bled or not, to fling myself into the sea and...escape. I wanted my feet to be hard and tough enough to take me across the oysters and the cungi, to be able to dive into the water, to be able to go deeply into the chasms splintered with crystal prisms of light, decorated with castles of coral. I fished and I swam, and once my father and brother and I were sucked by an enormous green wave from the rocks on the point, dragged over rocks as we clung to each other before we found ourselves in the sea, tossing like corks in whitewater...We would have made it back to the shore, strong swimmers all, but the sea flung us back on the rocks from which we'd been taken. After we'd spluttered and staggered to the sand, we walked the miles home in our swimmers, as Dad had lost the keys to the car in the wild ocean. We arrived at our house, cut and bleeding and somehow triumphant, into my mother's protection, which involved a lot of glaring at my father.

Incidents like that did not put me off. I wanted to stay in the water. I never wanted to be out of her. I wanted to breathe underwater, and I knew how it felt, I told myself, to be able to take water in and somehow manufacture oxygen through that place on my brow, the same place I drew crescent moons in dark blue pencil during the day.

I haven't heard of Atlantis. Not yet. Not of Avalon, or Lemuria. However, I know that there are magical lands that once were there, amongst we humans, long, long ago. Where are they now, I wondered to my younger self.

I have my first crush on a Manga cartoon character, Marine Boy. In my dreams, I am Marina, and he is my love, and together we roam beneath the sea.

But when I read the Little Mermaid, I cry in disgust to hear of her swapping her tail for legs, not only legs, but ones that are stabbed through with pain when she walks on the earth.

At seventeen I learn to surf.

But then at twenty three, I move away, into the city, and get very lost, before I begin my journey back to myself in earnest.

But all the while, I, who walk on the earth, wish only to return to the sea.

Now we're about to do so.

The Journey Begins

In our art, folktales, myths and legends, in the stories that we tell each other over centuries and centuries, and in the ones we choose to keep believing, the same names occur time and again. Atlantis. Ys. Hyperborea. Lyonesse. Avalon. Thule. Shamballah. Lemuria. Mu. There is an overwhelming body of evidence for civilisations that have been "drowned". And it is not only of Atlantis and of Lemuria. The tales are of Brittany's Ys, to Cornwall's Lyonesse, to the land off the south of India called Kumari Kandam. They are spoken of in our tales, made into some of our most popular movies, television, books and music, but more than that, the knowledge of them is held deep within our cells, just as they are firmly embedded in our consciousness. Our Mother, the Earth, remembers her children, and has longed for our return.

But none of us knows all. It is my hope, in creating this book, this guide through these lands, to stimulate you to take your own journey.

Lemuria, Atlantis and Avalon were all worlds whose lifetimes spanned epochs. While many scholars and mystics have fixated on a particular location, for example, the debates that rage over whether Atlantis is located in Bimini, Santorini, Easter Island, Vanuatu or the Caribbean, I feel that the truth is that all of these locations and more were part of the vast Atlantean Empire. Scholars have searched for Atlantis, faithfully following Plato's beautiful, considered and very detailed description. But it remains a description of a small snapshot of a much larger civilization, and a mere fragment of its magnitude.

For all of us, our experience will be our own. In this book, I wish to guide you through the places I and others have experienced, but the journey cannot stop there. For from that point, it will be your mission to connect personally and to understand the rich diversity of experiences.

I also have something of a confession. When I began to write about these Lands, I experienced a great deal of fear. I have a real block about coming across as too "out there", and maybe even too "new age." It's one reason I have hesitated so long. The writer's deadline was drawing closer and closer, and then passed, and I still had so much to do – I worried that my publisher would lose patience. I had so much to read, and every book or article I read led me to still more books and other articles, which led me to even more scholars whose works led me to yet more research that seemed absolutely necessary to understand and digest before I dared to write a word. Each person I spoke to had a list of must-read books or must-watch DVDs to tell me about. The task seemed endless, and instead of Alice Through the Looking Glass, I felt very much like Alice down a rabbit hole that had led her into a subterranean labyrinth. Eventually, after years of research, much travel, speaking to people and absorbing all I could, I just began.

Because in the end, it is my hope to introduce you to these places, and then to let you go on your way. To find your own path through the Lost Lands.

Much will come up for you. Take it easy, and pace yourself. For me, some of the times in vision, dreams or meditation, and even in discussion and while reading, I was simultaneously re-living and working through some past life issues. Sometimes it felt too intense, the discoveries – of enslavement, of a rigid caste system, of evil things done in the name of good – were too much for me to bear. But I know also that facing what you fear and doing the work is often the best and quickest way to work through our karma. So, all the information, despite my misgivings and fears, is here for you!

None of these places are truly lost of course – they are dimensional...they are like, in scientific terms, the matter that cannot be seen with the eyes of the physical, (known in scientific terms as dark matter – dark not being "negative" but meaning invisible, because some matter does not radiate electromagnetic light...) in other words, at this stage in our evolution, some things are hidden to our physical eyes.

And if they weren't? What sort of world would it be? Is Atlantis as I see her, a world of pyramids of crystal towers, beflagged with ragged deep green sea-plants, and antennaes, like long acupuncture needles piercing the sky, reaching up from skyscrapers shining with light? Is the truth as I see it, with hybrid, shapeshifting beings who are enslaved in the last days, and a world matrix of power being telegraphed from pyramid to pyramid, from this earth to other worlds beyond this star system? I see stones, carved and shaped with thought, which resemble hieroglyphics, but ones that animate and twirl and move about, and carry code. And, if you can imagine musical notes "singing", these symbols have tones that can reawaken us… We can't always see these details of the Lost lands with our physical eyes…

They can be seen with the eyes of the spirit, however.

Dimensional thinking is an interesting way of looking at the world – and some beings are just way better at it than others. I am an earth girl in so many ways – so strongly connected to Avalon and the ocean, and such a common sense person. I have a Cancerian solar influence, a fiery Aries moon, and one big way of approaching the world – grounded, maybe via my Taurean ascendant. Makes sense that I was born into such a wonderful and grounded family...well, they *were*, before I got to them! But when people talk about 3-D reality, the truth is that time is already long gone. We have been living as multi-dimensional beings for some time. There are the regular dimensions of moving to the side...moving forward… moving up and down...three dimensions! But then there is time. So that's a fourth – one that in many ways, we have created – we are very clever, we humans, but not as clever as we think. Science feels we may be living in seven dimensions now. It makes sense of what happens in the world, in our solar systems, in the other star systems we can now begin to explore. These added dimensions we are already living with are space. And we also need to add the dimensions of past and future...all of which exist. This is why the notion of parallel worlds works so well – and why some evolved folks already have reclaimed the power of slipping between dimensions...something shamans have known how to do for millions of years. Others, of course, have already activated their "junk" DNA to such an extent that they are time travelling and science now is exploring the idea (the reality) of what is termed exotic subatomic matter...which is what, I feel, the dimensional lands largely consist of, and will become visible to us when we begin to use our "junk" or deactivated DNA...but I digress. I could go on. But everything will unfold as we reach each of our beautiful, magickal and completely enthralling destinations.

It is time.

It's time for us to go...together, to The Lost Lands.

Where Are You From?

Are you a Lemurian, wise and earth loving? Or perhaps you are more a brilliant, creative Atlantean? Or you could be a passionate, magickal Avalonian...?

The sacred lands of Lemuria, Atlantis and Avalon have distinctive energetic blueprints that can be stimulated at various, usually pivotal, times in our lives. This can take place spontaneously, or we can choose to activate them. We are, at different times of our lives, "from" one land more strongly than another, though we have all lived lifetimes in each place.

Of course, all of us have lived many lifetimes, with the exception of some souls who have been born recently, predominantly post-2000.

It is important to note that if we are strongly resonating with a particular dimensional blueprint, it will follow that there are strengths and, well, certain challenges we can experience. Once we have tested and discovered which you are working with, and you have learned more about each land, you will be given ways to work with each that will maximise the wonderful qualities that you can bring to Mother Earth, and avoid the imbalances and misjudgements we have all made in what we call the past.

As Edgar Cayce revealed in his teachings, many of us have returned at this critical time to help the planet through her next major shift – returned from either the past, or from ventures into the future, too. We can better help Mother Earth, others, our loved ones and ourselves when we understand who we are, where we are from, and what we have learned. This knowledge sometimes assists us in understanding many dilemmas and challenges we are confronted with in this lifetime.

Please answer true or false to the following questions in each section below. Section four is multiple choice. Answers will follow!

SECTION ONE

1. I am an emotionally deep person
2. I care deeply for others
3. Plants have feelings
4. I have experienced more than one life changing experience
5. I have been so depressed that I have contemplated suicide, or attempted it
6. I sometimes long for my pain to vanish
7. My body feels uncomfortable. I feel my natural state is evading me.

8. I often feel surrounded by spirit beings

9. I am shy and prefer to be alone with my own company or my close friends

10. I see things as karmic, "meant to be"

11. People describe me as naïve, innocent – even foolish!

12. I am not sure I am the same person I was when I was born

13. I am strongly connected to my ancestral bloodline

14. I communicate with my ancestors and deceased loved ones

15. I am highly telepathic

16. I feel protected by divine beings

17. I truly feel I can talk to animals

18. My soul-family and friends are very important to me

19. Body work is something I am drawn to

20. I have an addictive personality

21. I love to sing and dance and chant

SECTION TWO

1. I am more drawn to energy work than to body work

2. I love angels and ascended masters

3. I have great discernment

4. I respect groups of people and their energy

5. I do not like my physical appearance. It feels heavy, dense

6. I am drawn to technology: the internet, computers and programming fascinates me

7. I am drawn to crystals and grids

8. I can heal people just by being with them

9. I often wish I did not need to eat

10. People have described me as cold or harsh

11. I am financially secure

12. I have rejected the mainstream path, although it could have been very successful for me

13. I have a background in higher education

14. I am drawn to the sciences, particularly physics and chemistry

15. I like order and calm

16. I can channel spontaneously

17. I am suspicious of those who believe everything is simple

18. There are negative forces in the world, I have experienced them

19. I am said to be inhibited and slow to reveal myself

20. I am claircognisant. I just "know" many things, even before I am taught them
21. I have dreams and premonitions of natural disasters

SECTION THREE

1. I wanted to be a nun, monk or priest growing up
2. I am very sexual, but wish to be free
3. I find conventional relationships attractive, but stifling
4. I feel drawn to the land
5. I bless my food
6. I work with essences
7. I love each element; earth, air, fire and water
8. I know more than I should about herbs
9. I create close-knit groups of friends
10. I am drawn to ceremony, ritual and spellwork. I believe in magic.
11. I have an individual style
12. I do not trust conventional religions
13. I have experienced persecution, bullying
14. I have been described as passionate
15. I know I have something that is needed; but I do not know what it is exactly
16. The idea of enslavement is terrifying
17. I am creative, but I have a tendency to start projects and leave them incomplete
18. I feel safer with my own gender: people of the opposite sex are mysterious to me
19. I mistrust structure, it can seem dangerous
20. I long for a sisterhood or brotherhood, where we live in harmony with the earth
21. I wish I could find my soul family

SECTION FOUR: GOING DEEPER

1. If you could work with one of these sacred tools, which would you choose?
    a) A drum
    b) A wand
    c) A chalice

2. Choosing from the three below, which time of day most appeals to you?
    a) Dawn
    b) Sunset
    c) Midnight

3. I feel most drawn to wearing
   a) Natural fibres, organic cotton, hemp, skins with symbols
   b) White, pure clothing, nothing accentuating my gender
   c) Flowing gowns or robes with rich colours

4. The land I would most like to visit
   a) Hawaii
   b) Greece
   c) The British Isles

5. I feel our souls are most influenced by
   a) Our bodies
   b) Our thoughts
   c) Our emotions

6. If you could curl up on the couch and watch one of the below, which would you choose?
   a) A movie like Clan of the Cave Bear, 10,000 BC, or a fascinating documentary on ancient tribes and peoples
   b) A film like Star Wars, Star Trek, or a TV series like Battlestar Galactica
   c) Mini-series like the Mists of Avalon, Merlin, or a film like Harry Potter

7. The beings I am most drawn to are the
   a) Plants, birds, whales
   b) Crystals, dolphins, dugongs
   c) Horses, cattle, trees

8. The being I am most drawn to is the
   a) Mermaid, shapeshifter
   b) Angel, Ascended Master
   c) Unicorn, dragon, griffin

9. I connect most strongly to
   a) My tribe, the elders, my ancestors
   b) Council, High Priest or Priestess
   c) Priestess, Goddess, Druid

10. The environment I would most like to experience is
   a) Wild, untamed jungle, underground passages
   b) High mountains and sea with temples
   c) Green countryside rich with stone circles and sacred wells

RESULTS

For sections one, two and three, tally up your answers to discover if you are resonating with Lemurian, Atlantean or Avalonian energy. Section one investigated and tested the intensity of your Lemurian connection, section two your Atlantean, section three your Avalonian. Now you can see which of these you are most "at home" with. As you will find, the section under which you have received the most TRUE answers indicates that you are most likely experiencing that energetic influence most profoundly at this current time. Again, remember that section one refers to Lemuria, section two to Atlantis and section three to Avalon. To discover more about how this energy works with you, just keep reading. Each section of the book will give you exercises and magickal work to do. Wherever you have the MOST true answers is your energetic truth for the moment.

Now for section four. Please add up the amount of A's, B's or C's you chose. The more A's, the more predominant is a Lemurian influence. The more B's, the more Atlantis is with you. And if you chose mostly C's, you are resonating most greatly with the Isle of Avalon at present. This cross-checks your current dominant influence, as section four tells us more, and so serves as a final checkpoint if you have experienced very "even"results.

It is important to acknowledge that present day Lemurians, Atlanteans and Avalonians are all individuals and have many influences. There are many sub-groups within each land. And, as individuals, we have different families, grow up in different geophysical places and can come from diverse and rich cultural backgrounds. All of these play their part.

However, there are predominant themes running through each group that hold true and consistently show up. As such, we are very much going through a cycle when predominant energy shows up. It would be more helpful for a person experiencing predominantly Atlantean energy, for example, to fully activate their discernment, withdraw from the energy of judgement, and engage in understanding all beings. They could benefit from testing the information they receive from powerful individuals against their own inner integrity-detector. Each energy has these polarised opportunities.

I do not ask that you radically change your modality, but to understand the various areas that may need dissolving, and others that could do with strengthening.

We have all lived in these three places, and none are "better" or "worse". There are distinct vibrational patterns, though – and discovering these will assist us on our own journey, as well as assisting Mother Earth.

When we understand our Lost Land imprint that is currently activated, we then know what we need to do. Know who you are, and you will know what to do...

If you answer this series of questions from time to time, you will notice shifts and changes. This is to be expected, as we are in the process of personal and planetary evolution.

LEMURIANS

General profile

Current time Lemurians tend to be very gentle, innocent and sometimes naïve. They do not understand structure and hierarchies, and can seem extremely subversive to people who have more time for the way in which workplaces and social structures are organized. They certainly are very egalitarian, and kind. Family matters greatly to them; however, they often feel they were born into the wrong family. Thus Lemurians can search for their clan, or tribe, and feel most at home when they lose a sense of individuality and create a sense of community. They know that what happens to one of us, happens to all of us, and respect and venerate their elders, though they may experience some challenges in finding these elders! They also love children – all children, and animals. They are very likely to be vegetarians or vegans, and even find it difficult to eat plants at times, due to wishing no-one harm. They tend to be strong and sinewy people, and if unfit they feel most uncomfortable. Rarely, but at times, I have come across Lemurians who have padded themselves with enormous amounts of protection in the form of weight. This is an extreme method of self-protection and denial of the current time.

They often have long hair or an unconventional appearance, dreadlocks and can also have a free approach to relationships. They often sport beautiful tattoos! They are very hard working, often enjoy physical work, and love to do outdoor work for the clan, with a purpose, in something that they revel in. They excel as musicians and shamans, gardeners, drummers and percussionists, have an innate sense of rhythm and dance and, while they understand they have connections beyond this Earth, they feel blessed to be here, and are very much protectors of Mother Earth. They often become passionate animal advocates, or environmental protectors. They tend to have more than one life partner, and feel confused as they no longer have a clan to support the extended family. They will recreate this whenever they can.

Strengths
Innocence and wisdom, fluidity in relationships, acceptance of their brothers and sisters and various permutations of sexuality.

Challenges
If unawakened, they can be drawn to drug and alcohol or substance addiction as a way of escaping from what seems to be a harsh world. An inability to recognise danger to themselves; collective danger is understood and acted upon, but they can put themselves in rather dangerous situations as they tend to only see the good in all.

Where they can excel
In healing modalities working with sound; the arts, agriculture, organic farming, alternative energy housing, bringing a group together, creating family, teaching, spreading tolerance for alternatives, shamanic work, housing communities, collective needs. Great at hosting parties, raves and gatherings! Wonderful at assimilating digital and traditional culture. See no conflict there, and use technology wisely and very creatively. In creating their own companies, like record labels for example, that do not allow others to exploit them, but offer a fair share for all. (Successful Australian musician John Butler is a perfect example of this kind of brilliant Lemurian.) They understand that the group of people they will be working and creating with will change over the lifetime, and can intuitively pick the right groups to come together with to fulfill their vision. They do not appear to be "successful", no suits and ties, and they seem like rebels, but they are visionary and creative free thinkers who change the world by living out their truth and their dreams. They are loyal and true: but they are best served by being most loyal and true to themselves and their dream, rather than being consumed by the group. They are often exceptional body workers, with healing touch. They excel at massage therapies and at kinesiology.

It is important for Lemurians not to hide away from the mainstream – a desire that sees them often "disappear". But from time to time Lemurians will almost be forced into successful positions and structures in order to change the mainstream. This may be difficult, however, you will be changing your very large extended family for the better by doing so.

ATLANTEANS

General profile

Are often very charismatic with hypnotic eyes: they almost have the ability to mesmerise with their attractive personalities and find themselves with numerous friends, many of whom they may not feel particularly connected to. They can be early adopters of technologies and they can suggest innovative improvements to many things. While they are very forward thinking and creative in some respects, they can often have rigid parameters, and can be harsh judges of other people. They are aware that they are different and in fact somewhat brighter than others: they do tend to conform and can be easily persuaded to detach.

Some people are wary of Atlanteans as they can be critical-minded, a little like Virgos in the zodiac (in fact, many Atlanteans are Virgos and other earth signs this time around...). They often seem to be experts, and have an astounding affinity for sacred geometry, codes and languages. They can develop stunning ideas and theories and present them convincingly and intelligently. They often take refuge in mainstream professions or become brilliant and eccentric scientists. They can also become successful media personalities, actors and performers – they have a way of almost scientifically understanding what is required and can adapt themselves to suit the occasion. Some of the world's most ardent sceptics are Atlanteans, but so too are some of the most brilliant philosophers, scientists, new-thought advocates and spiritual beings. They are exceptional energy workers, and can understand complex concepts and sciences with apparent ease.

Atlanteans are often very good looking, tall, well-dressed and have an innate love of luxury. They struggle when their circumstances or life path leads them to walk the path of lack for a time, and they have a sense of injustice. They truly do need people to "assist" them in many tasks. They are brilliant, and very sensitive – they often forget to create relaxing down time for themselves, and therefore they are especially influenced by others' thoughts and emotions. If they work in an unpleasant environment, they can feel quite overwhelmed. They may suffer when in large crowds whose thought patterns may be negative. They are gifted, telepathic, and are able to communicate brilliantly, and swiftly. They are, however, considered to be quite high maintenance, and are very concerned for their immediate family. They do tend to suffer headaches, can be physically less robust due to the ingestion of thought forms, have a fear of water and natural disasters, and feel a sense of urgency in terms of completing their work.

They are very sensitive to what people may describe as dark energy, and they actively avoid people, beings and places where the energy does not feel right. Many can be conceptual artists, and a high proportion are reiki masters and healers. They understand how energy works absolutely intuitively, and create methods of working with this, which they teach selectively. They closely guard certain parts of the knowledge and wisdom. They are manifesting geniuses, are working towards the "future" and feel they suffer psychic attack. They have a high level of possibility to have entities attach.

They often develop physical issues due to physical disassociation, are sensitive to psychic attack, can experience asthma and other respiratory difficulties. They just know they are different, and can feel very detached from most people. They are always doing courses – that's if they are not teaching them. They are very attractive and beautiful, and develop their own methods which they are meticulous about maintaining. They make excellent scientists, healers, reiki masters, colour therapists, light beings, angel therapists, astronomers, astronauts, mathematicians, physicists, doctors and surgeons, and have enormous impact when they meditate. A group of Atlanteans praying creates powerful results on all planes of existence.

Strengths
Their incredible charisma can be worked to influence people in positive ways; they are extremely attractive, they are brilliant and technically no-one comes near them. They can understand and teach about crystals and other forms of life. They also make excellent mediums and channels and intergalactic communicators. Nothing is too "out there" to consider!

Challenges
Their desire to go to their real home can be overwhelming at times. Feeling held up by the mundane can frustrate them, and when frustrated these sensitive beings experience physical symptoms such as migraines. They tend to work to such a high level of brilliance that they can seem a breed apart: people may often wonder if they are human! Physicality can be very challenging, and using their extreme power wisely is also a challenge. They are often motivated by the highest concerns, and yet their detachment can make them seem cold and cruel at times. They are neither, but they do need to interact with people who just love to laugh and eat! They can develop eating disorders as a way of control, and quite often they develop weight issues to ground them in this reality for now.

It is important for Atlanteans to work with their heart energy, as their crown and third eyes are so very powerful...working with the other chakras as a system and loving their body will assist them in fulfilling their important life purposes.

AVALONIANS

General profile

Avalonians are often Celtic in appearance (golden or red-haired, light eyes, pale skin. They can be rather tall and big-boned.) Or they can be small and dark, with dark skin and blue eyes, quite little and delicate and deceptively frail-looking. Nothing could be farther from the truth! They are strong and very fiery of temperament, these small ones. The taller ones often have red hair, or hair that is dyed or streaked with red highlights. They often feel drawn to that colour without knowing why. They are frequently what I would call mystics and misfits: they have a wandering tendency, and hate the idea of being trapped or enslaved or giving their personal power away. They feel like "orphans" or castaways in their lives, and are most strongly drawn to Lemurians, falling deeply in love with them. They often work as solitaries, having mistrust of group activities and group minds. They are extremely sensual, but again, they are often quite unconventional and wonder if they will ever find their soulmate. They adore history, stories of King Arthur and of his court, and have a kind of ancient feeling to them, no matter their age or their workplace. They are intelligent but often they are impatient and can be quite fiery – they have a warrior imprint on their temperament that leads them to be rebellious, even when it seems there is nothing to rebel against.

They are deeply spiritual people and often contemplate joining the priesthood, or becoming a nun, or joining a monastery. There are times when they wish to withdraw and only live on the fringes of what others call the real world. They tend to be romantic, and love is what often draws them into their friendships. They feel they would die for love.

They often have a skill at healing with herbs, and connect strongly with the divine feminine. They mistrust technology, unlike some of the Atlanteans and Lemurians, and thus need to bond with their Lost Land brothers and sisters so they can come to grips with changes in the world and not isolate themselves. They are often the very last to update websites or send emails, or adopt technologies. They do not care for status, and actively dislike people who consider it important to have the latest something-or-other. They long to find a group of people who is their family, as their own family sometimes feels quite alien to them, and there can be a high proportion of broken homes, adoptions and estrangements with this soul group.

They adore meaningful sexual relationships, but while they are deeply romantic, they mistrust the idea of love that is dominant in our culture at this time. They can, however, develop infatuations that feel very much like "true love" and will go to extreme lengths for this "love." Once they awaken, they feel enspelled, like they have awoken from an enchantment.

They are deeply attuned to the moon and her cycles, and often grow their own food or make their own clothes. They are not willing to compromise their freedom by relying on the grocery store!

They live in towns, but feel very trapped in them. When they live in the country, they search for their kin.

They are often eccentric, sculptors, painters, artists, and can be reclusive writers. They have the gift of prophecy and a talent for protecting the earth. They are less interested in the heavens than they are in the here and now, and they are passionate and loyal to their friends.

They tend to handmake presents and gifts, or select them carefully. Avalonians also care deeply about water, and are able to work with that element to a highly proficient degree. They are adept as disguising themselves amongst crowds, even shapeshifting, and are able to go unnoticed, and then dramatically draw all attention to them when the moment is right. They have special gifts and talents in spell and ritual and energy work involving all the elements. They sometimes take on the characteristics of the Goddess they are most affiliated with, and are often drawn to the Goddess path, Witchcraft, Wicca, neopaganism. They make brilliant fantasy writers and artists, and can bring through on this plane the worlds beyond the mists.

Strengths

Very intelligent and practical-minded – except when it comes to love. Believe in the power of good food and a hug over sending someone energy. They are very compassionate and can calm people with their presence and physical touch. They have a wonderful sense of humour and are adept at charming others. Can be delightful company, and brilliant cooks. Tender hearted and deeply sensual, they are romantic partners who nevertheless are searching for freedom. They are independent, strong minded, and have excellent discernment. They have clear, bright energy. Some have self-worth issues when it comes to money, but most are adept at creating income, though they value money less than they value their independence, which is what money is to them – the opportunity for freedom. They can galvanise public help, and are charitable.

Challenges

Are often stern when parenting or have authority issues. Need to find the causes that they can be effective in, rather than engaging in pointless rebellion (as an Avalonian for much of this lifetime, I understand this trait very well!), refusing to adopt new technologies that may support and assist their cause due to tendency to mistrust technology. Suspicious of others, and quick to temper. Commitment issues. Must be very cautious not to estrange others with their fiery temper. Must understand their energetic impact when "venting."

Water soothes them. Often have circulation issues, feel cold and heat intensely, can be moody and dejected unnecessarily. Often quick to take on others' causes as their own, and thus disable their own purpose for a time. Give in to distraction and procrastination, and often run off after the classic red herring!

The Timeline of the Pre-Ancient World

Do not forget me… I will come back for you…

These are the words I would hear over and over again upon awakening. My dreams were so vivid. Sometimes they seemed on this planet, but in ancient times full of futuristic technology. At other times I was surrounded by a circle, dancing, of friends and wild ones, all of us in harmony. And at others, I was standing on a hill, focusing and levitating standing stones into place. In others, I was underwater, yet breathing… each voyage was an Imramma, a wonder journey, a voyage across the seas of time into an ancient past that resonates so strongly within the present.

While you are making your own Immramas, you may encounter places and peoples that are difficult to pinpoint. Here is a timeline that reconstructs the happenings of the pre-ancient world, so you can map your experiences, your former lives, and trace the memories flowing through to you in the present day.

1,000,000 BCE HYPERBOREA

This great colony was said to exist in the far northern climes. Unknown whether it succumbed to a forced "abort experiment" order, or whether the natural earth changes brought about her non-viability.

800,000 BCE AVALONIA

Massive continent known as Avalonia in the northern hemisphere. It formed what is now Belgium, France, north Germany, much of Poland, England, Wales, all bar the far north of Ireland, the Avalon peninsula in Canada, Nova Scotia, New Brunswick and New England in the US – including, of course, Salem.

This means that there are pockets of Avalonian culture far beyond the traditional England/Ireland/parts of Scotland historical structure. There was an ancient land, in which the traditions of Avalon as we know and understand her today seeded and took root, and grew into the mighty oak forests. And while one oak stands, so does Avalon.

First trees are born. Part tree, part, well, us really. Fae beings. Nurtured hybrids. There is less differentiation between the land, the sea and the sky in the Avalonian world, with marshy, salty bogs, and thick, viscous mists.

900,000 BCE LEMURIA FOUNDED

True mother civilisation. All of us are from Lemuria.

* Fully conscious human earth angel society.

* Ethereal and physical in appearance, extremely large and luminous light bodies.
* Double firmament – inner and outer earth. Many tunnels beneath cities.
* Crystal clan system. These crystals either seeded into shamans' bodies (shamans being both men and women) or into secret locations on the earth.
* Inner earth still exists … crystal cities.
* Dancing, chanting music each day.

500,000 BCE ATLANTIS RISES

Peaceful, fascinating and respectful interactions between the three great cultures. Atlurian culture is what is often called the Golden Age of Atlantis.

100,000 BCE LEMURIAN MIGRATIONS

The survivors and shapeshifters head to Atlantis, some say led by Prince Idon.

Atlantis takes in these survivors from the gradual sinking of Lemuria. There is initial optimism, with hopeful interactions between the two groups, who are determined to learn from each other.

60,000 BCE ATLANTIS AND LEMURIA

Tensions grow as Atlanteans seek to enslave shapeshifting Lemurians, who are disparaged and believed to be primitive, childlike and savage, compared to the technocrats of latter Atlantis.

Atlantean attempt to create shapeshifters themselves in genetic experiments that result in individual tragedies and a group of slaves.

Further experiments undertaken to shut down the shapeshifting capacity of Lemurians and Atlanteans in mass DNA inoculation.

Lemurians begin to secrete themselves into the land, beneath the land, beyond the land, taking into that land with them sacred stones and symbols. Prepare to leave in the form of whales, dolphins, birds and other beings. Some head to the surviving colonies in Hawaii.

25,000 BCE LEMURIA GOES UNDER

* Destruction of Lemuria.
* Experimentation on Lemurians and the hybrid beings continues. Atlantean hierarchy enslaves mer-beings and many other hybrid beings, who evade their captors by shapeshifting into dolphins, swimming vast distances, and settling in far off lands and places across the planet.
* Survivors escape to Avalon, Ireland, Ys, Iona, Lakota people, Hopi people, Mayan people, Aotearoa (New Zealand), Australia, Easter Island, the Caribbean, Central

America, the Four Corners region of the current day United States.
* Vast exploration of other lands, including Africa, Dogon people come from Sirius. Or the Dogon is colony set up.
* Some go north...huge migration patterns, particularly to South America, China, Tibet and central Australia. Departure from New Zealand and inhabitation of Hawaii, various parts of the Philippines, Malaysia, Borneo, Ys, Lyonesse.
* Atlantis fragmented, survivors to islands of Greece, Persia, Egypt.
* Colonies from earlier time in Australia, Mongolia, Tibet and Hawaii continue.

20,000 BCE ATLANTIS EXPERIMENTS INTENSIFY
* Experiments to fully switch off DNA and enshrine the enslaved Animals, humans and Hybrids begin. Slave culture commences, continuing in many forms to this day. Kept in enclaves for their safety: then put to work. Then herded away. And killed. Some vanish or shapeshift into ordinary "animals" to avoid this persecution.
* Mishandling of crystal and pyramid energies, appropriation of symbols. Lemurians shapeshift, or exodus, or assimilate into Atlantean culture, working undercover.
* Dragonfae depart dimensionally, ripped apart by genetic experimentation, become the unseen in much of the planet. Still exist in dimensions beyond, and in Avalon and in areas such as Bali, China, Japan. Propaganda flourishes about these in-between beings.

18,000 BCE LEMURIAN CULTURES RISE IN NEW LOCATIONS
*The rise of survivors' cultures.
*Gateway of the Sun constructed at Tiwanaku, Bolivia. Attributed to the Inca.

15,000 BCE SPHINX CONSTRUCTED
Sphinx created in 15,000 to mark the oppression of the hybrid animals by the beings that had left Atlantis and set up residence in Egypt, including Thoth, who watched from afar and knew he must keep the secrets alive. Beneath the Sphinx, which is as yet still very far from being "correctly" dated, are records held in a medium we have yet to fully understand.

According to the "sleeping prophet" Edgar Cayce, there is a secret chamber between the paws of the Sphinx, and a series of tunnels that run deep beneath, containing secret documents and hidden records.

15,000 BCE THE FALL OF ATLANTIS
Egyptian colonies in Lemuria established. Atlanteans go there to establish trade links.
Survivors head to established colonies in Egypt, some make it to Avalon, others to

south America, present day Americas, Australia and islands of the Pacific, and Tibet.

11,000 BCE DESTRUCTION OF ATLANTIS
Massive tsunami, creates a widespread migration pattern.
 Rise of Sumeria, Arkadia, Ur, Egypt, Greece.

7000BCE – 8000BCE BIBLICAL FLOOD
Confusion induced through survival of biblical great flood. People begin to forget where they are from, and who they are.

3113 BCE MAYAN CALENDAR BEGINS
Mayan Calendar begins.
 The Mayans locate the galactic centre, which they call the Galactic Butterfly. They believe that from this place, all life emanates. It is a point of creation and destruction on a vast cosmic scale. From this galactic centre are born planets, worlds, physics, time, space and the shape they take. Into this point, they are also taken, to be destroyed and recreated.

5,000 BCE RISE OF THE ANCESTORS
Ancient civilisations continue to rise, many interacting with and overseen by ascended masters, angels and deities.
 Avalon flourishes as a powerful spiritual culture across Britain, Ireland and Europe.
 Age of priestesses and wizards. Druid bards keep the histories going.
 Hybrid beings again find safe harbor in Avalon's embrace.
 Newgrange in Ireland begins construction. Aligned to catch the first ray of light of winter solstice.

3,000 BCE STONEHENGE
The great healing temple of Britain, this powerful energy centre is a place of sun worship, calendar timing of the wheel of the year, and of transformative power. The stones are aligned to catch the first rays of light of summer solstice. Convergence of healers at summer solstice each year continues to this day.

3,000 BCE AVEBURY CONSTRUCTED
The greatest stone circle on the planet, Avebury became a healing centre and ceremonial centre of Ancient Briton and the Avalonians. Each stone records history and has a song or vibration. Stonehenge, Newgrange and Avebury, as well as the natural formation of the Tor at Glastonbury and Silbury hill behind Avebury (a man-made hill) anchor

galactic energy into the landscape in a kind of energetic acupuncture, or geomancy. Leylines converge and run through these monuments.

355 BCE PLATO'S DIALOGUES ON ATLANTIS
Plato's dialogues, Timeaus and Critaeus, with their detailed accounts of Atlantis, said to come from an Egyptian priest named Solon, create a sensation. To this day, they are still considered one of the best sources for information on Atlantis.

55 BCE AVALON INVADED
Roman invasion of Britain: enslavement of indigenous peoples of Briton, including the Avalonians, who were said to be shapeshifters.

300 AD STONE CIRCLE AT GLASTONBURY DESTROYED

1,000 AD MORE HEALING TEMPLES CONSTRUCTED
Chichen Itza said to be constructed: venerating the feathered serpent god Quetzalcoatl, it is a celestial observatory and physical calendar of great sophistication.

(Note: Quetzalcoatl is the feathered serpent god; in Australia, we speak of the Rainbow Serpent, in Avalon, the Dragonfae – are these beings the same?)

1,000 AD ANGKOR TEMPLE CONSTRUCTED
The Angkor temple complex in Cambodia said to be constructed.

Angkor Wat is a rebuilding and recreation of Heaven on Earth. Largest temple complex on Earth, it is said if you climb to the top of the steps in the centre, you will burn through karma!

While it was "found" by the west in the 1800's, in fact Angkor has been revered and cared for by Buddhist monks for centuries, and has been an important pilgrimage centre for hundreds of years.

1,000 AD CHRISTIAN MONUMENTS BUILT OVER TEMPLE LOCATIONS
Europeans construct Christian churches over ancient temple locations and leyline convergences.

1150 AD VITA MERLINI (LIFE OF MERLIN) PUBLISHED
Official court historian, Geoffrey of Monmouth writes his history of Britain, and then his Vita Merlini, the Life of Merlin. In this he recounts the Arthurian folklore as history, including his own take. Includes mentions of Morgan le Fey as healer, necromancer, or medium, and shapeshifter (able to change into raven).

1190 AD ARTHUR AND GUENEVERE'S GRAVE

Monks at Glastonbury uncover a grave while working on the Abbey: the grave includes evidence suggesting it is the resting place of King Arthur and Queen Guenevere.

1882 AD ATLANTIS THE ANTEDILUVIAN WORLD

Published by Ignatius Donnelly.

1888 AD BLAVATSKY'S THE SECRET DOCTRINE PUBLISHED

Blavatsky described in detail how the Atlanteans' misuse of power and technology led to a cosmically ordained downfall. She expanded on Plato, describing a secret priesthood who migrated from Atlantis in the Atlantic to the Gobi desert in Mongolia, before creating new lives in Shamballah in the Tibetan Himalayas.

1923 AD SLEEPING PROPHET EDGAR CAYCE

Edgar Cayce's predictions about Atlantis begin to gain notoriety.

1931 AD THE LOST CONTINENT OF MU PUBLISHED

James Churchward publishes "The Lost Continent of Mu."

1935 AD NAZI PARTY EXPEDITION TO ATLANTIS

Nazi party search for Atlantis.

The Nazi party sends scientific expeditions to Tibet to search for Shamballah. "Atlantis was the mythical homeland of the Aryan race."

The theory of Welteislehre, or "World Ice Theory" gains popularity in Germany. They asserted that six moons once surrounded Earth. Five crashed into the oceans, triggering ice ages, the last of which coincided with Plato's date for the destruction of Atlantis.

Because of the shadow cast over Atlantis by the Nazis, many were turned off searching or questing for it, rejecting the notion of Ayran superiority.

1960s AD PEACE MOVEMENT

Environmental movement and peace movement begins. Indigo scouts come through. Meditation and alternative lifestyles flourish. Tarot decks become widely available. Woodstock is held in 1969.

1971 AD GREENPEACE FORMED

Indigos being born in more numbers. Public awareness of their power growing. Organisations to combat nuclear testing, like Greenpeace, form.

1972 AD GREENPEACE LAUNCHES FIRST WHALING PROTEST

1984 AD HARMONIC CONVERGENCE

Harmonic Convergence initiates and unites international movement for peace. On August 16 and 17 1987, sacred sites like Stonehenge play host to gatherings of thousands of people calling themselves "lightbeings". They gather to welcome in a new era of peace, love and harmony. These dates were chosen as they are the end of the "pain" or "hell" cycles of the Mayan calendar. Shirley MacLaine declares the Harmonic Convergence a "window of light" opening us all up to change, and a massive shift in awareness.

2002 AD STONE CIRCLE ON GLASTONBURY TOR

Remnants of a stone circle found on Glastonbury Tor by Nancy and Charlie Hollinrake of the Glastonbury Antiquarian society. Found on 22.2.2002

2004 AD OCCULTATION OF VENUS JUNE 8

Venus occults the sun (the planetary equivalent of a lunar eclipse). Signifies the resurgence of the feminine, the Goddess Aphrodite and her associates, Ishtar and Pele.

The Goddess principle becomes natural, growing recognition of the sacred feminine and her influence, power and healing energy.

Dan Brown's novel, "The Da Vinci Code," based on the Grail line and the feminine sacred, becomes a runaway best-seller.

March 15, 2004 AD SEDNA, TENTH PLANET DISCOVERED

Sedna, named for the Inuit Goddess who created the dolphins and whales, and transformed pain into creativity and rebirth and protectiveness, energy enters our world.

December 21, 2012 AD END OF THE MAYAN CALENDAR

End times of Mayan calendar. Solstice.

December 21, 2012 AD FIFTH WORLD BEGINS

Beginning of the fifth time on Earth. The beginning of a new 5,125-year energy on this planet.

Immrama One:

DISCOVERING
LEMURIA

Immrama: An otherworldly voyage over water to island destinations that sparks our cellular memory, ancestral wisdom and enlightened awareness. (Irish)

Lemuria

The Lost Continent and Settlements

ANCIEN

OBSIDIAN ZONE

GRASSLANDS

FOREST OF GIANTS

woodland

GREENSTONE

Woodland

GRASSLANDS

Lemuria
Motherland of the Pacific

EUROPE

ASIA

JAPAN

MIDDLE
EAST

INDIA

SOUTH EAST ASIA

EQUATOR

NEW GUINEA

INDONESIA

AFRICA

MADAGASCAR

INDIAN
OCEAN

the kimberley

uluru

AUSTRALIA

BYRON

movement between the
australian and african
plates caused the further
displacement of india and
madagascar from the
lemurian landmass

KERGUELEAN ISLANDS

N

north america

hawaii

PACIFIC
OCEAN

OCEANIA

EQUATOR

south america

movement here caused by
the nazca plate helped to
seperate the most easterly
parts of the lemurian
landmass

zealand

EASTER ISLAND

ORIGINS OF LEMURIA – THE STAR IMMRAMAS

Some of us, they say, are from the Pleiades. Others hail from the Sirian star system. We have received so much from the Arcturians, and from those who inhabited Sumeria, called the Arkadians...

But what if many of us are *of this Earth*... and it is our ancestors who went forth, inhabiting new star systems, and waiting there for us to be ready to be returned home – to ourselves? Are there human colonies of the Atlanteans, the Avalonians and the Lemurians, returning home in incarnations now?

Perhaps. Just perhaps it is not that we are being visited by others.

Perhaps we are being visited by our own selves.

From the heart of the Mother.

GALACTIC ORIGINS

"Mu Mu Land (Ancients of Mu Mu)
Mu Mu Land (Ancients of Mu Mu)
We're all bound for Mu Mu Land
Mu Mu Land
Mu Mu Land
We're all bound for Mu Mu Land"

–International hit song by the KLF, 1993

THE MU PROJECT

A long, long time ago, in a galaxy far, far away, a group of voyagers were preparing their second venture to a place that we now call Earth. These beings were very happy and curious and beautiful: some were of pure light, others were sound, others looked very much like you or I might look, if we were six feet tall, fair and wide of eye... but all of them were intelligent and kind, and quite serious about their mission. Some only knew what it was it was to be a spiritual being. And they wanted to experience physicality.

You see, for many of these voyagers, where they lived and how they existed was in and with such bliss and comfort that they sensed that they had reached a point of stasis. And they knew that stasis would be the death of their kind.

In order to develop, they knew they needed to have an entirely different experience. And so a collective of galactic societies and civilisations gathered together, and chose ambassadors from each of their worlds. Some were Pleiadian, others were Arcturian, and others still were from a place called Sirius. There were beings from Orion, from Lyra, and from constellations our telescopes have yet to reveal to us. All were given personal names reflecting their mission, names that would be very familiar to you if you were to hear them today, and each being agreed to undergo a radical metamorphosis. They would transform from a light body into a physical body, a being of both matter and energy. They would travel through time and space and create a world in which they could grow beyond their experience, where they would know both the pleasures and the pitfalls of being alive, and in a body.

And so they came. As each being transformed from energetic entity into physical creatures, they were at last differentiated, one from the other. But they all had some things in common.

They had chosen and created bodies with long extending skulls, skin that was tinged different colours, and glowing masses in what we would now call their third eye area. Their limbs were long, and their ability to transform their physical self was radical and subtle. They could create and transform all kinds of energy, and knew that in these times, on this journey, they would interact with beings whom they had never before met. Beings who were of stone and wood, and sea and sky. They would feel, and cry, and love, and die. And they were glad of it all.

They were set to travel in craft that were silver, barely discernible, that would vibrate to harmonics that would be on a scale far higher than that which we can hear right now, but one which our souls vibrate to nevertheless. On this voyage, they were prepared to establish a colony on a natural landmass that had been identified in the vast southern oceans on the third planet from a star in the solar system that contained planets known as Mars, Venus and Saturn. They called their mission Mu, or Motherland, and these tribes ventured forth, some for the first time in physical form, to establish the second Earth colony, and the first that would survive for eons, the place from which we all have been birthed. From these beginnings, of wanting to understand and learn and grow in physical form, we have developed. And they are our ancestors, and we are still working with their energy. We are the children of Mu.

When we speak of this homeland, this colony of this Earth, we are speaking of the Lost Land now known as Lemuria.

And that's the story I have been told, by beings I now call the Arkadians.

I really should explain myself here, before I go too much further.

Whenever I used to hear the word alien, a little ripple of fear would snake its way down my spine. It's not a nice word, or a positive word. It means other, and thus it keeps beings separate. Whatever we wish to separate from, we often fear. And thus it was with that word and its vibration. Whenever I *feel* (and I do mean feel, as I'm empathic) what most people truly mean when they say the word "alien" I literally have a physical reaction; that little shudder I often experience that tells me there is strong fear beneath the surface of dislike, prejudice and hatred. For when many people talk of aliens, their fear, resentment, paranoia and determination to be victimised comes to the fore. Therefore, because I was intuitively tuning in to the fear and hostility we had for these beings, when I was younger, I felt completely turned off by the exploration of encounters with alien, soaked as that word was in fear and paranoia. However, I grew up in the decade fascinated with neophyte UFOlogy: Erik Von Daniken's Chariots of the Gods was a documentary series screened on television that I watched as a child… and it both fascinated me, and completely freaked me out. I could not read Whitney Streiber's Communion, as I could feel the fear coming off the pages, and I did not at all relate to the concept of the androgynous, hair-free, disturbingly described idea of the "alien" or other. Lost in Space and Star Trek left me kinda cold. The Daleks on Doctor Who *really* scared me. Fear was not a thought field I was very interested in exploring, pondering and increasing in my young life, struggling as I was at times to make sense of my own magickal experiences. So I turned my attention elsewhere.

However, I had two experiences with star-beings that I can recall. One was just after becoming verbal – I was tiny, and had just learned the rudiments of beginning to talk. However, I was also experiencing night-flying, astral traveling and visitations from beings, predominantly ancestral spirits, deceased loved ones, goddesses and angels. One evening, however, some very different beings showed up in the back garden of our small home, examining, it seemed, plants in the garden. (The plants were agapanthas!) They were small, friendly-faced, and very…different! Despite their being in the garden, like other beings I saw, I knew they were different from fae beings: but at that just-learning-to-talk-stage, I had no words for them. I was slightly wary, and very curious, and they were very gentle.

Later, I had a visitation in my room. A small being, quite ET-like in its appearance, akin it seems to the beings interested in the plants, came to me and talked…in another language entirely. I know that this information is being slowly absorbed by me now…it is rapidly accelerating these days, but for a time there, I felt quite frustrated by the fact that so much was shared, but so little, it seemed, was available to me. Not now! Now it's all flying in, and sometimes I need to meditate just for a little informational peace. They are very kind, though, and they will turn it down and slow down a little if I am not absorbing joyously. We simply need to ask them, and it is done.

So, you can see that personal experience has led to the fear I held being replaced and released over time with love and eagerness to learn: my own explorations and answers I was receiving during meditation suggested that our own DNA is indeed multi-dimensional and multi-galactic. In other words, this planet is host and garden and home to many beings whose origin is beyond this particular solar system. We are all extra-terrestrial. Some of us have such a beautiful diversity of DNA material that we are indeed crossovers with other beings – fae and mer-folk, dragon and other dimensional beings.

It was my fascination with astrology that initially drew me closer to my new understandings of what I term Galactic Consciousness. The sun is not simply fixed in the "sky" with planets moving around it...the sun, too, has its orbit, and we are all involved in this beautiful cosmic dance. Learning of planetoids and other systems through astrology opened my eyes and mind to a more cosmic ecological consciousness. What we here do on the Earth does not simply affect us: it affects the balance of galaxies, as we are very significant in the galactic ecosystem.

I feel now too that perhaps many of the abduction and implant experiences were in fact premonitions on a mass human scale of what is being proposed by our governments on a grand and inhuman, mechanistic scale. Microchipping is, of course, commonplace with our pets, and technology has developed to such a degree that we will be confronted with these proposals over the coming 18 years. So if you fear microchipping or implants by extraterrestrials – well, I feel we are in fact in most danger from ourselves. I believe that many of the sightings and experiential contacts taking place now are freeing us from the paranoia of the other, and will assist us all in standing our ground and repudiating attempts to microchip us, and create a control centre for our minds. But I digress.

The channellings of Abraham, Kryon and Seth all indicated that what had previously been termed "alien" and frightening was in fact kind and powerful, compassionate indeed. I find that though David Icke's theories are admirable, and he is a passionate advocate of the planet, much of his thinking is fear-based. The notion of reptilian "others" does not resonate with me – we are in fact the "others" and our determination to control each other, to dominate each other and the planet is the true falsehood.

And then I began seeing them. And they began to tell me about our origins, back in the ancient, and oh-so-futuristic past.

Seeing them, for I had no other name for them at the time, is extraordinary. These beings proved to me that there are as many star-beings as there are human beings, and elemental and angelic beings, for example. When it first occurred, I had a strong impulse to protest. "Hey – I'm an Earth girl – I love this planet – what is it that you want? I communicate with Goddesses, fae and dragons – what are you guys about?" It was completely mind-blowing, empowering, loving, amazing...all those words. I felt awestuck but not overwhelmed – just so grateful and uplifted and elated.

To date, as telepathy is the form of communication these beings most frequently use with me, I cannot clearly discern the messages, except they are those of intelligent love. When I hear them, they predominantly "speak" in tones, in musical notes. The music that they speak in contains information, that then is translated by me into information that I can more easily comprehend, much of which is contained in this book.

There is a definite opening between worlds/dimensions occurring, and thus I feel more akin to the dimensional being visitation theory than the "extraterrestrial". They are not exactly opposed in any case, as dimensionality explains time shifts – and time travel, and covering enormous distances via thought transportation.

As time is non linear, surely these beings are literally simply moving through time and space in ways that we have yet to formalise – though many highly psychic human beings are already travelling these roads.

In Somerset, travelling with two wonderful beings, Crystal Academy founder Rachelle Charman, and author of Seven Sacred Sites, fellow witch and healer Serene Coneeley, we saw an enormous Pillar of Light in the distance. We had been pondering the origins of crop circles, and here, in the sky, at a distance, was an enormous pillar or column of vibrating light...I did not know it at the time, but it was to bear a resemblance to beings I then began to meet.

Exploring time and dimensional reality has given me some tools by which I can begin to see these beings by moving into their dimensions, and opening portals through which they can enter mine.

After carefully meditating for answers on what was happening, I received a flow of information that indicates we are in the midst of a fifty-year shift in cosmic consciousness, and we are in the midst of first contact with beings that are profoundly compassionate, intelligently loving, and enormously wise. Not only that, they in many ways are us: and they have formed a part of the planet we now call home.

So, maybe I'm one of the fortunate ones. I have not experienced abduction or implants, not to my knowledge. The crossover between ascended masters and these compassionate wise ones who I experience fascinates me, and we will explore it together through this book. During readings with clients, I have been stunned to see more and more frequently galactic beings with the people I am reading with/for (it's always a co-creation). I am even more surprised, being the level-headed witch I am, that people are very open to galactic consciousness, and the web we are all a part of. They are eager to learn of their off-earth origins and friends.

Meeting people whose origins are clearly from other galaxies is always a pleasure, and fascinating. Clearly, these people display interesting characteristics, and are not easily able to assimilate into current Earth culture. However, they are among the most peaceful and loving of beings. Strange? Well, as a person who has had that word flung at me more times than I care to remember, I'm cautious about labelling another. But yes, they bring to this planet a different perspective, and are assisting us in managing the challenges we are currently facing. My belief is that technological geniuses – Bill

Gates, for example, Einstein in what we call the past, are being guided by star people and dimensional beings. That the people who are assisting us with developing solutions to carbon-neutral business and technologies to help the planet make it through the global warming creation are many of them, star beings.

Are goddesses and gods, angels and other beings simply articulations of galactic consciousness? Is God an alien? Are we all composed of a perfect combination of stardust and earth?

Both celestial and terrestrial we most definitely are. And both are divine.

I look forward to many more beautiful experiences with interdimensional beings, who are extraterritorial, and who, in many ways, are *us*. I look forward to your experiences, as we reach out beyond our seeming limits, and become truly infinite.

ATTUNING TO GALACTIC CONSCIOUSNESS

Crystal Workings

Particular crystals have affinities with particular realms of the Universes. A grid utilising clear quartz and rose quartz in the shape known as infinity can connect you with the galactic beings wishing to reach you. Many galactic beings, predominantly the Sirians and the Arkadians have contacted me to inform me that crystals contain information regarding time travel and interdimensional portals that we are on the verge of beginning to work with in a more conscious way. Selenite is another crystal that de-layers time travel consciousness. Holding selenite above your head, towards a star system with which you wish to connect, will send a conduit of light and time energy outwards, and you will begin to receive information in return. Consider it a kind of radio transmitter – or, as in the archangel, an Ariel.

Recognising Intergalactic Beings

There are many different groups of physical and non physical beings. They represent other galaxies, other dimensions as well as other aspects of time. Very often there are groups of different beings working together to help us, such as with the Intergalactic Councils and with Ashtar Command. The main groups that assist Planet Earth and the starseeds here are the Sirians, the Pleiadians, Ashtar Command and the Arcturians, and coming in now the Arkadians, the Hathors, the Venusians. All of these groups have deep connections with Planet Earth and this is why they regularly step forward to assist us.

Each star system and Galaxy has its own energetic flavour and focus for consciousness. They each offer different skills and gifts to humanity.

Arkadians

These beings are towering...around two metres tall, they are composed, to my eyes and senses, of light, primarily white and pale violets. They are enormous, are like us, in that they have a large head, torso, arms and legs, and they are very, very kind. Light sort of "spills" from and around them, like a fountain that is constantly moving within a fluid form that is identifiable. They have rather large heads, a little like they are wearing helmets of this unique light. They bear a strong resemblance to other teachers' description of angels. For example, Sylvia Browne's, but my very strong information suggests, and my feeling is that they are not angels, not in the traditional sense at all. We have much to learn, and they are on the verge of revealing much to us. We simply need to take the next step, to be prepared.

Where are they from?
They are a pre-civilisation of Sirius, from Sirius B.

Why are they here?
To assist us in moving into the understanding of the galactic part we have to play, and to release our fear of continued cooperation and contact. Their domains are lawmaking, building, and they are the architects of matter.

Arcturians

In my meditations, and in "person" the Arcturians are very interesting to me. They appear as pure geometric form and colour – almost as symbols themselves – and arrange themselves into shapes to convey meaning. They almost appear like 3-D crop circles, and can create physical matter and holographic-style imagery with their moving, kaleidoscopic energy. They feel very dynamic and strong to me ... colour and shape is their modality for communication. Some of the most highly developed beings known as the Arcturians are from a star system and star called Arcturus. Arcturus is a fifth dimensional civilization, a prototype for our future Earth. It is an energy gateway through which humans pass during death and re-birth; it functions as a way station for non-physical consciousness to become accustomed to physicality. Arcturus is approximately thirty-six light years from Earth and the Arcturian starships encircle the earth to monitor our progress and help us with our spiritual evolution. These beings are pure love, they have advanced knowledge and are of an extremely high vibrational frequency. They often communicate with humans through telepathy, and they have some of the most advanced healing techniques available to us. They can be called upon by anyone who so wishes for healing, they will take you to their healing capsules on their planet and work on your etheric, mental and emotional bodies if you ask for them to. They are very powerful healers. Their average life span is 350-400 earth years because there is no sickness at all on Arcturus.

Where are they from?
They are from the Arcturus star system, located in the Bootes constellation.

Why are they here?
The Arcturians tell me that they wish to help humanity through conveying the healing energy of shape and form – sacred geometry is how I interpret this. They can purify energy, ground us, increase our perspective on galactic matters and work with each chakra. They seem to be intent on making shapes in forms that awaken us to information that we seem unwilling to accept in the form of language...

Pleiadians

Pleiadians resemble humans to such a degree it is said that we can rarely tell one from the other ... they are very beautiful, tall, well-formed, and fair in skin and hair, blue in eyes. They have incredible skin ... absolutely radiant, and are extremely long-lived. They have very long fingers, feet, hands and limbs, and look faintly bizarre due to their size which is very tall and large. They are slim, small-breasted and are quite straight up and down. They are very beautiful, almost like a kind of superhuman ... their third eye area is often decorated. Their eyes have a strange, far-away gaze and their eyes are slightly almond shaped, tipped up at the far ends and are placed far apart. They are slightly "strange" to gaze upon, and very appealing. They have suffered their own destructive times and tell me they wish for us to avoid their mistakes. Language is like water running over rocks, natural sounds. Heartbeat is able to be heard from the outside. Their energy is strong and bright and their presence can create physical healings and sometimes pain as their frequency is so high. We share a great deal of our cellular matrix, or DNA with them. They express themselves simply, without embellishment, and have very large eyes and faces. Slightly giant-like! The Pleiadians come from a star cluster in the constellation Taurus, approximately five hundred light years from Earth. They are one of the most advanced races in this galaxy in terms of music and dance. They subtly bring through music to those musicians who are spiritually attuned, which in turn raises the vibrations of all those who hear it. They are also helping to bring in great advancements in the use of light, holograms and laser technology. They were the first humanoid society to develop hyper space travel and claim that their technology surpasses ours by about 3,000 years.

Where are they from?
They are from the seven star system known as the Pleiades, and have been worked with by the indigenous peoples of our planet since pre-ancient times.

Why they are here?
To help us avoid the consciousness that can lead to seismic disasters. To help us into the next stage of our development, the reclaiming and reactivation of our dormant, or our sleeping DNA.

Sirians

The Sirians are the "professors" of the galactic web – they are very advanced in their ability to reach and transmit information, and set up many academies where beings from all over the galactic web can train and learn. They have wonderful insights into past, present and future – they are the masters and mistresses of time travel – and can describe even now hidden worlds. Sirius and our beautiful planet have long had a strong and valuable association, with many of us training with Sirians in meditation or even while we sleep and dream. They are strongly associated with many tribal peoples, including the Dogon tribe of Africa, Egypt, and the Mayan civilization. They are another wonderful civilization. They are more advanced in the metaphysical sense as Sirius is one of the more advanced training centers or universities to which the Ascended Masters travel. Sirius has a direct link with our solar system and the Sirians have been amongst us since the time of the Mayan and Egyptian civilizations. They gave the Egyptians much advanced astronomical and medical knowledge, and created levitation techniques that work on earth (each technique varies according to the geophysical space in which the methods will work...) They colonized Mars at one stage of our solar system's history, and can help us create such clear, bright intentions that we have a laser-like impact on the world around us. The creation of calendars is a Sirian art: the Mayan and Egyptian calendars rely heavily on the movements of Sirius. Sirians are creators, and assist us with our own creations. The Dogon tribe's tales of interactions with Sirian beings – some 700 years in the making – speak of dolphin-like beings originating on that star system.

   They are said to be creating a time-travel vehicle which ressembles a throne.
Sirians are very like us in many ways – they have very long, extended craniums that stretch out from behind, are very tall and wear headpieces to cover and protect this fine cerebellum they have. It lights up conspicuously.

Why they are here:
To help us into the next time period that needs mapping; with positive time interaction.

What they can assist with:
They are here to help us to work with the notion of time – helping researchers, scientists, doctors and lay-people, including mystics, create a new concept and experience of time and cycles... Instead of a linear version of time, know that time is indeed layered and looped, interwoven. Thus when we begin to explore our own being and its existence in time, you may find these beings more able to connect with you, or you with them. In my workshops, we are working on this, travelling the streams of time for advanced psychic development and the development of Galactic Consciousness.

Ashtar Command

I kept hearing the name Ashtar for quite some time before I began to receive information about this body of beings, who represent the existing Universe. They are a body of representatives from each sentient civilisation, and their mission is to protect threatened civilizations, and to teach us all the ways of each other. There are both members of the group with physical humanoid bodies, and others who are tones, sounds and beings of shape and light... an interesting and very diverse group indeed! A being called Lord Ashtar is said to be their leader... though the voice that comes through for me as leader is distinctly feminine. They have large spaceships, and teams on these which represent the diversity of the galactic web of life. It's like an outer space UN! Earth is already a member, with representatives from various times of earth history and civilisations. They assist starbeings currently incarnated adjust to life on earth, and to their life mission and purpose.

Why they are here:
To protect, serve and guide. They are intergalactic lightworkers of great discernment and high intent. They are also not infallible – but have great integrity! They cannot interfere with human destiny, individually or as a mass, without invitation.

How to work with them:
They are great doctors and physicians: They love to be consulted for their insights on etheric medicines and healing modalities. They are adept diplomats, and can work with us to promote peaceful interactions between diverse beings. They encourage us to work with the power of starlight, and star-generated forms of power, including solar energy. The purpose of Ashtar is to assist humanity in going through the transition commonly known as Earth Changes, Apocalypse, Armageddon, and/or Rapture, depending on the source of the information.

The Galactic Confederation

This is an amazing cooperative venture that is the basis of Ashtar Command, which is essentially the roaming representatives of the Confederation. Its base shifts every 1,000 years, and is presently situated in the constellation known as Lira in the star system known as Alcona. They are not at all to be confused with missionaries as we here on earth have experienced them: they do assist, but have a strict non-interference policy, and hold intentions that are grounded in co-operation and the preservation and development of emerging civilisations. They are helping many of us on earth move through these changes. They are varied and diverse groups of dimensional beings and they are, literally, regrouping the relationships of the Universe.

Where they are from:
Every "corner" of the Universe. They are an intergalactic council representing incredible diversity and the possibilities of non-dualistic polarities coming together. In other words, we can retain our differences and work in harmony. Their symbol is the infinity sign.

Why they are with us:
To help us through this very erratic and seemingly dangerous time on earth – as our negative thought forms gather and create changes, they are assisting us in healing the planet in both practical ways and in healing our thinking.

Venusians

Are very beautiful light-beings who can move between physical form and light-being with ease. They are very happy, very musical, and offer a kind of way-station or resting point for space travellers. Venus is a kind of stopover point for the long journeys between star systems. It also helps light-beings assimilate into material density, which can be very tough for them. Likewise, for those going from purely physical form into a more etheric form, it serves as another acclimatisation station.

Why they are here:
Beauty, music, love of life and self.

What they can help with:
Balancing spirit and matter, moving from one state to another without the accompanying transition sickness.

Note: There are also many terms used by new age groups and theosophists, such as the Great White Brotherhood, that do come into play with the story of the Lost Lands. The Great White Brotherhood is, similar to Ashtar, a collective of beings who once walked the planet Earth, and who have agreed to assist us through our Earth changes from the spirit plane. They include beings such as Maitreya, Ghandi, Princess Diana, Jesus, Buddha, Yogananda, Saint-Germain, Sanat Kumara (more on him later!) Lady Portia and many others. They are not, however, named because they are a collective of white males, they are named for the white light that they emanate. The brotherhood aspect is a little misleading, as they do indeed have many beings who primarily identify as female in their midst. They include feminine and masculine, as well as androgynous beings. Some agree to incarnate several times again, though they are past the incarnation processes, to assist in earth matters. They are devoted to the service of Love and helping humanity understand the truth – that we are all One.

LEMURIA... THE ANCESTRAL HOME

"...Now I see the secret of the making of the best persons,
It is to grow in the open air and to eat and sleep with the earth."

- Walt Whitman, American poet

I am about to dive, from an immense natural rock platform jutting out over a turquoise ocean. Carved into the cliff face behind me are faces, what look like huge, stone carvings: except here, they move and speak...they urge me forward. I smile and give a nod of assent.

I run along the platform and launch myself into the abyss, feel the air rushing past, then plunge into the watery depths, so clear I can see all the way to the bottom... The water is my home, and I swim, moving through this element with ease, feeling myself change as I become the water...my skin alters, my third eye opens, and I begin to breathe...through my skin I can transform the water molecules into oxygen, and this is as natural to me as taking in the breath is to me now... I have an actual third eye...it looks around independently of me... My third eye also converts oxygen...it is akin to a dolphin spout and I can feel it breathing in and breathing out...

My hair is long, beyond what appear to be my legs, but which are so different from human legs, as I have small fins at the end of either foot, which is webbed and thickened, and a powerful means of moving swiftly through the warm waters.

Each length of my hair is long, and each tendril moves almost independently, like snakes through the water. My hair moves in patterns sending out electrical energy underwater, like that of a nautilus...it is a kind of antennae, and it can trace the movements of energy around me, sensing the whereabouts of what I am searching for.

I am in a world of vibration, and my ability to locate objects through the sensitive interpretation of this vibration is a kind of echo-location...I can see through the sound bouncing back to me... three-dimensional diagrams of places and spaces, and rich deposits of minerals... my voice carries underwater for thousands of kilometers, effortlessly, joyously, and with purpose.

My fellow beings are in the water...my hair reaches out, and speaks its own language. I look down and I see my legs are long, shining and faintly blue...they are finished in feet that have fins on their heels... I am like the mermaid Eurynome...

I am a child of the Mother. I am a child of Mu.

Mu is the motherland, our off-earth home from which a band of explorers from different worlds gathered together to assist some off-world beings to experience the Great Adventure – that of being in a body. The colony that emerged here was founded by a collective of beings: some of light, others of sound, some in humanoid form, and all who had a love and a longing to experience life as it could be experienced on this planet. With food, and animals, and beings, and challenges. It was the ultimate learning program: full of joy, and pain from time to time, and struggle, and bliss and laughter and tears. It was amazing – they were, many for the first time – experiencing what it was to be alive as an individualized being.

The land they colonised and the civilisation they created is called Lemuria, and what a beautiful world she was – and is. For there remain many fragments of her in the world today, and when we connect with her, we feel a sense of strength, solidity, peace and power.

When the Mu-project starships arrived, they did not find an unpopulated earth. Pre-existing this colony were remnants of a first colony – of primarily Pleiadians, called the Hyperboreans. In addition there were pure creatures and beings of this planet – the fae, elementals, and many beautiful creatures, including land animals and sea creatures. Many of these were in-betweeners... the new beings of the Mu project dubbed the lands they settled in Lemuria. The earth beings were very open, innocent and friendly, and indeed had nothing to fear.

From these beginnings, and from incredible diversity, Lemuria soon grew into groups of civilisations, lands of fully conscious beings of great diversity, beings who lived in balance and harmony with the land, the water, the sky, and the healing element of fire, working elemental magic and maintaining this balance and harmony between all that is. Who felt that being alive and in physical form was the greatest blessing, and one through which they could learn and have revealed to them great lessons. And they lived this way for close to one million years, until the balance came to be altered by those who believed that these ways of being were too simple, too "primitive", too unsophisticated.

But before that time came, before the fabric of ourselves was altered and we slipped into amnesia, we had a different world, and we were fully ourselves. Authentic. Real. Available. Innocent. Wise.

We all were there. You were there, as was I.

But no matter how far away from us in time, the remnants of our beautiful, peaceful culture of Lemuria survive. Because Lemuria and her consciousness is rising again, and we are becoming more aware, more peaceful, more loving, more kind, and more aware of ourselves as beings of the Universe. We are beginning to once again revere the sacred nature of our mother, this planet Gaia, and so Mu comes again.

Welcome to your home. That which lies beneath the core of us all. Lemuria, our motherland.

WHERE IS LEMURIA?

Lemuria is vast! Her location lies between and beneath the land mass we now know as India, and the west coast of Australia, throughout its north west, middle areas and north-east, through to the most easterly point of Australia and Indonesia. It includes parts of present-day Burma, Cambodia, Laos, parts of Vietnam, Thailand, Borneo, Japan, some parts of China, New Zealand, Madagascar and parts of South America. Its remnants lie like green jewels smattering the blue velvet of the Pacific on its coral atolls, making them lush, loamy, fertile...all of these are the present day traces of the once-upon-a time land mass of Lemuria.

Lemuria sometimes seems overlooked to me. We have seemed to be more easily fascinated by the tale of Atlantis, more obsessive about the search to "find" this place spoken of by Plato in his dialogues, and referenced by such esoteric giants as Helena Blavatsky, Edgar Cayce, James Churchward and Ignatius Donnelly. Atlantis seems so brilliant, so intellectual, so tragic – so close. It seems to lie just beyond the veil, and tantalises us with its proximity, and its mystery.

But beyond, beneath and behind Atlantis there lies the motherland, Lemuria, a place from which we sprung, where elements and rocks and mountains and sky were formed. Lemuria, which existed from perhaps millions of years ago, reaching a brilliant moment some 80,000 years ago.

As we approach a time of earth changes, I can sense the energy of fear and panic that stirs at the thought of change... It can be wise to contemplate that our mother, Gaia has already passed through the crystalline crucible of three ice ages. Of a time of fire. Of a time of flood.

Over her vast and powerful lifetime, or cycles, our Mother the earth has experienced vast cataclysms that have swept her surface, clearing and shifting land masses, bringing forth or destroying lifeforms, and she has been the cradle of galactic energies and experiments. These geological cataclysms created massive shifts in the sea level – land masses were changed, rising seas covered entire continents. This shifting took place over thousands of years, resulting in the planet as we know her today, and encompassing the lands and wisdom teachings of Atlantis, Avalon, Ys, Troy, and Lyonesse and Shamballah.

And then there were other cataclysms that came about due to interference without respect. And this is an important thing to remember. The planet has her own heartbeat, her own wisdom, her own cycles. Things will change. But when beings attempt to force the change to suit themselves, via genetic modifications, DNA experiments, weather control and artificial cooling and warming of landscapes, and the poisoning of her bloodstreams and oceans, we do indeed walk in the well trodden steps of others who thought they were also doing the right thing.

Which is why Lemuria is so exceptional in her energy, and why I wish for you to truly feel what it is to be at one with all that is. To know what it is to live and breathe and be in balance and harmony with the environment. With your body. With all sentient beings.

But before and beneath the time of the experiments lies the bedrock of Lemuria. Our foundation, and our Mother. We are poised at a point in our history where we look likely to walk in the footsteps of our ancestors yet again – where we may repeat the tragedy of fear-based interference. But the solution is so simple. And my guides tell me that if we re-embrace the beautiful, simple yet very powerful magic of Lemuria, of the elements, of our selves and our nature, we can pass through these changes as we are meant to. Like birth, there can be transition, and a narrowing, and intensity, and a pushing forward and forth. But we will, and can be born again, healthy and well, and whole again.

And this neglect of Lemuria, and of our diverse galactic origins, is an oversight in our nature and philosophy – and says so much about us. We turn to the tragedy of Atlantis, sifting over what we know, and remain unaware of her sister, the beauteous and pacific – literally peaceful – Lemuria.

If Atlantis is a diamond, Lemuria is the physical Motherland – all loamy soil and rich earth, a sustaining land mass, driven up through the watery origins of the planet through massive volcanic explosions, the land masses created from cooled lava, or obsidian, the powerful black transparent crystal that takes, to this day a powerful energy to handle, and one which makes the places built upon its cooled fires extraordinary.

It is a place of shamans, healers, telepathy. Elemental magicks and oracles, seers and amazing beings and creatures who defy our classifications of today. A place of living rocks and speaking trees and a whispering, sentient ocean, and of communication between all of these beings, who are all considered children of the Motherland.

Her peoples have been described as one-eyed giants leading dinosaurs about, as etheric beings without a physical experience, as egg-laying beings with three eyes. Deep in meditation, many other pieces of the puzzle were revealed to me. But we shall get to that later...

Thus, we have Lemuria. A miracle-place where stones agree to be moved, and then are transported via sound. A place where temples are carved out of existing rock platforms with pure thought, where holographic projections of self across the thousands of miles facilitates understanding and dialogue. A place where sexual differentiation shifts throughout a lifetime, and where those lifetimes are ages old in comparison to our shortened spans, even of today. A place where visitations from our family off-earth was a regular and systematic occurrence. On equinoxes and solstices, we had the meetings. Four for the earth each year, and four for the galactic beings. And together, they formed the wheel of the year, still recognised today from the Hopi to the Celtic tribes, and one which has formed the basis of what we call shamanic earth lore across this beautiful blue and green planet.

LEMURIA'S FINGERPRINTS

It is not as though we do not know of Lemuria. She is referenced in much of our folklore and oral traditions. She is spoken of as the Pure Land by the Hindu, and is revered by the Inuit, the dreamtime peoples of Australia, the Mayans, the Polynesians, and the people of south-east Asia. Lemuria was, and is, vast: remember, her territories stretched from coastal eastern Africa, and incorporated South East Asia, Madagascar, Australia, New Zealand, islands of the Pacific, and of north-west South America. These places were not separate, but were joined by land bridges, creating a culture that harmoniously integrated differences spanning thousands upon thousands of miles. This was achieved due to two overarching principles: The first, the implicit belief that we are all one, and we are all children of the Mother.

MAPPING OUR CELLULAR MEMORY

One of the most challenging aspects of writing this book is in many ways its vast scope – and Lemuria was soon proving to be an amazing challenge – testing me, perhaps, to see if I could honour her. It soon felt clear to me that Lemuria was and is immense, and that many hours would be spent researching, meditating and communicating. One aspect was the mapping of Lemuria! How to map and chart a land mass that shifted and changed over such a vast amount of earth-time! But map her we would... Poring over present-day maps with Kylie McDonough, my friend, a visionary artist who is a powerful intuitive, who I had been told would be perfect for the maps for this work...I kept feeling that Mu was not so much a large continent in the middle of the Pacific, as a large continent that stretched from the Pacific through to Madagascar in the west, to the Easter islands near South America. She is a massive continent, a motherland, from which split off the African, Australian, South American and European areas. When reading the Secret Doctrine, I was fascinated to read Madame Blavatsky's words on Lemuria.... She believed the area she described as Lemuria to be vast, and extended from *"...the foot of the Himalayas, which separated it from the inland sea rolling its waves over what is now Tibet, Mongolia, and the great desert of Schamo (Gobi); from Chittagong, westward to Hardwar, and eastward to Assam. From thence, it stretched South across what is known to us as Southern India, Ceylon, and Sumatra; then embracing on its way, as we go South, Madagascar on its right hand and Australia and Tasmania on its left, it ran down to within a few degrees of the Antarctic Circle; when, from Australia, an inland region on the Mother Continent in those ages, it extended far into the Pacific Ocean..."*

Interestingly, science backs this up. Geological studies tell us that for hundreds of millions of years, all the land masses on Gaia were one: this super continent is called by the scientists Pangaea – all-Mother, in Greek. The Motherland. According to scientists, this Motherland broke apart into two masses. To the north was found the continent named by the geologists Laurasia, to the south, Gondwanaland. And we know that even scientists believe that Gondwanaland (from the Sanskrit – the mother tongue of earth-dwellers!) included Africa, Madagascar, India, Australia, South America.

Over millions of years, these two land masses – Lemuria and her northern counterpart, which one day would be revealed to be Hyperborea, which was partially refounded as Atlantis, moved farther apart. Glossopteris, a fossil plant can be found in all of the locations that were originally Lemuria.

Lemuria was warm, and dry, with rainy seasons – tropical, and life-sustaining. There were tree ferns and coniferous plants, and a civilisation. There have been some thrilling discoveries over the last decades which are pointing to the existence of this Motherland. In 1999 a research vessel for the Joint Oceanographic Institutions for Deep Earth

Sampling (JOIDES) found something mysterious in the Southern Indian Ocean, about 3,000 km to the southwest of Australia.

The researchers found that an underwater plateau, almost a third of the size of modern-day Australia, known as the Kerguelen Plateau, was actually the remains of a lost continent, which sank beneath the waves around 20 million years ago. The team found evidence of a forest in the fragments of wood, seed, spores and pollen they dredged up from the depths, containing soil over 90 million years old...

The rock samples have the same composition as those of India and Australia, perhaps proving they were connected in the Motherland continent. Ongoing research has led to scientists believing that this super continent had tropical flora and fauna – including small dinosaurs... could these be the creatures Madame Blavatsky saw in her visions?

Present day Lemurians have distinct ideas about its location! "Many people speak of Lemuria in books, saying North America made up a large portion of it. This is not what I have seen and know. Mu is the Pacific Atlantis... taking in South America, Latin America and Mexico and the smallest portion of North America, Hawaii, the Pacific Islands, Papua New Guinea, New Zealand, Australia, India and finally Mauritius and Madagascar. You could almost say very much like Gondwana," says Allyson Tanner, a healer, geology student and present-day Lemurian living in Sydney. She feels her own lifetime on Lemuria was lived in current-time New Zealand. "I know when I finally step onto New Zealand that I will be home," she explains. "Particular spots which exist today existed long ago and hold energy of great wisdom, knowledge and spirituality."

Clearly, the land mass of Lemuria is remembered as being enormous by earth standards. Her civilisation also spread to other parts of the world – including Atlantis in the Atlantic Ocean, China/Tibet, Egypt, India and meso-America. Her civilisation thrived for nearly 900,000 years, and some modern-day Lemurians know they have experienced lifetime after lifetime there. "Both of us lived through much of this span," says Dr. Ralph Ballard, an author and expert on Lemuria, who has researched both his own past life memories and those of his partner, Sushi. He believes its location to be in the Pacific, stretching from Indonesia and the eastern border of Australia, through all the Pacific Islands including Easter Island. The capital was located in Hawaii, which was at the eastern border of Lemuria.

If we had this common motherland, it may help us explain why across the planet we share the same symbols, why our languages have the same words, why we have the same stories, told over and over again. We were torn asunder, we went forth and created new colonies, but at the root of them all, is Lemuria.

SHAPESHIFTERS OF SEA AND SKY

As we have discovered, some of the first people in Lemuria were elemental spirit in form, and then went on to become the land itself.

One of the traditions of Avalon is to see the embodied Goddess in the land herself, and many tales tell us if the leader of the people sickens and dies, the land too sickens and dies. Perhaps our original ancestors were in fact all that we continue to be sustained by, today.

The Lakota tell a story of how our ancestors of flesh have become our bedrock – quite literally. They tell a tale of rising waters, of land being covered by this flood, and of a great chief who led his warriors to the mountains in Arizona. "When it became clear that even the mountain peaks would be submerged, the chief told his braves that, rather than let them drown ignominiously, he would turn them to stone. They are there guarding the heights even today."

It is so like the story told by the Maung people of Arnhem Land in Australia, where they attribute the formation of a huge reef to a spirit being made flesh called Blanket Lizard... The tale says that Crow cut down a big paperbark tree, which divided a creek. The crow then called out in its lonesome voice, driving the creek further and further apart, until the waters rose and the people drowned. A man named Blanket Lizard swam, looking for his wife , but halfway across the chasm dividing the drowning lands, he tired and went under, and his bones turned into a reef.

In September 22, 2008, newspaper articles around the world, including AAP, the worldwide syndication agency based in Australia, reported on the finding of an ancient reef. Right in the middle of the Australian outback.

Scientist, Jonathan Giddings, told the reporters of a 650-million-year-old reef which existed during a period of tropical climate. The reef is located in what is now the desert in South Australia.

"This reef is an internationally significant discovery because it provides a significant step forward in showing the extent of climate change in Earth's past and the evolution of ancient reef complexes – and it also contains fossils which may be of the earliest known primitive animals," Mr Giddings said.

"From a climate change point of view, this reef provides an important record of what was happening in the ocean 650 million years ago."

"The chemistry of the reef and other sediments forming in the ocean at the same time show the ocean was poorly mixed, and this may have had an effect on Earth's climate at that time by allowing carbon to be trapped in the ocean's depths."

Could we have lived and breathed beneath the water, as the chemical mix of the ocean was very different to what it is today – and the existence of Lemuria – a place where we both breathed over and underwater – seems less and less in the realm of legend? I know she existed – I have been there. But to know that science too is travelling the same path – 'tis miraculous indeed.

So there is much wisdom in the dreaming tales, and in the stories and legends (which are mythic truths) of all ancient cultures. Other Dreaming tales tell of a snake who swallows the people escaping from the drowning. The snake later vomits them up, and their bones become rocks and mountains. And the people of the Badlands of present-day South Dakota tell that the incredible landscape of the Dakotas are the bones of a water monster, who fought the Thunderbirds for the Earth... These are all variations of the journey of that mothership from the off-earth colony of Mu to the Earth colony that we know as Lemuria. Beings of essence and of ether, or spirit and not of matter consciously chose to incarnate here, to be here, as physical beings. And in doing so, we were all given life – the most incredible blessing of them all. We were the rocks, the very mountains of the sea themselves. We dwelt within all the elements, and in a very tangible sense, we are now those elements.

And yet today, we seem so far away from that understanding of interrelationship with nature and all of her forms.

Too many of us, safe within our buildings and cars, supermarkets and massive malls, are living in a state of deep disconnection from the cycles of the planet. We feel but one temperature, which does not allow us to feel the light of the sun, its variations, programming us to awaken at sunrise, and to sleep and relax at sunset. Instead of the sunrise, the sunset, and the arc of the sun's journey throughout the sky, we have artificial light, hard, midday light shining down on us at all times, and we are being impacted seriously by this. We become ill, sleep poorly, our appetite for sugars and caffeine increases, and our growth becomes imbalanced, as it does with obesity, or we feel tired, lethargic... Simply reconnecting each day with natural light can change all this.

We, like the Lemurians, can choose to be sustained by the incredible animals and plants, with whom they had such intimate relations, and they had ceremonies and skills that we can learn from now. Because we are now in a time of earth changes, just as they were. And they are our ancestors...we must talk to them. And learn of their ways to avoid repeating the mistakes of the past.

I knew instantly that I had to speak more to my friend, Scott Alexander King, whose work on animals and spirit is beautiful and complex. Scott, to my surprise, had already written about Lemuria in his latest book, *Kids! – Indigo Children and Cheeky Monkeys.*

MEMORIES OF LEMURIA

Scott Alexander King is a funny, warm, emotional and caring man...and a dear friend. We see each other throughout the year, having formed a fast friendship at various MBS festivals – we are part of the roaming people! We arranged to catch up, and he told me that the word 'Lemur' actually means Ghost, while the Roman translation Lemure refers to 'Ancestral Spirit'. It was thought that, on a set date each year, Ancestral Spirits rose from their resting places to attend The Festival of Lemuria or "The Festival of the Ghost World" (the term Lemuria literally means 'Ghost World')."

How fascinating, given that all our earthly ancestors are said to spring from Lemuria!

"I know it sounds crazy," Scott told me wonderingly, "but I believe I was there, in some form, at some time. I don't have many memories of the place, but I do have flashes of green, lush wilderness. And I know it's from a time before "our time", if you know what I mean. I have memories of creatures like Pan being there – half man/half goat – and other creatures, like Centaurs and Merpeople. I can't remember if this was on Lemuria, or after, during the time of Atlantis, but the memory is very clear."

No, I didn't think he was crazy – these in-between creatures had always seemed so natural to me! He nodded. "They looked nothing like we see in books – they were quite wild, animal-like and dangerous (or, for want of a better word, unpredictable). They lived their life in fear, confusion and discomfort, being that they lived in two worlds, or were driven by two sets of emotions, instincts and impulses – that of man and that of beast. I think I either tended to these creatures, or was somehow responsible for them. I didn't create them, but I remember it happening."

"I knew I was connected the very first time I saw a centaur. I saw a picture of one while reading a CS Lewis book, I think it was *The Last Battle*... not sure. Anyway, although I didn't know about Lemuria, I did remember, in fine detail, working with these animals. I only realized it was Lemuria I was thinking (and dreaming) about when, as an adult, I read an article about it. When I was a kid, after seeing my first Centaur, I used to say to my mother all the time, "Why can't I speak to the animals? Why can't I hear their voice or understand what they're saying"? And, now, I believe this was because seeing the Centaur triggered a memory of a time when I could…"

I also thought of my own love of centaurs, which I'd written about in my book White Magic. Masculine and kind, musical and full of healing wisdom, the Centaur Chiron is one of my guides... I wondered if this was the truth of the being known as Chiron – the being who brought medicine and healing to the world. Could he be one of the founders of Lemuria? I returned my attention to Scott, who was explaining his deep love of animals...

"I have always loved – no, actually … been obsessed by (that's a better way to describe it) animals. And anyone who knows me well would attest to that. So, after reading about the Centaur, I wanted to know more about "mixed up animals" and so I read anything I could find that even slightly hinted at crypto-zoology. I stalked the garden for faeries and played in the forest that bordered my home as a child looking for Yetis. And the rest is history … what with the path I follow, my books, and so on … "

Everything he was sharing made so much sense to me – not just in a mental, or "thought" sense, but at a deep and knowing level, where his words seemed like a story he was telling me about my own life, too! I at once felt that Scott was on to something profound, with Lemuria being a motherland for animals and magickal beings that have since populated the entire world. I also feel that many of the Lemuria-people became the land itself; the mer-people; the elves of the inner earth worlds; and sky-beings... They could travel across time, which to me is the explanation for why we cannot find traces of their civilisations – until they choose to reveal them to us. They have been transported to a different dimension, like the tales of faerylande with beings who can change from tall, giant-like elves to the tiniest of sprites and pixies.

Wondering if my ideas were too strange, I mentioned this to Scott. What did he think of the notion of giants, for example?

To my surprise, Scott had similar views! "I remember, very clearly, being visited by a giant once. I was about five or six and he loomed over me as I stood looking up into his eyes one evening in my cubby house. He had to stoop right over (he was about 9 feet tall) and his upper back sat firm against the tin roof of the cubby house."

"And on another occasion, when I was about eight or nine, I remember seeing "monkey-like fingers" clutching the edge of the air-vent that sat in the ceiling of our bathroom. Whatever was attached to the fingers was watching me through the vent, and when I spotted them, I gasped, and the fingers quickly withdrew and were gone … "

"I have memories of waking alone, at night, outside, and then waking to find myself back in bed, with mud up my legs and covering my feet … but being that we lived in tropical Queensland at the time and I was wearing summer, light-weight pyjamas, I can't begin to imagine where the mud came from … "

As Scott told me his story, I wondered whether he had travelled in time... I checked in with my intuition, and it relayed back to me that yes, he had experienced a kind of dimensional slip, where Scott had walked back into his own past life, and his previous self had given him a sign of what he was to do in this lifetime. It was something I had experienced myself as a child, with my waterfall hideaway which I had never been able to find as a grown-up. Children, truly, can navigate these dimensional slips so easily, because they are not yet consciously looking, or full of doubt.

I was excited by this possibility. What if civilisations that seemed to "disappear" –

leaving behind massive structures like the temples of Angkor Wat, had time-travelled out of that place, and exist elsewhere now. What if they were taken home?

I too had memories of an amazing place...where food was plentiful and life peaceful, where we partook of meaningful movement and ceremony daily, and where some kind of glowing mineral was consumed... It was time to ask more from the present day Lemurians about their memories of daily life!

A SACRED SOCIETY

So what was daily life like in the world of Lemuria? Perhaps the nearest word we have to describe the experience of being a member of Lemuria is *tribal*. Tribal cultures most often have a sense of family that extends well beyond the idea we have of family today. In a sense, the tribe is the extended family, with defined roles and each member of the clan caring for the others, with totems and signs that distinguish each role, and each tribe, one from the other.

In Lemuria, each and every person and being was considered a brother or sister to the other...there was no sense of having a separate self, and thus the notion of mirroring, or projection of our problems onto others, which creates disharmony in our time, was absent. If we saw need, or lack, we helped. We had a duty of care to one and all, and all had that in return too.

According to Dr Ballard, we "were all manifestations of the father and mother, and life was lived tribally, simply, with shamanic practice the bedrock of the culture. Lemurian society was based on a clan system.

"There were no vertical hierarchies – no better than or less than. People followed their heart's calling and lived their deep inner passion – in regard to relationships, "work" or vocation, and in what form they honoured The All and The Earth Mother. All was done in joy, creativity and harmony.

"They came together in groupings for a particular purpose they were called to at a particular time. A leader would emerge to focus the project until the task was completed, and would then step down. This was a fluid, natural, organic coming together of like resonances for particular purposes, and then a dissolving once completion occurred."

LIVING IN LEMURIA

Lemuria, with her waterfalls and lush forests impregnated with fruits and flowers and wild, peaceful beings, was a transparent society, and an extraordinarily innocent time – indeed the garden of Eden. Lies could not be told for most of its history, as the highly psychic and telepathic peoples could see exactly what was happening, moment by moment. Thus there was a kind of honesty and transparency that we can only imagine.

It's important to understand that the innocence of Lemurians was not always to their advantage. As Ralph Ballard says, "Lemurians tended just to see the Divine Light at the core of a person and could disregard any unconscious, ugly or damaged/damaging outer aspects of the person. It was like only seeing the divinity within Jack The Ripper, and not perceiving his wild, damaged aspects which could murder you."

The physicality of the Lemurians was both of the flesh and the spirit – they were the perfect marriage of both. Lemurians did not consider the body a shell; nor did they revere the intellect above the body, nor did they pine so for the spirit that they neglected the physical self. They had integrated spirit, matter and mind...they were One Being. The body was considered to be the perfect articulation of the mind and the spirit... a healthy form created beautiful minds. Physical pleasure was a spiritual past-time. There was not this separation, this dualism that we today seem to so struggle with.

A site which retains strong and vibrant Lemurian energy to this day can be found on the beautiful northern east coast of Australia. The area known as Byron Bay is one of the counterculture capitals of the world...it too is built on the obsidian left behind from the outpourings of the sacred site now known as Mt Warning. Casting out all that is negative, shielding these sacred lands from destruction, Byron Shire is a magnet for people wanting to explore who they really are. It has attracted people who are passionate about organics, sustainable living, harmonious relationships, healthy bodies, minds and souls for many years. My family lives near this area, and I've spent many years in this town and its surrounds.

One day, while gazing out at Mt Warning, I felt I saw it shift and move... it seemed an energy was radiating out from the very top of the mountain, which is a sacred site to the local Aboriginal people. But it felt alive, like it was communicating, and it brought home to me the fact that the Earth herself is sentient – is intelligent and aware, and is communicating with us all the time. We are, now, somewhat out of touch with this communication with the Mother. We have forgotten to listen to her heartbeat. We have tried to change her pulse, and move faster. We are interfering with her sonic rhythms and her song, so her voice is muffled to her creatures.

Some say the original beings of Lemuria were giants...and this makes me wonder...could the giants of Mu now be the land itself, now. Is Mt Warning one of the Lemurians?

THE LAW OF ONE

Lemurians were, and still are, peaceful, tribal people who are advocates of mutual responsibility and caring. Their nature was and is social – not in the sense of wanting to be around people all the time, but in terms of community. Lemurian communities were organically developed so that each person had others they could rely on, and be helped by. As everything was exchanged by barter, and as each person had something to offer, Lemurians thrived, and lived on an earth that was peaceful, and plenteous. Vegetables and fish were the predominant diets, and many Lemurians were purely vegetarian. Their DNA strands were fully activated: they could shapeshift and see far into time.

Lemurians were balanced beings: in betweeners, if you like. They were not competitive, nor were they interested in definitions of difference: they nevertheless delighted in diversity. Their hair was long, on men and women, and was worn locked, actually no – this is the natural way in which their hair grew. Each of the locks received information from far away, and as stated before, each could unfurl and live quite independently. It's a function of our DNA-deactivation tragedy that we are no longer able to truly activate our hair – though this is becoming more likely as time goes by and we approach a sort of timelessness … They could breathe underwater via their third eye, and in many ways Lemurians are more akin to mammals of the sea, than the land-dwelling creatures!

As Lemurians did not experience stress, they did not experience disease. Thus life to them was very simple…seasonal eating, building non-permanent homes, living outdoors for as much time as possible, able to work with sunlight and moonlight extremely effectively without becoming "wired" as we are often by moonlight, or becoming burnt and dehydrated as we can be by sunlight. We still need both.

Homes were round, with open sections for sunlight to pour into…darkness was welcomed and they could move about easily, simply by using their sight and sensitivity. Lemurians slept for between four to five hours, and conducted a great deal of dream travel and communication. Their dreams were extremely lucid and vivid, and sometimes accentuated by the judicious and wise use of powerful plants and herbs. There was a very fluid and harmonious relationship between the dream state, the waking state, and the deep sleep state for Lemurians.

They watched and ritualised sunrise and sunset, and the rainbow was their symbol and sign. They did not develop machines or any kind of transportation – completely unnecessary as they could move (transportations) if they wished.

The first and most important lesson of Lemuria is that the land itself is what is sacred, and is considered to be alive. This is a concept that "modern" "progressive" peoples may think they have grasped, but we need to reach back into our own ancestry to fully understand this.

When speaking with what many would call the Old Gods, who I believe are the way in which we can communicate with these times, I am often shown beings that are huge, of the mountains and the sea, with animal parts for heads, or wings, for example. (They are reminiscent of Thoth, Sekmet, Sedna and other such in-between Gods and Goddesses.) But they do not *say* that they are angels...or Gods. They say their names, and that they are what they are. And that what they are is all of the elements. They have such power, and yet have a gentle sense of humour.

One being who feels this way is White Buffalo Woman. She appears as a woman, and as buffalo, and as land. She appears in white, and from a star.

All of these beings remind us that we are here courtesy of the mother of us all, the Earth. And that though some of us have come from other star systems, we remain here thanks to the generosity and nurturing of this blue and green planet.

Lemurians were not competitive or liars or deceitful and cruel, and lying was in fact *inconceivable*. That's why we were able to work clairvoyantly – we were actually transparent. People and spiritual folks have taken this to mean that we were physically transparent – while we were certainly light-bodied human beings, we were not completely transparent or etheric. We were fully, in fact MORE fully physical. It was that we were clear and transparent in our whole selves … unable to be artificial. All shone out, and all was known, and we absorbed a great deal...

In Lemuria, each and every person and being was considered a brother or sister to the other...there was no sense of having a separate self, and thus the notion of mirroring, or projection of our problems onto others, which creates so much disharmony in our time, was absent. If we saw need, or lack, we helped. We had a duty of care to one and all, and all had that in return to us. The difference is that this law, or reciprocal care, was fulfilled without the thought of anyone taking advantage of it. So anyone who may be injured was made whole. Anyone who was hungry was fed. Anyone who was unwell, was healed. This healing took place via energetic transformations...the physical bodies of the Lemurians were far more mutable than those of present-day humans. They were able to work with whichever of the elements would most assist in the healing process.

One of the more alarming memories that had occurred while in my meditations was of being a slave in Atlantis – but I appeared in my vision to be my Lemurian self. While trying to pinpoint the timing, I realised my experience as a slave could not have taken place during the days of Lemuria. You see, in Lemuria, slavery was abhorrent. I was able to shapeshift, and breathe underwater. Finally, I escaped Atlantis by shapeshifting with the help of dolphin friends...and became what is more commonly known as a mermaid... I realised after much searching and questioning that this vision related to an Atlantean experience of my Lemurian self. You see, in Lemuria, slavery was abhorrent... These concepts, such as servitude, really were unheard of in Lemuria, and would have been the closest thing to sin these beings, our forebears, could have imagined. But life, day to day life, was simple. Allyson Tanner remembers her time as being full of laughter and community.

"Life was good, peaceful, simple but plentiful. I lived in a hut-like dwelling with a small farm attached near the ocean. It was just Father and me, but we were happy. The people in my village were like a big family, all helping each other and supporting everyone. No one was ever poor as all people lived much the same way and only places such as temples were adorned, or buildings of significance."

"Every week our village leaders would walk throughout the village and welcome people to speak with them. They treated everyone with respect and didn't see themselves better than anyone else. They would also organise a weekly celebration in the village for everyone to enjoy and many other celebrations would follow for special days. During the celebrations, we would give thanks to each other and to Mother Earth for all she provided us. During these celebrations I would meet up with other young people, dance, play instruments and have fun."

It sounds wonderful in some ways, familiar in others. Lemurians lived for thousands of years, in many diverse areas and clans, so the distinct nature of our memories is only natural.

The homes of the Lemurians worked with the light that was available – as we are designed to. In each home, many of which contained the number five in its making (the basis too for the pentagram), homes were illuminated with sunlight, sunset and sunrise, and starlight and moonlight.

The tribes of Lemuria communicated telepathically, and there was a central form of tribal elders, each a representative of the tribe of their place...agreements and disagreements were not uncommon – but violence and war-like solutions were not an issue.

I received a lot of information about Lemuria whenever I was at the ocean's shore. Either there, or in a deep forest, information would flow through to me in waves, like pulses from another time. I could see pictures, hear words, see symbols. Grasping it, translating it has proved very difficult at times! But the more I connected, the calmer I became, the more able to handle the pulsing informational waves. I worked in the garden. The visions were lengthy, but they were wonderful. I felt so grateful to have this connection, and to be receiving the answers from a place growing more and more familiar.

Out in the garden, or by the ocean shore, sometimes just with the bountiful dolphin energy of saltwater, and the sacred lake of the Biripi people, more and more visions were streaming through. Memories, of a land before time.

This hot, tropical environment, where we lived on land and in the sea for at least equal amounts of time meant clothing as protection against weather was not necessary. So decoration, and communication was the purpose of "wearing" clothing. There were natural fibres woven from plants, dyed with indigo and stained with ochre. When insects were more plentiful, and could no longer be talked from attempting to feast on us, we simply covered ourselves in thick, damp ochre from the rivers that flowed so plentifully into the oceans. When we did this, the soothing comfort was beautiful, and after washing it off under freshwater waterfalls, we felt so blessed and purified that this ritual worked its way into our lives.

SEXING LATER

"Our nature of old was not the same as it now is. It was then androgynous...
...Hence Zeus divided them into two."

– Plato, 429-327 BC

Lemurians are and were extremely long-lived, gentle and wise. They were not polarised beings, and this was reflected in their sexuality.

You see, many earthkeeper cultures do not have a dualistic system of gender classification: just as there are various sexes within the animal kingdom, including among sea creatures, deer population and many birds, humans too have long had more than two categories. To this day, despite many attempts to make these amazing people conform, with either operations, drugs, or going into hiding, there remain the Fa'afafine in Polynesia, the Hijra in India, Xanith in Oman, Fakaleiti in Tonga, Phet thee sam in Thailand, Muxe in Oaxaca, and two-spirit people in some of the native American tribes.

My guides explained to me that these people were of Lemurian descent – as we all are – but that these people are returning to show us all that there is much more to being human than what we think.

In the first times of Lemuria, there was very little sexual differentiation...lives were long, and procreation was not such an issue. But then the Lemurians began to experiment with the form that their physicality could take. And thus individual souls had the choice of whether to be "male" or "female" but for many, this was a differentiation and choice that was made after adolescence – and sometimes several times during the one lifetime.

Lemurians experienced sexual differentiation: ie, they were what we describe as men and women, but they did not sexually differentiate until later in life. Their language, was not their primary mode of communication – telepathy was often used – and sound was a healing and sacred vehicle for the soul. However, language did develop, a spoken and written language.

In Ancient Sanskrit, we find the interesting anomaly of three genders being referred to. (This pattern occurs in German, and some other languages...) Could it be that the Sanskrit language, the keeper of the sacred sounds of Lemuria, refers to the way in which Lemurians lived in a less gender-oriented culture than ours?

Not until twelve or thirteen did young people take on fully defined sexual characteristics, and the change which came to them was beautiful, and gentle, and an awakening into their next self. They experienced a name change and ritual at this stage, but the ritual was to recognise the biological and spiritual shift which they had been through. To this day, we humans need ritual to acknowledge our own coming into manhood, into womanhood. This ritual need, anchored deep within our own genetic history and our bloodline, and remembered by our spiritual cycles, creates a yearning for this choice and recognition.

LEMURIAN CRYSTALS

The Lemurian crystals are programmed by the inhabitants said to be priests, with love and healing vibes, with the knowledge that we are all one. There are striated edges that resemble a code, which will activate with the coming earth changes. We can activate by touching and holding this surface and feeling the codes.

During the last days of Lemuria, special seed crystals were planted where crystalline growth was expected to form over the coming millennia within the Earth (millions of years ago) in order to transmit frequencies to other crystals that were created throughout time. The special messages transmitted are of equality and are excellent for channeled work. They create the energy of love, unity, and equality for all. The specialized purpose created by Lemurian seed crystals is to open up clear conscious telepathy and assist in creating a holographic connection with the outer multi-dimensional universe.

Seed crystals, sometimes called star seed crystals, are predominantly mined in Brazil. Lemurian crystals can be recognised by the striations running horizontally across the facets. These striations are said to contain codes – for healing, wisdom, knowledge, which once connected with, can activate ancient knowledge with the crystal's keeper. They are called "seed" crystals as they are here to seed the ancient knowledge – they are the point of origin for the growth and return of Lemurian wisdom. They literally "grow" other crystals and grow our knowledge, wisdom, balance and understanding of our planet, our collective galatic and earthly history, and awaken our DNA. Some believe that these seed crystals were not actually planted by the Lemurians, but by galactic beings seeding the galaxies – thus they are called star seeds by many.

It is also said that the Lemurians left this planet and "returned". But my feeling is that they originated here, and some survived and stayed and others went elsewhere.

Others still went below the planet – into what is known as middle earth. The elves.

However, many of the Lemurians also went into inner earth and it is from within that domain that they still care for the earth and are responsible for these crystals surfacing now. One of the main purposes of these seed crystals is to create complete holographic unity. It only requires one Lemurian Seed Crystal to holographically connect to all seed crystals. This energetic connection forms an energy grid around the earth which links us to inner and outer worlds.

Many people believe that there were two moons at this point in earth…one smaller than our present sister-self. Her silvery light refracts and works with sunlight and light from other galaxies, pouring crystalline beams into us…olivine, the black crystal onyx and labradorite…and of course, an abundance of volcanic glass – or obsidian…

Lemurian crystals are said to be located in Brazil … one particular mine has brought forth many seed crystals and wands. They are said to be energetically linked to all other seed crystals, and create a kind of Lemurian web. They are said to have been planted in the last days of Lemuria beneath the earth's surface for protection, as they were so powerful.

When we examine the shamanic initiation ceremonies of indigenous peoples (and we are ALL indigenous peoples!) the vital importance of the power association with crystals and sacred stones becomes very clear.

The elders of the Arunta people of Australia tell how the potential wise man goes to a cave, where he waits. If he draws the energy of the dreamtime spirits to him, he undergoes a series of tests. A spear will be thrown at him, passing through his body at specific points. When he "dies" he is taken into the cave by the spirits, and his internal organs are removed and replaced with quartz crystals.

"Among the Wiradjeri people of western New South Wales the power of the crystals stems from the fact that they are believed to embody the essence of Baiame, the All-father or Great Sky-God of the people … two great quartz crystals extend from his shoulders to the sky above him, and Baiame sometimes appears in their dreams, causing a sacred waterfall of liquid quartz to pour over their bodies. Absorbing their bodies, and they grow wings instead of arms. Later the dreamer learns to fly and Baiame sinks a magical quartz into his forehead to enable him to see inside physical objects. Subsequently an inner flame and a heavenly cord are also incorporated into the body of the new shaman." These words are from Nevill Drury's fabulous book, *Magic and Witchcraft*. So the shamans of the present and of the past are an actual blending of the celestial and the terrestrial. No wonder so many of us are passionate about our relationships with crystals!

LEMURIAN CRYSTAL HEALING

In more visions, I was shown clearly that there were many sacred stones in Lemuria. Some were worn, and each clan was the protector of a stone: within this stone was the collective wisdom and information of the tribe. Bring the stones together, activate them, and you had a power source with infinite knowledge: an energetic library able to be connected with. These sacred stones were protected, highly taboo for any but the most sacred to work with, and eventually were sought after. Jewels were not worn just for adornment in Lemuria...however, this was a very beautiful society, and there was such joy and honour in wearing one's clan stone! Every adornment had a ritual and special function. For example, there were the crystals worn by clans, and as a signifier of that person's skills and training and affinity with a star-group, too. The crystal clan system was as follows:

* Rose quartz worn by beings working with unconditional love.

*Clear quartz for beings who communicated frequently between species, and intergalatically (clear quartz is a neutral amplifier and was best for this practice at that time).

*Peridot for beings working with plants and growth and foods and moonlight and tides and growing cycles (the lunar geology is primarily peridot in its crystal construct).

*Larimar for those working with the oceanic beings; stone for those working with shapeshifting into the earth to renew her.

*Obsidian for those who were the protectors. Obsidian throws up a natural shield that is deeply protective. It is a stone that has a huge impact on our nervous system: until we adjust to working with it, we can experience some light-headedness. However, over time, it is very grounding, protective and shielding.

*Turquoise for moving more deeply into the ways of the earth – beings who were ambassadors into the dryer areas wore this to protect them when they were far away from the vibration of salt water.

Though this was not a hierarchy as such, it was indeed a clan totem, or web.

The crystal healing that took place was very natural, simple and powerful. Sacred spaces were chosen for their inherent healing energies to conduct the healings within. These were often forests or sea shores, where negative ions abound. Negative ion-rich environments are naturally healing and uplifting, and very simple to work with.

The healer and the being to be healed sat opposite each other. The healer generated their crystalline self, and beamed out light. Their hands transformed into long tentacles that could go into the auric field and remove woundings. Sometimes, later in Lemuria, it became clear that psychic attack was taking place. The Lemurian response, to send love, was sadly unable to stop the flood of illness that swept through the clan system... while they maintained their purity and beauty, many Lemurians died from this soul-sickness. Dealing with hate and envy, literally, killed many Lemurians, or caused them to transform out of their first forms, which were too easily detectable, into other, new forms that allowed the Lemurians to continue to do their work undetected. For example, many beings shapeshifted into merbeings. Like me!

A LIVING CHAKRA SYSTEM

In Lemuria, it was simple to see and read chakras, and auras – they were absolutely visible, and considered as normal a part of a person as your head is to you today. To walk about without a fully visible auric field and chakra system was as unthinkable as walking about without a head!

These chakras and auric fields were therefore as "real" as an internal organ, and we ALL were able to see each chakra, able to discern an individual's wellbeing and state of "mind" and emotions visually. Add to that telepathic communication and we have a very clear and honest culture.

We also developed hand signals at this time, as the voice was primarily used for sacred work. In my visions, water beings had teardrop shaped chakras and auras, others star-shaped, others lunar-shaped, which is where the sacred Avalonian symbol of the crescent on the third eye region comes from. (Mine was higher, and I believe that there was a series of them on my brow representing lunar phases ...)

Star-beings had a star-shaped third eye region... those of the Earth's were rounded, and solid. A crystal was sometimes found in the body at each chakra point...and often at the third eye chakra. These crystals were a natural part of the Lemurian's body, and developed there over time from the interaction between beings and crystals, and their interaction was cellular...thus we were truly crystal beings.

In Lemuria, connection to the elements was natural. Working with each element was a very natural way of life. Each morning, the dawn was greeted. Each evening, the sun was farewelled, and each member of the clan was bathed in the light of the sunrise and sunset, which activated and cleansed each chakra.

Ritual and magick were as natural as breathing in Lemuria – and as natural as breathing underwater, as my memories showed me... Ritual was conducted in large, regularly timed gatherings, of which the medicine wheel and the moon times of the first Americans, and the wheel of the year in the Celtic tradition both sustain that practice today.

As we work with this wheel today, we begin to again support and honour our mother the Earth, and acknowledge ourselves as both celestial in form and terrestrial. As above, so below!

And honour the wheel of the year, wherever you are.

EATING FOR YOUR LIGHTBODY

I have long felt that living simply: eating locally, organic where possible, growing your own food and food sharing were simple, but not unrealistic and unsustainable behaviours for us to aim for as humans in evolution. My own memories of Lemurian living informed me, along with my guides, that when I lived there I experienced certain food types and diets: but I knew that by following these broad principles I would reawaken the memories and maintain wholesome wellbeing this lifetime. My memories of Lemuria were vivid: eating outside communally, gathering foods in clan groups, including harvesting sea-kelp, growing and tending plants by talking to the herbs and fruiting stems, and knowing I *was* food, food *was* me, that what *I* ate *I* became, that food was a living organism with its own intelligence and sentience and way of knowing the world. I absorbed these too, when I absorbed and gave thanks for the energy exchange between plant and myself.

In Lemuria, then, what did we eat? I personally know I ate sparingly, and communicated fully with the plants I was to eat. I have no memory of eating meat or flesh at all – and I do remember supplementing my food intake with mineralised waters and crushed sea pearls...shimmering minerals and a liquid gold. Initially the only food requirement was a kind of liquid gold, an alchemised form of energy that, as Ralph Ballard says "provided all the nourishment that was needed. Sometimes other foods would be eaten purely for the pleasure and sensations of the experience – this would sometimes also be done as a form of ritual to honour the Earth Mother and her creations. These foods were mainly fruits, berries and other productions from plants."

My memories veer from this a little...perhaps this is an earlier memory of the Mu-beings' food needs...for in Lemuria I recall, food was important, as we were, remember equally physical and spiritual beings – we were fully balanced matter and soul... and I can remember the joyful gathering of the kelp and seagrass. We crushed pearls and seasoned our foods with this trace mineral, ate them, and coated our physical bodies in them...We created tattoos from our thoughts...their symbols would appear on our skin as a sign we had received the rites of that particular message...

We drank water from mineralised springs. Each spring had a distinct energy, an energy signature, and a healing quality and purpose that was unique.

One thing is for sure – we were able to absorb the rays of the sun, each of those seven rays of colour, as we do now – and my instinct tells me there were additional colours to the spectrum we see now. You see, we still require sunlight for so many purposes. The sunlight we absorb each day creates chemical transformations in our physical bodies that enable us to be healthy, confident, vital and brimming with energy. With the replacement of sunlight by, for example, electric light, our health is being seriously degraded. We still absorb the light source we interact with, despite the fact that we are not so "open" as we were in Lemuria. But rather than shut down, we need to reconnect with natural light sources, and cleanse, balance, ground and protect – that way we can absorb fully, without fear, and shine out brightly, lighting up the world.

I feel there were also much higher oxygen levels, which led to an incredible feeling and reality of well-being... All around us was the discernible heartbeat of the earth, that all seemed to "pulse" with, and over and through this beat was woven a beautiful song of harmony made up of all the individual voices of beings and creatures. The song of life was alive and well!

Foods were eaten mostly as they grew – in other words, a predominantly raw diet was followed. This was not done "consciously" – foods simply did not need to be cooked. Fresh fruits and vegetables were delicious, as were seafoods, which volunteered their lives, and were a source of necessary protein. The incredible energy of the fresh and raw food diet created a group of beings who were physically beautiful: lustrous hair that had its own life force and was certainly not the dead protein we often consider it today... and this explains our own modern fetishism with hair. When we dye and chemically poison our hair, we tend to reduce our own intuitive facility and our telepathic range. Our sensitivity is still impacted upon by this poison.

Fortunately, we are blessed to have with us many foods that the Lemurians ate, and benefitted from. I received clear images and information about this food during a powerful but very relaxing and peaceful meditation in my herb garden.

MEETING KHUMARA

One of my dreams has long been to grow a sustainable herb garden, from which I would eat, treat via herbal poultices, tinctures, teas and medicines, and grow herbal sources for smudge sticks which I would use in my space clearing work.

There was no "need" for this, except the urge, the message, the drive and a real longing to do this – and to do it within a time frame.

Digging and planting the garden helped me enormously: all of it becoming a beautiful metaphor for living a life full of meaning. Finding the right natural soil that would work with the local climate ... choosing my herbs, oregano, thyme (several varieties to bring fairies more closely into my life, as I adore them), basil for memory and focus, rosemary for past lives and peace, sage, for smudge, lavender for smudge, and several varieties of indigenous herbal plants gifted to me by a magickal horticulturalist at the Goddess Conference have all found their way into this garden. Preparing ground, nurturing with water, blessing, and seeing the bees, whose hives I hope to visit one day to taste the sage honey, the wisdom honey. This garden became devotional, and hours spent there were in service to the Goddess and to the divine. Fairies, insects of multiple hues and varieties visited me there, and then came the beings.

It was while working with sage that a certain being came to me. This future friend and trusted guide delivered information during his companionable visits, which were primarily about the connection between our physical and energetic wellbeing, and our chosen food sources. I had put it out there that I specifically wanted to connect with a Lemurian food expert … and so when one came through, who called himself Khumara, I was very happy, if a little wary initially.

Khumara was very wise-looking, with long dark hair streaked with silver that whirled about him, and long white robes. They may have been robes – they may have been light! He had a very bright and fully activated chakra system and he radiated pure health. Most bizarrely, he had a shining third eye region, like a beam of light radiating out. It wasn't exactly painful to look at: it was more like trying to stare at the sun!

Right away, he got down to business, telling me about foods I – we – needed to be eating for the health of our entire being. First up was garlic – something I was NOT planning on growing. But he convinced me otherwise!

"Dear one, you can benefit from this superfood, as it has within it something your nutritionists call allicin. This, which gives your garlic its strong and powerful odour, creates healthy levels of blood pressure; it thins your blood and also can reduce blood pressure." He chuckled, at my surprise. "In countries where people eat much of this food, there is a lower incidence of heart disease," he revealed, smiling. "If you have poor circulation," (I smiled – it's something I suffer from, with cold hands and feet) "eat more garlic – it will improve your blood circulation. It has antiseptic properties and can cleanse your system of germs and viral beings if taken raw. One clove, up to four or five times a week will make a difference," he said firmly.

He insisted that it is best NOT to take supplements, except in cases where we know well the area the garlic is grown in. Khumara was very concerned about GM modified varieties, insisting that we avoid these foods, as their impact on our bodies and on our insect and animal friends is profound. "If we are to help the honey bee continue its evolution and spread its wisdom and happiness," he said with what looked like concern, "we must turn from these foods that restrict their lifespan."

The next big "talk" from Khumara happened when I was at the beach … wondering and feeling slightly woeful about the masses of kelp rotting in the powerful sunshine. Seaweed, which I had seen so many of us eating in my visions of Lemuria, and my yearning to collect and eat seaweed found on the shore, turns out to be a modern-day Lemurian superfood! Khumara laughed when he saw how I wanted to collect the seaweed, but had been dissuaded by friends who thought I was, to put it mildly, a little more delusional than they usually thought I was. "You were on, as they say, the right track. This fruit of the sea mother contains many minerals – iodine, iron, copper, magnesium, calcium and potassium – for those of you whose power station is down, it makes the perfect food."

Okay, he lost me there. Confused, I asked him to clarify power station. "Your thyroid," he explained, making coughing noises. "It also protects you against what you call cancer and heart diseases. Eat this at least weekly," he recommended warmly, "and look how much we have provided for you."

"And yet here it lies rotting on the beach," I said, a little sadly.

Khumara laughed and said I should cheer up, and make use of what I had, rather than despairing over what had already passed. I could see the wisdom of his words, but I still found the waste sad, just as I find the sadnesses of war and harshness to each other almost unbearable at times. He looked kindly at me, as though reading my thoughts – which, of course, he had.

"On that," he said, "I have more to tell you," but that would be sufficient for that day. He faded from view, but his presence was easily felt, like a warm soft breeze, next to me. His energy was very warm, yet fresh and vital. I felt protected and calm, and very "well", full of well being – when he was around. I am blessed more and more with radiant good health as my life is lived more and more in alignment with my guidance, but being with him was truly an experience of heightened vitality and pure powerful energy.

I headed up the beach, looking at all the food, literally laying there, and wondered about we humans and our apparent belief in lack! All around me were people complaining about food prices, and yet here was Mother Earth and the sea Goddess offering us so much. And yes, it was going to waste.

I didn't have to wait long for Khumara to nudge me into further action.

For a while I had been receiving urgent intuitive messages to plant even more of my own vegetable garden: the words coming through were very clear ... "The most radical action any of you can take now is to nurture and grow and sustain your own food through planting, prayer and care. Do not hesitate!"

So, within days of Khumara's advice on the beach, there he was again one morning, out in the garden."Look at all this land he said, gesturing. "Can you not see you can create bounty?"

I nodded and got to work. Within days, the next stage of the garden had been dug by my beloved, soil turned over, and more herbs and vegetables based on Khumara's advice selected and planted.

EATING LIGHT

The pleasure I found in doing this simple thing was so profound and deep – it seemed foolish that I had not followed my intuition before.

"Because you are all so separated from the earth," Khumara explained, while I dug and planted in the early morning sun, "you think this work is not spiritual. But it is one of the greatest spiritual acts of all – and the act the first voyagers found great pleasure in when they arrived here."

I wiped the sweat from my brow – it felt good to have my hands and feet in dirt, to be out under the sun, to be tending my small crop. "Do you mean, the intergalactic beings grew their own food? How did they know to do that?"

He gestured at the aura of a plant nearby. Around it were bright lights, hovering and tending its energy system.

"Aliens were taught to plant by the fairies?" I asked.

"Who else," he smiled. "Who else knew the secrets of the plants and the growing things?"

I smiled, as I had just planted some more thyme – a herb I had been told by the fairies themselves was a signal – a sign for them to come on in! I now had three varieties, and all of the established thyme was thriving – as were my connections to the fae! They were stronger than ever, and I was loving the intensity and vivid nature of our interactions. They also seemed to ground me... quite the opposite of being "off with the faeries". I felt strong, powerful and at ease after my interactions. Better still, I could eat the foods I was growing in their honour!

While I dug and planted, visualizing and dedicating my garden to eating well and in blessed energy, Khumara continued with his lecture on Lemurian foods.

"Do you know what you're eating right now?" he said, teasingly. He certainly has a sense of humour!

"No," I answered, looking at him with a smile.

"You're EATING LIGHT."

"Oh. I hope you're not going to tell me to be a breatharian," I grinned. "I don't think I could do that. I love being in a body, I love my body, and I love and am grateful to be able to eat... I love this interaction with all that is!"

"No," he said, shaking his head. "Breatharian? That would be foolish indeed! You have not yet evolved to that stage."

I rolled my eyes. "I feel so... so *unevolved* when people and beings say that," I said. "I feel like you think or feel it's less to be in a physical body," I grumped. "I love this planet, this life, this form. I feel blessed!"

"Not true," he said, chuckling at my discomfiture. "We in fact love physicality, and many of us wish for this experience again. Oh no – we advise you to relish it. There will be time enough as a pure energy body. But you do, nonetheless, drink the light, much as we do. Much," he said, pointing at the herbs I was planting – this time a grandfather sage – " as they do, too."

"Have you not thought about what they breathe out, you breathe in?" he continued.

"Of course I have," I harrumphed. I must admit, all the toil in the garden was making me less patient with my guide. "I know every breath is a blessing. I know they can drink what I breathe out."

"But you transform light, too – into vitamins and minerals. You need the light. That's one reason," he said, just a tad smugly, "I got you out here."

"Tell me more about food," I said, to distract him.

"Well," he said, "let me start with something that's going to regulate your hormones."

"Are you saying I'm premenstrual?"

He raised an etheric eyebrow. "You KNOW you are!"

At that point I jokingly flung a clod of earth at him, which of course sailed right through his etheric body, and made him laugh harder. "Oh, I had forgotten what pleasure there is in teasing you!"

"EAT LIKE A DOLPHIN!"

Soon after our light-eating discussion, we moved onto more "earthy" topics!

While I was struggling with the weeds near my spinach (Khumara didn't need to tell me about her benefits!) my Lemurian friend showed me a small grain, only a little larger than sesame seeds, and I frowned, trying to make sense of the speck in his golden hands. I gave up.

"What's that?"

"It's what you people call linseed," he explained. "It helps to regulate you females with your moon times – and when those moon cycles are undergoing change. It contains," he said, screwing up his handsome face, "phytoestrogens – yes, that's correct, and they help regulate the hormone you call oestrogen. It also has omega three fatty acids."

"I thought they were in fish," I said, slightly puzzled.

"Oh they are – and we'll get to that," he said. "You are going to eat like a dolphin!"

I frowned, feeling irritated. Maybe I *was* hormonal!

"They're also in this powerful little seed," he explained, holding up something I could barely see and looking serious. "It alleviates infection, it is an anti-inflammatory, works to regulate the bowels, lowers cholesterol and, er, reduces breast tenderness at your moon times." He had the grace to look slightly abashed.

"But let's not forget fish," he went on. "You know you ate seaweed and grains and fish, of course, in Lemuria. The trick," he explained, "is to eat like a dolphin."

"I'm hot. I'm going to be like a dolphin and get into some water," I said, gesturing towards the house. I walked to the back of the house and stood under the outdoor shower my beloved has rigged up. Khumara appeared in the sunlight, and continued talking to me as though I hadn't just walked fifty metres away!

"Your body cannot create the EFA's you need," he explained peacefully, "so you must ingest them – another reason complete absorption of light only is not advisable right now. If you eat them, all your organs benefit, and feel revitalized, your skin plumps up, looking firmer and thus what you call younger, and your hair and nails become the sensory antennae they are meant to be."

"Are you saying I'll be more psychic if I eat these foods?" I asked, wrapping a towel around myself before turning off the shower.

"I can see through that anyway," he pointed out.

"Never mind," I said. "I'd prefer if you didn't look. So, if you eat oily fish three times a week, you will have a healthier skin, hair, nails, heart and immune system, your brain will function better AND you will be more psychic?"

"Indeed."

"All that from fish?"

"From fish," he sighed. "You know you ate them when you were a mermaid."

And with that, he vanished, faster than it would seem he should have in the drenching sunlight he stood in. I sighed, headed inside, still dripping, grabbed a notebook, and wrote everything down as rapidly as I could. (I left quite a puddle on the couch!)

Interestingly, when I have these visitations, it's not like I have to remember anything, it's more like I have put the information on a memory stick, and then plugged it in. Out it poured, just as he'd said it. I felt relieved, as so much was valuable, and I looked forward to being able to share Khumara's wisdom about food in Lemuria – and experiencing its power myself!

Of course, fish are now endangered due to trawling and our indiscriminate taking from the ocean. Initially after receiving this information I felt at peace with the idea of eating fish. But now, I choose when I eat fish carefully, and choose fish from sources that have been hunted in ethical ways. I am currently planning on creating the right balance of EFAs through plant based foods for now. Please do as your conscious advises.

At the time of this experience I had a working knowledge of the notion of ascended masters, but it is not, and was not, an area of particular interest or expertise. I felt my connection to God and Goddess energy very strongly, and my interaction with them had been primarily through dear friends sharing their experiences of them. I was interested, but not eager for interaction, I guess you could say. So I was amazed when during a Lemurian workshop a participant shared with me that Sanat Kumara is an ascended master, who has long been revered in Hindu and Zoroastrian paths. He is also said by theosophists, who I also have kinship with, but less interaction, that he is in continuous telepathic communication with Gaia! And the consciousness of the sun. When I thought about my interactions with him later, I realized that they had all taken place in the sunshine. Was "my" Khumara and the ascended master known as Sanat Kumara the same being?

After the first draft of the manuscript was complete, Kylie McDonough, who was working on the maps, asked me whether the being called Chumara (who has spoken with me throughout the creation of the *Oracle of the Dragonfae*) and this being (surely not coincidentally called Khumara) were related.

As Chumara's domain is akin to Spider-Woman's, her realm is about interconnection and "taking off our false face." And being ourselves. At no stage did the Lemurian being Khumara mention this, or a connection.

But I think there is more to that story than I currently am aware of. I await Khumara and Chumara's wisdom on this – as patiently as I can!)

LEMURIAN ENERGY CENTRES

Lemurians like Khumara, the shamans, and the hybrid shapeshifters are the ancestors for the peoples of the Hawaiian islands, the current people of New Zealand, who say they came from a sunken island named Haawiken, the people of Australia, whose sacred dreamtime spirituality has remained active, though compromised by colonization, for some 60,000 years, those of Peru, the Maya, and of the Atlanteans.

There are Lemurian ruins in Hawaii, Easter island, and the very body of the earth itself is created out of the mass shapeshift of Lemurians. Many went to the sea, as dolphins and merpeople when the event took place. Others became the land itself, resolving themselves into elements that could thus be disguised from the starseed people. They were not all transformed: others remained, to ensure their bloodline remained and became a part of the new breed of beings who would soon be walking the Mother planet.

The people of Thailand's coast, Vietnam, Borneo and the people living on the land within and on the edge of the Andaman sea retain much of their Lemurian nature, as do the beings of southern Sri Lanka, and those of Vietnam, particularly around the crystal caves of Ha Long Bay.

When in Ha Long Bay in Vietnam, my Vietnamese friend Zhung told me the ancestor story of his people, of the dragons coming from the sky and meeting with the Gods of water – and the land masses of Ha Long Bay and its crystal caves are their children, their offspring. The people grew straight from there, and they were beautiful, peaceful, and happy.

As Lemuria is the motherland, and Shamballah one of her outposts, the Bon-po shamanism of Tibet, Mongolia and the first tribes of the Americas conserve kernels of this original wisdom to this day.

Lemuria was – and is – a tropical paradise, that was home to millions of beings, who grew and developed out of this planet's earths and oceans, evolving from sea beings, and able to genetically tap into the memories of being sea beings. The Incas are aware of the Mu, as are the Australian Aboriginals, Peruvians, the Maya and the Hopi.

Places where Lemurian energy exists today are many, and particularly dotted throughout the vast ocean known as the Pacific (which translates to "peaceful"). Throughout much of Melanesia, Micronesia and Polynesia, we can find these energies in pockets that are so strong, they are almost like stepping, very literally, into another world. The energy varies from island to island: from the bare, masculine energy of New Zealand to the feminine, lush energy of Phi Phi in Thailand.

Australian locations of Lemurian energy
Uluru, Darwin, Byron Bay, Bunbury, W.A. and Mandurah. Bellingen, Blue Mountains remnants. South Australia's inland tropical reef.

South East Asia
Much of Thailand's island region is dotted with wellsprings of this energy. In particular, the islands of Phi Phi – Phi Phi Don and Ley (large and small) and Krabi. The energy at Lana Bay, even after its devastation by the 2006 tsunami, is peaceful, magickal, wild and otherworldly.

New Zealand
Much of New Zealand is Lemurian, either in form or ancestry.

Malaysia
Borneo, Sarawak, Kuching area. The great apes of Borneo, the orangutans are holding a great deal of this Lemurian energy for the planet.

Japan
In 1985 off the southern coast of Yonaguni Island, the westernmost island of Japan, a Japanese dive tour operator discovered a previously unknown stepped pyramidal edifice.

This rectangular stone ziggurat, part of a complex of underwater stone structures in the area which resemble ramps, steps and terraces, is undated. These remains of a submerged civilisation connect Japan with Lemuria.

Gulf of Cambay: (off west coast of India)

In December 2000 a team from the National Institute of Ocean Technology (NIOT) discovered the remains of a huge, lost city, thirty-six metres underwater in the Gulf of Cambay, off the western coast of India. This has the foundations of huge structures, pottery, sections of walls, beads, pieces of sculpture and human bone. One of the wooden finds supposedly from the city has given a radiocarbon date of 7,500 BCE, which would make the site 4,000 years earlier than the oldest known civilisation in India.

These are only some of the global sites of Lemurian energy. Anywhere there is tropical vibrancy, peaceful people, and open hearted ones, there you encounter the magicks and the truths of Lemuria. But oh, to combine that and to step on her shores – that power is truly life-changing!

THE MAGICKS OF LEMURIA

Many people have strong, vivid memories of the way in which Lemurian spirituality was expressed, including science student and animal shaman, Allyson Tanner. Allyson remembers a lifetime as an assistant to one of the high priestesses in the central healing temple in a large village, where people from all around Lemuria would come for deep treatment to purify their physical and etheric bodies. "The temple had an opening to allow for ancestors, guides and universal information to enter and leave," Allyson explains. "It also allowed for the sun and moon to shine their light in and directly onto the crystal healing bed. The bed was not like today's crystal beds but rather a beautiful cradle of clear quartz, with softened points which the patients lay down in. Other crystals were used and healing mandalas were drawn onto the patient using pigments."

As our shamanic remnants teach us, we are part of an enormous galactic web of life. When the planets, and galaxies are in particular positions, we are able to communicate, build energy, and release energy from both our physical body and our lightbody. In Lemuria, we could see, very clearly, any stains, damage or toxins building up in our light body. In fact, seeing the light body was as simple as "seeing" the body is today. We did not simply see the person's physical being – we always saw their soul.

Healings were conducted at specific times: conjunction with the sun's position in the sky or the astrological alignment of the moon to give the patient the maximum healing effect. It makes sense. You see, at eclipse time, for example, the atmosphere is absolutely loaded with positive ions, shifting the electrons in the environment, charging the atmosphere so that it has a tangibly different feel. And in Lemuria, there were many priestesses – "The priestessess were women of great integrity and never once did they abuse the healing power they received. They also prescribed everyone in the village their primary crystal for them to wear. This crystal would change if the person visited the temple seeking guidance and healing for whatever they were going through or about to go through. So, an external signifier was always worn, linking one with their villages. When these clans came together at the great gatherings, the power of the stones was immense, and safely worked with," says Allyson.

WHY PRACTISE LEMURIAN MAGICKS?

In these times, there are so many modalities to choose from. We are told which way to spin our merkabas, who exactly inhabited Atlantis, why we must follow certain gurus.

And to all of it, the old ones laugh quietly. There is no cruelty in their laughter. There is wisdom. You see, they have seen it all before.

There can be an arrogance to those who believe they have the one truth or way: they feel they must keep pace with a changing spiritual landscape, and must have the way to ascend and become higher, and greater, and more evolved.

When we begin to look at the deep shamanic practices of peoples as diverse as the Hawaiian, with their beautiful Kahuna, to the Mayan, to the aboriginal people of Australia and the animists of south-east Asia, there are some very strong themes all these practices have in common.

From observing these, and by drawing upon the reservoir of ancient knowledge, we can then create globally relevant forms of magick that speak to the human spirit. I feel that it is these very simple and profound practices that will reinvite the magicks of Lemuria into our lives today.

What results will these practices have? In my own experience and observations, they result in the following.

   *A sense of who you truly are
   *Acceptance and activation of your own truth
   *An ability to discern quickly and with wisdom
   *Movement away from anger, fear and other pathologies
   *Humility and heart-centred living
   *Increased self-reliance: ability to manifest what is truly needed
   *Honour without force

LEMURIAN MAGICKAL PRACTICE ONE: ELEMENTAL HEALING

Working with each of the elements creates a wonderful connection to our selves, and can strengthen and reignite many of our dormant powers – even "switch on" our dormant DNA. As the Lemurians knew, our relationships with the elements is crucial to our healing, and our healing is surely the purpose and focus of much of our spell casting.

Each of the five elements are sacred: earth, air, fire, water and spirit. Each element has a unique energy and resonance, and all are in balance. We work with their energies, and the various blending of their energies in spells, rituals, and when we cast circle, within which is our sacred "world between worlds". In circle, we ask the elements to join us for our sacred work. Spirit, the fifth element which holds all else in balance, has not the definitions of the other elements. It is unique and personal to each person working with magic.

The five elements which I work with are by no means universal, or absolute: it is the model with which I most resonate. When I meditated on the Lemurian way of working with the elements, they were very encouraging. They explained to me that unless we can absorb and internalise the lessons of each element, it is difficult for us to come from our wisdom while we are in physical form!

Elements are associated with the directions of the compass, however in meditation it was explained to me by some Lemurian elders that it is a matter of personal preference whether you work within the model they proposed as a galactic standard, or whether you adapt these associations to reflect the natural features of the region you are working within, or whether you work utterly intuitively... The most important aspect of working with the elements is learning their unique qualities – honoring them as the sacred expressions of the planet and the Universe that they are.

Please note that these are traditional northern directions, which I sometimes work with intuitively. Intuitive it may be, but is often wise to adapt the direction you place an element when casting circle according to where that element can be found in your location. This truly honours the spirit of place. So, if I was working for a particular reason – to connect with the locality or the Spirits for example, in the east coast of Australia, I would place water in the East, the air in the South, the fire in the North and the earth in the West. Note that this circle is cast in the direction the sun moves in the Southern hemisphere – anti-clockwise. We open, or close the Circle in the opposite way to which it is opened, so it is an unwinding. This can seem very complex and tricky but is actually very practical and simple once you think it, feel it and walk it through several times, so don't let the challenge put you off! It is well worthwhile doing, as it brings us closer to understanding the land we find ourselves walking on, and gives us the opportunity to honour the land, the sea, the sky and the fire in a very real and connected way.

AIR

When we work with air, we are working with our intellect, our ideas, our ability to stay light, and our own breath. If we have experienced past life trauma via the abuse of the element air, we may have trouble with our breathing. To bring air into our spell casting, focus on the breath during ritual, and explore magickal methods of breathing to raise energy, and to change consciousness.

Air: Mental faculties, thinking, ideas, conceptualizing, swift, subtle, light, unpredictable.
Direction: East (traditional northern hemisphere)
Colors: White, pale blues, gray, the colors of clouds
Altar tools: Athame (a short knife worked with to cut cords, to distinguish space, to detach entities. It is *never* used to cut on the physical plane.) Incense, oil burning (the vapor represents air), feathers
When to work with air: When we feel "heavy", for writer's block and inspiration, for original approaches to solving problems, to "lighten up", to release attachment to the material. When we need to bring our "head" into a situation. A Lemurian healing featuring air would focus on breath work, and utilize fresh air, breathing in concert with others, feathers, and calling up the winds to blow away whatever was causing us to feel out of balance!

FIRE

When we work with fire, we can be reunited with our power, our sexual fire, and our ability to tell the truth. It can be as incandescent as rage, and as gentle as a warm heart. Its variations determine its purpose and its outcome. To bring fire into our spell casting, concentrate on discovering your passion, and work with fire through candles, your cauldron, and your physicality.

Fire: Sexuality, strength, the urge to action, purification, our instinctual nature, our urge to move and express our natures physically. Its energy is extended, extroverted, and desires to find passionate expression.
Direction: South
Colors: All the variations of flame...
Altar tools: Wand, candles
When to work with fire: When our sexuality is diminished, when our desire feels flattened, when we are depressed, when we no longer care, have ennui or apathy, when we have relinquished the desire for passion, when we have stale life circumstances.

WATER

When we work with water we are feminine, sensual, and powerful. We can be strong as a wave, or persistent and annoying as a dripping tap. We can be clean and pure and refreshing, or muddy and carrying toxins. We can be crying, or we can be moist with desire. Water is a beautiful element to work with in bathing, our fluids, liquids and drinking ritually. Potions are strong water magic.

Water: The nurturing, cleansing, psychic and emotional element, its energy is receptive, feminine, flowing, tidal, surging, in sync with the moon.
Direction: West
Colors: Blue, blue-green, green, gray, indigo, aquamarine, white
Altar Tools: Chalice, cauldron, mirrors, scrying bowls...any receptacle that can "hold" water
When to work with water: When we are running dry emotionally, when we feel thirsty or dehydrated, when we are rigid and lacking the ability to flow or change, when we feel we have been "sucked dry". Can assist with depression and infertility. Bleeding, menstrual issues, issues of cleansing. Lemurians often worked with water and the moon to recharge and cleanse their very visible auras.

EARTH

To introduce earth to your Lemurian connection, consider what you may wish to bring into the material world, what you may wish to realise. Earth magic will help you to create, in a solid three dimensional form, thought forms that exist on other planes. When we work with earth, consider the food you eat, the clothing you wear, and the form of your body itself – all of these are expressions of earth magic.

Earth: Internal, shifting, yet stable, the feminine element of earth is the practical element that is expressed in the material...it can create food, and it can forge jewels.
Direction: North
Altar tools: Stones, crystals, jewels, sea salt, earth itself
When to work with earth: When we are unable to commit, when we wish to lose weight or similarly reshape our body, when we work with environmental issues. For assistance with animals, our instincts, prosperity and handling material goods, working with silver, stones, metals and gold. Consider what minerals may assist you, just as the Lemurians did!

ASTROLOGICAL MAKEUP

When working with the elements, which element I may wish to work with depends on many things, but none less than the relationship I was born to have with an element. For example, as a Cancerian, I have a strong affinity with water: a fire-sign may feel drawn to working with candles, for example, an air sign with breath-work.

A person who is an Air sign may also have interesting ways to work with other signs when there is conflict. For example, take Aquarian witch and lawyer Phyllis Curott's famous example of working with a controlling, sexual and angry fire sign in her magickal story, *Book of Shadows*. She surmised that her "air" approach literally fed his anger, just as fire can be fanned by wind. If you are a water sign, you may find that interactions with earth signs go "muddy" and unclear at times. Lemurians would always tailor their elemental healing to the direct needs of the individual. Individuals who were suffering were not seen as difficult or threatening, but as beings working through an imbalance in their elemental makeup.

To discover more, your astrological chart will reveal much of your own elemental makeup. A person with a large proportion of one element in their chart may wish to work with the other elements to understand more about those aspects and how others interact with them. Because of the diverse ways in which we can express our elemental selves, solutions can be found through understanding and bringing into harmony these elemental parts of ourselves.

PAST LIFE

Some people have dilemmas working with particular elements, no matter how drawn they are to them, and even though their soul tells them that they are rightfully a part of them! Many people who identify as witches or spellcasters, for example, may have suffered abuse at the hands of a person or theology who deliberately misused an element against them – the most powerful way to break a continuing line of witches' power. For example, when we gaze at a Beltane fire, we see it is life-sized, and beautiful, and roaring. We leap over it to grow closer, hand in hand with our beloved. We may "feed" it with grain and fallen wood, to symbolise new growth and fertility. This beautiful symbology and power was twisted during burnings, when the purifying quality of fire was twisted and misused by those wishing to break our love of the elements, and thus many of us have fears around fire.

To overcome this fear, which is not our truth, we must re-invite the element into our life. I have worked with many people who fear fire – so we start with candles. For those who fear water due to drowning and the ducking stool, we work with blessing with water. Earth was used to crush the life from us, so we work with stones on our body during crystal healing, and some were hung – so our breath and fresh air becomes the healing tool.

CONDITIONAL PERSPECTIVE

Where we grew up, what our parents taught us, what our environment has contributed to our beliefs regarding the elements.

GENETIC PERSPECTIVE

Our bloodline will have much to teach us about an element. Explore this – if we are of Polynesian descent we will have a different relationship to the ocean than, say, a person from a hill tribe of China. Similarly, a person with Nordic blood will experience different tendencies to a person whose lineage is from the deserts of Australia. This too will influence our relationship, and thus our spellwork with an element.

DEITIES

Each element is associated with Goddesses and Gods, as well as elementals and magickal beings. Pele is a strong fire Goddess, whose sexual power is immense. Aphrodite is a love Goddess whose element is water. Explore these beings, and call upon them as part of your spellwork, never forgetting to thank them for their assistance. Unicorns are associated with water (as their horn can purify bodies of water) and gnomes with earth, for example.

LEMURIAN MAGICKAL PRACTISE TWO: CREATING SACRED SPACE

We can recreate personal sacred space within the world by calling on the four corners of the world...and of the Universe. This is an essential part of magick...and as a tradition it is inherent in the magick of the Celts, Mayans, and the tribal peoples of all four corners of this sacred planet.

The great difference here is that rather than individualising Spirit, it is more in keeping with the Lemurian way to call simply on the directions, the elements and the Great Spirit. We keep it simple. Now this is simple – but for many of us, we wish to make things complex. My sincere recommendation is when establishing this energy within us, and regrounding it, please call in Spirit, rather than the traditional Wiccan way, for example, of calling in God and Goddess in individualised forms.

First step, then, is to acknowledge the directions, and the elements. The second is to create personal sacred space – sometimes known as casting circle.

CASTING THE CIRCLE OF ONE

"It was all a circle. The important thing in our life was to be near the fire, and telling stories. Sharing our songs and our stories and most of all listening to the sounds of the earth when you sit near the fire. You listen to the sound of the fire when it's burning too, when the wind's blowing. So you listen to everything. The spirit of the earth is always there all right around. West, north, south, east, west, wherever."

– Bunna Lawrie, Songman of the Mirnum people, South Australia

A circle represents many things. One world. One planet. No hierarchy, no beginning, no end, zero, a place of infinite potential. In modern day practices all over the world, circle is "cast" or created to designate sacred space: what is within is safe, and private and between worlds. Within that space there is no past, no present, no future. There just IS. Casting circle is a tradition that has been kept alive by witches, and indigenous peoples of the planet, and one which originated in Lemuria as a method of protection in the later days of the continent.

LEMURIAN SACRED SPACE

To protect themselves from negative thoughts and energies that were so harmful to them, the highly-sensitive and intelligent latter-day Lemurians (remember, who were VERY long-lived, so many had been on the planet for thousands of years) bravely chose to stay amongst the earth creatures displaying fear, negativity, hate and envy. To enable them to continue their work, they created a system whereby powerful sacred space was created, inviolate as long as the intention was held by all participants. After circle was complete, the energy was sent out into the world, and changed the energy, like a flood of negative ions being released after a storm. Weather often changes when circle is cast and weather can often be different within circle, as opposed to without. I have cast circle and been within, and rain has fallen gently around us… Individuals can create sacred space in this way too, but Lemurians were highly social, and so preferred to create sacred space in groups to continue their work together. In time, however, these circles were often infiltrated by others wishing to harm them. Discernment is necessary – but paranoia is not! Sometimes, it can be difficult to remain balanced when working with energy and energy discernment. I KNOW I am loved and protected, and so I set the intention when working in circle that only beings with reverence and positive intent, who are light of spirit, join me. I also ask for agreement before doing circle work in public space, such as the Mind Body Spirit festivals. I can't control who attends, but I can clearly set intent and ask for wonderful beings to join me. Together we create beautiful energy!

When you work with sacred space with others, it is important that all participants agree to the intent and integrity of the circle. Otherwise, work alone or with trusted others until you find those you can trust.

Casting circle is one of the most essential aspects of working Lemurian magic. It is the sacred art of delineating space: a space within which connections can be safely made, with nature, with deity, with elements, with ourselves, with all that is...the circle encompasses everything, and yet it is a place where only those who are pure and in agreement with the principles of the circle can enter...

In the Wiccan tradition of witchcraft, a reconstructed form of European shamanism, before one could enter the circle, often a blade was held to the heart or solar plexus chakra, and the circle's creator would say "'Tis better that you rush upon this blade, than enter this circle with fear in your heart".

It was then asked: "How do you enter?"

And the answer was: "In perfect love and perfect trust."

Only then would that being be permitted to enter circle.

BETWEEN THE WORLDS

There are many ways of casting circle, and I would like to state clearly that each person working with Lemurian magic will need to work with themselves in order to understand what works for them. For me, my technique varies depending on the purpose, and the energy, and the intention. They have been both given to me through meditation and vision, and through study, research and long practice I have developed safe, pure, methods that visibly energise, change and protect a given area. It is almost impossible for anyone of impure heart to enter when this methodology is used, and I can vouch for its safety.

I've written a truly fundamental guide to circle casting and calling in the elements here, which can be used as a guide which you can work with....consider this guide akin to a blank Book of Shadows and Light, a structure, but it is up to you to create the colour and texture and flavour, the unique energy and personality of your circle.

To add Lemurian touches, work with sea symbols: I often include shells, sea water, salt collected from rock pools and dried in the sun, feathers of sea birds gifted to me. (Thank you, Pelican! Thank you Sea-eagle!)

What is casting circle?
Casting circle is a powerful rite of protection. The circle keeps power and energy and intention within a sacred space, and keeps any other energies out. These energies can be mundane, or they can be magical, or etheric in nature.

Because you are often working between the worlds, you want to make a statement of intent that your actions are for the highest good of all, and prevent anything else affecting your work.

Like all true magic, your circle may be simple, or highly formal and ornate.

How do I cast circle?
You can simply use your finger to trace the line of the sacred space around you, or you can visualize a circle of white light surrounding you, or you can mark out a physical circle with salt, candles, chalk or water or wine. If you have more time or prefer to go deeper into this sacred art, you can use your athame (a sacred blade used to delineate space, cutting harmlessly through dimensional and energetic doorways into other worlds) or wand (a wand tends to colour and flavor the energy, unlike an athame which cuts through and delineates very clearly. Just something to be aware of.) So, use athame, hand, or energy beamed out from your solar plexus, for example, for power.

Draw the circle, chanting your intent as you go.

When casting a circle or raising power you move deosil – with the sun – which in the northern hemisphere means clockwise but in the southern hemisphere means counter-clockwise. This can get very confusing, but the most important aspect is to delineate space...

So, move with the sun's natural direction in your hemisphere to open and create circle.... When closing a circle or "banishing" power you move widdershins – against the sun – which means counter-clockwise in the northern hemisphere and clockwise in the southern. It's important to note that closing circle is sometimes termed "opening" circle, ie, casting sets up the space, opening marks the ending of that magic circle.

I feel it is essential to set this space physically, by using your finger, wand, athame or other tool.

It is important to not break the circle, but it is equally important to not worry if someone crosses the path, or moves about in circle...

If you are working with others, please have an agreement in place that people may not break the circle and depart for toilet breaks, or if they become emotional, for example. A break in circle is a break and a tear in the energy. It is sacred space, and leaving means not coming back during the ritual, a little like sweat lodge.

If you need to depart the circle, to maintain its integrity, you may "cut" a dimensional portal within the circle with an athame, and then return. But simply walking in, and walking out, disturbs the energy, and can weaken the power which has been raised. Intent does "hold" the circle, but please keep it as intact, and in as deep integrity as possible. So, before beginning, be sure to have voided, and be ready to focus. Sometimes, too these "urges" are simply the ego playing tricks on us. We need to stay in integrity, and keep the circle intact to the best of our ability.

Once I've cast circle, what do I do?

After casting the circle (primarily, by physically casting, then visualising a sphere of white light above, below, and all around) it is traditional to welcome the elements. This is sometimes termed "calling" the elements, or "summoning" the elements.

It is important to note that there are many variations to this technique. Some magical practitioners working today, out of their own ancient traditions, prefer to call the Guardians of the Watchtowers, the beings who are the caretakers of the powers, aspects and etheric being of each of these elements. Others simply call in the element itself, allowing an intuitive energetic presence to be felt.

My own method varies from circle to circle, but of late it has tended to be along the lines of: "This circle is blessed by water, and then making an offering of that element to the earth...others may prefer to raise the water to the sky...others may scatter the water on each person in circle." When working in the style of Lemuria, know that the power of One, zero, the infinite, is what is most valuable to you. Calling in each element itself would be my recommendation.

How to invoke the elements

Here are some simple words to invoke, call, summon or bless with the elements:

Hold your bowl of spring water aloft and say: "I welcome the spirits of the water."
Hold your bowl of sea salt/earth/sand and say: "I welcome the spirits of the earth."
Hold your incense stick, alight, aloft and say: "I welcome the spirits of the air."
Hold your candle, aflame, aloft and say: "I welcome and rejoice in the spirits of the fire."
Raise a candle, and say: "This circle is blessed by fire."
Hold up the incense and say: "This circle is blessed by air."
Hold up the bowl of salt or earth and say: "This circle is blessed by earth."
Last, hold up your bowl of water (dew, collected that morning, would be powerful) and say: "This circle is blessed by water."

The order you invoke the elements in is, in my understanding and practice, dependent on your purpose. There is no element greater or lesser than another.

As I have stated, sometimes my preference is to pour the water to earth, hold the fire to earth, and so on. Sometimes I wish my circle to be earth-sacred, rather than celestially energised, which is why I sometimes use this method. I also tend to work with the five element system, and include "spirit", which is by no means "correct". (Some Celtic traditionalists work with a three element system, some eclectic practitioners invoke up to seven, even more. The choice is yours, but for me, based upon my own research, earth, air, fire and water are essential for the feeling of a balanced circle. Especially water, sea water, when working with Lemuria!)

Elements are associated with the directions, and often follow this pattern: air in the east, fire in the south, water in the west and earth in the north – however, this can be influenced by where you are casting circle. For example, here in the southern hemisphere earth is usually in the south and fire is in the north, as that is where the sun is. It can also vary depending on your geographical location, for instance if you live south of a major lake or ocean you may wish to put water in the north. If you are calling in the elements, I feel it is of most value to follow your intuition and the features of the region you are working in. For example, I often speak these words...

I call upon the spirits of the east...of the air...of your mind. I then allow Air to let me know what needs to be spoken. I then wait for a sign... perhaps a brush of air upon my cheek, the wind rising slightly... As a symbol, I may use a pelican, or sea eagle feather, or perhaps a censer filled with incense with a pinch of sea kelp!

I call upon the spirits of the south … of the fire...of your passion, your intent, your motivations...I may use something volcanic, but fire is such a pure element – you cannot go past a cauldron or a flame itself! Again, a sign. Warmth...an inner flame being lit.

I call upon the spirits of the west...of the water...of our emotions, our intuition, our psychology... and again, I may feel thirsty, or alternatively, tearful, or perhaps experience some insights at this point. Water is beautiful to me...I have no fear of emotionality. I believe it to be a valid and beautiful path of wisdom. As a symbol when working with Lemurian energies, I would be inclined to use sea water! I also collect moonwater at particular times, to work with specifically.

Finally, I call upon the spirits of the north...of the earth. Again, for Lemuria, I would use a rock such as obsidian, volcanic and from that deeper time of the birthing of the planet's creatures. It holds such energy. Salt, too is of the earth, and nothing can equal rockpool salt for its cleansing qualities! Of the land, of my body, of my food and form... and again, a physical sensation bringing me a message may arrive.

Now compare the directional attributes to the medicine wheel...and of the way in which indigenous cultures gather in circle, with fire so often in the centre. Tell me there is not something ancient happening here. And I will ask you, with a smile, to look again and allow yourself to feel the not so faraway ancient self you are.

Who calls in the elements?

Well, if you are working alone, you do.

If you are working with others, you may wish to take turns in leading, or assign one person to call in each element. Again, you may make this process as simple, or as elaborate as you wish.

Raising energy in circle

Raising power is to give your magic energy and strength...it is magic itself. How can we do this? At times, particularly with many people in circle, I have felt an urge to say nothing, and raise power with silence and stillness while in circle. It can be very powerful, particularly when outdoors, when the moon is rising. Allowing the elements to whisper to me has created vast aching reservoirs of pure energy.

Other, more active methods include chanting, singing, drumming...sometimes clapping... I like to hum, or softly chant... Just as power can be raised in stillness, it can also be created in movement, so some prefer to dance the circle and raise energy in that way.

In my visions of Lemuria, particularly the ones I experienced while in trance, I "saw" the circle being danced from the outside, by Lemurians, who were twirling and leaping, holding fire, flames pouring forth from their body – amazing, and so powerful. In this first vision, I was an outsider to the camp, watching, but oh so longing to join the circle. In time, in my visions, after being rebirthed by the Lemurian tribe, I have been permitted to enter the circle.

Welcoming the Goddess and the God

Depending on the circle's purpose, you may wish to work with particular Goddess and God energies, though this was not, strictly speaking a Lemurian concept. They would invoke the masculine One and the feminine One, and then all the in between beings, as we are all one.

Opening Circle – Completing the Ritual

This is the point at which you can release the energy you have raised so it may go out and do its good in the world. The pulse of energy often felt as these times is palpable, a circle rippling out into the world, so powerful, cleansing all in its path, and having an amazing, strong and purifying effect even on mass consciousness.

Often a little confusing, understandably, as this can also be called closing circle. Farewell all who you have welcomed in, and close circle in the direction opposite to that in which you cast your circle. So, if you cast circle, or began in Northern hemisphere style, close in that style. If you chose to work in Southern Hemisphere style, open circle, or finish in that manner. Simply put, be consistent, and certain of your intent.

Know that your circle is open, but never broken. Its energy continues to work beyond that moment.

Ground afterwards by eating, earthing, and taking good care of yourself. To connect and seal those Lemurian energies, why not eat of juicy mangoes and glorious figs – if you are in an environment where these cannot be found easily, try tropical juices! Stay well hydrated, and eat healthily to gain maximum benefits, and remain working within the best of all possible energy.

By working in these simple ways, and by tuning your intent, the connection with your innate Lemurian wisdom will be strengthened. You will reawaken to your saltwater being powers, your body love will grow, and a sense of connection, of a beautiful, peaceful planet being truly possible will become a part of your daily life, thinking, feeling, knowing, being peace, love and understanding. Being Lemurian. Being a shapeshifter.

And that blessed state is well worth the simple practice it takes.

You do not need to widely broadcast your practice – your energy will speak for itself! Please, do not fall into these places where confusion and your own discernment will be held to ridicule.

You are all that you need, and being simple, and knowing the land and her ways is the place to begin, quietly, to redraw your relationship with yourself and all that is.

Do not feel you must redraw and remake this land and place in your image: your time is not over. You will evolve and change by simply being. Breathing in and out. Being kind. Succeeding and living a good life, as a good person.

What is the point of all the talking if it is too complex and competitive and ego-bound for us to hear in our hearts? And much of it, I cannot hear in my heart. My intellect can strain and yearn for "understanding" but my heart remains untouched.

LEMURIAN RITUAL

It can be so helpful for all of us who seek to bring meaning and purpose into our lives to begin to engage with the sacred art of ritual. When connecting with Lemuria, simple ritual conducted on a day to day basis programs us for maximum well-being and health, prosperity and happiness. Ritual is simple: it is to do something, something physical, emotional, spiritual and mental, in a sacred way, at the same time, over time. That is of course putting this very simply. My rituals vary: but generally I greet the sun each day with gratitude, turn to the four directions and offer thanks.

At sunset I do the same. At the major festivals I observe and acknowledge them, and make an offering. I have altars set up throughout my home, and they are beautiful, natural places. They are mainly very intuitive: I change them as the energy and the feeling around them changes. So, for example, on what others may see as my coffee table, I have a beautiful blue statue of Gaia, made with pure clay from the earth, her beautifully pregnant belly adorned with a turquoise. Around her I have looped sea shells, small dolphin statues, and rose quartz, for unconditional love. I am not a very formal person, and everything I do and create has a flow, it has meaning for me, but it is constructed from guidance and intuition, and is not ritual in the sense of having a great deal of preparation and decoration. I wear what others might feel to be ritual clothing most of the time in any case!

When connecting with Lemuria, the first aspect that I would see as very important is to connect with the water element all around us. Of course, I would do this as a part of honouring all the elements and directions: but water and earth were not divided in Lemurian times…we are "on shore" and "off shore." My father and mother go to the ocean every day. For some people who dwell in deserts, for example, if you are in Arizona, you may be wondering how you can connect with the oceanic magick of Lemuria without traveling an enormous distance. To me, this is simple!

First: Drink more water. Most of us are dehydrated. Simply drink beautiful, fresh water throughout the day, and give thanks for this water.

Bathe with awareness: Awareness really is the key: the key to, well, everything magickal. Awareness is being awake: feeling out the nuances, not needing to rely on others. Knowing that timing will be right, having trust, feeling the sacred heartbeat that pulses through every exquisite moment of being alive! And yet, we are so often numb. One way to awaken is to bathe with awareness. So, run your bath. Light a candle (please, consider working with pure soy or beeswax candle – they ionize the air, which stimulates feelings of bliss.)

LEMURIAN RITUAL BATH

Pour a handful of sea salt into the bath ... now, sea salt can come from dried rock pools if you are blessed to live close to the ocean and wish to gather the salt. I have done this on occasion and the experience becomes deeply significant, and links us to ancient people's who gathered salt in just such a way.

Your friendly organic supermarket will have wonderful varieties – be sure to use SEA salt, though! Glacier salt, while potentially containing ancient sea water, and even ancient sea life, may not be a reliable source. (The exception is Tibetan glacier salt, which holds energy and information of and on the earth's major shifts. This is almost a different exercise, though ...)

For your first Lemurian immersion, raise your left hand (if this is your receptive hand – if you are right handed, it is, if you are left handed, it is not!) to the four directions and ask for this blessing on your water cleansing. Place the handful of salt against your heart, bless it "I bless you with the love of my opening heart" will do, and then cast the salt into the water. Swirl the water gently – keep the water tepid, lukewarm, too please. This is not deep heat ... the waters in Lemuria were very warm, but they were not boiling hot – that is for deeper cleansing in the mineral springs!

Bless the east, for air and birth

Bless the south, for fire and warmth

Bless the west, where water flows

Bless the north, the earth she knows

Now, some of you may wish to honour the directions in a different manner: one that is more in keeping with the geographical features of your own area, and that is absolutely fine. The associations here are a suggestion, a starting point, but I can confirm they work beautifully, as a foundation. When I travel I sometimes alter the directions and their associations, a change which helps to ground me surely in that environment. (I am often guided to do this, rather than doing this as a matter of course.) Especially helpful after lots of plane travel, this is a wonderful way of having a sense of who you are, where you are, when all about can seem topsy-turvy! Ultimately though, this is one planet, and as we are working very much with the lesson of Lemuria – that we ARE all one, this foundation can synchronize beautifully with that Law. It works beautifully – for me. However, the intent is what is important, and the energy and emotion in which you immerse yourself before popping into the bath!

So, after you have called the directions and honoured them, and thus your place in the world, bathe. Wash yourself well, simply with the water and cloths … allow yourself to soak and float for a time … allow the memories to come forth. You may find yourself floating in the sea-salty amniotic waters of the womb before birth. Another time (because you will do this more than once!) you will find yourself in the warm salty waters of the Lemurian sea shore, simply floating. Saltwater is especially buoyant, and is associated strongly with mermaids and women, and with amniotic fluid. Before we are born into the "land" and breathing world, we all dwell within our mothers, in a sea salty ocean, and we all at this point ARE mermaids, as we grow through our ancient states and then are born into our current forms and selves.

The water will bring through memories of your own womb-time, your Lemurian time, or the days spent by the ocean you may have experienced this lifetime. Part of you is a saltwater being, and this bathing ritual will reconnect you strongly, leading to healing of the past in the present moment – in a very simple and peaceful and sometimes blissful way.

This Lemurian Ritual bath is so very healing, you will be astonished at how light of mind, spirit and body you will feel afterwards. This gentle bathing practice will allow the sea salt crystals to gently dissolve any "dirt" or toxins in your auric fields, and cleanse any hurts or wounds or microbes on your body.

My daddy always said to me whenever I gave myself a cut or scrape, usually after dashing about madly on rocky shores, trying to toughen up my feet so I could be a "wild girl", "Salt water will fix that."

He's right – and it applies to the physical scrapes and cuts and to the psychic ones too. It is the single greatest and most beautifully simple remedy for psychic sadness and old wounds.

We can all be healed by the natural energy and power of salt water.

EASY WAYS TO CONNECT WITH LEMURIA

Lemurians were very diverse, but they understood each other very well, as they communicated telepathically, and lying was as yet unknown. It truly was an age of innocence, but not in the sense of naivety.

As we approach the dawning of the fifth world, or the fifth sun, which is said to take place after the shift, we too can experience wonderful benefits from reclaiming some of our ancestral magicks, including the ways of the Lemurians.

*Hula: This sacred dance is a beautiful connective rhythmic movement that stirs the sacral and root chakras, aligning the posture of the dancer and creating blissful serenity and sensuality. It effectively links the body, mind and soul. Belly dancing has a similar impact, as does the tribal dancing style. For inspiration, seek out a belly dancing class that has a sense of the sacred, the sensual – and of feminine delight!

*Tattooing: To commemorate your Lemurian connection, you may wish to explore body art. Symbols include the spiral, round, encircling motifs and three lines. Tattooing is ages old, and when done with sacred intent, is a powerful way of moving forward and shifting your sense of identity.

*Eat as raw as possible: As already covered in the food section with Khumara, food is an essential component to life, in this incarnation. Bless food. Gather it yourself when possible. Share food. Offer hospitality.

*Watch sunrise and sunset to activate those chakras!

*Draw symbols on your body from the earth...clays and ochres are perfect and will help your own body vibrate to the energy of the Earth, to feel her heartbeat clearly again, and to be able to sing the leylines.

*Always gaze at rainbows to connect to past and future lives, ancestors, and deities.

*Hold gatherings or join gatherings to celebrate the four galactic energy points (the solstices and the equinoxes) and the four Gaian energy points (the four festivals, called in the Celtic systems Beltane, Samhain, Imbolc and Mabon).

*Practise and develop your innate intuitive gift of telepathy.

*Meditate outside in nature.

*Turn vibrations from a distance into a picture...

THE END OF LEMURIA BEGINS...

"I remember much fear or trepidation being centered on the sky, so perhaps there were 'gods' that visited or somehow controlled the movements of the people, but I can't be sure. I don't remember." I am speaking with Scott Alexander King, who is describing what he remembers as the end times of Lemurian society and culture. "I want to say religion was somehow linked to the celestial bodies (stars, suns, moons, etc.), but then I also remember it being a very nature-based society... with the seasons, elements, etcetera, playing a large part. But, I can't remember how or why..."

Not everyone feels the end to have been brought about the same way. Many people in workshops and in interviews gifted me accounts very much like this one, from Allyson Tanner. "The partial sinking of Lemuria was not due to abuse of power like Atlantis, Mother Earth was evolving and changing naturally so parts flooded and she left only what she wanted found. I feel this was to protect the integrity of the wisdom and energy Lemuria had. I feel that also it was because there was no "hierarchy", so to speak, that the energy that was brought to Lemuria was treated with reverence and deep respect as it was coming from a source of purity and something much greater than Lemuria was, however, no one feared this. I don't know if this is the right word but when I think of Atlantis I get arrogance and a thirst for power...thus ultimately their demise. However those who didn't agree with what some in Atlantis did, found their way to Lemuria..."

"People say that Lemuria (and Atlantis, for that matter) "sank". "They didn't," Allyson says emphatically. "The water rose and engulfed them. I remember there being an attack or a war or a cataclysm that shook the entire planet and shifted the way it sat in the heavens. Something hit the planet that caused it to rotate differently or to shift on its axis. However you look at it, the climate changed and the waters rose ... I remember lots of fire, wind and water... and then nothing."

"It only took three days ... " she said sadly.

As the sophisticated psychic attack began, there was a very definite energetic and physical impact. Lemurians begin to sicken. To feel fear. To hide. To feel shame.

Some souls from Lemuria would eventually go on to become studied and enslaved by the Atlanteans. Other Lemurians shapeshifted – becoming whales, dolphins, mermaids, and swimming to other shores, far, far away.

And it is at this sad place where we begin our journey northwards, to head in an easterly direction from Lemuria...

We are going to the place where intellect became King.

Where life was Golden.

Where Slaves were born.

We are going to Atlantis.

Immrama Two:

VOYAGE TO
ATLANTIS

IRELAND
including
TARA, NEWGRANG

NORTH
ATLANTIC
OCEAN

N

the
AZORES

open plains

LAND BRIDGE

the

LAND BRIDGE

fertile delta region

LOST
CONTINENT
OF
ATLANTIS

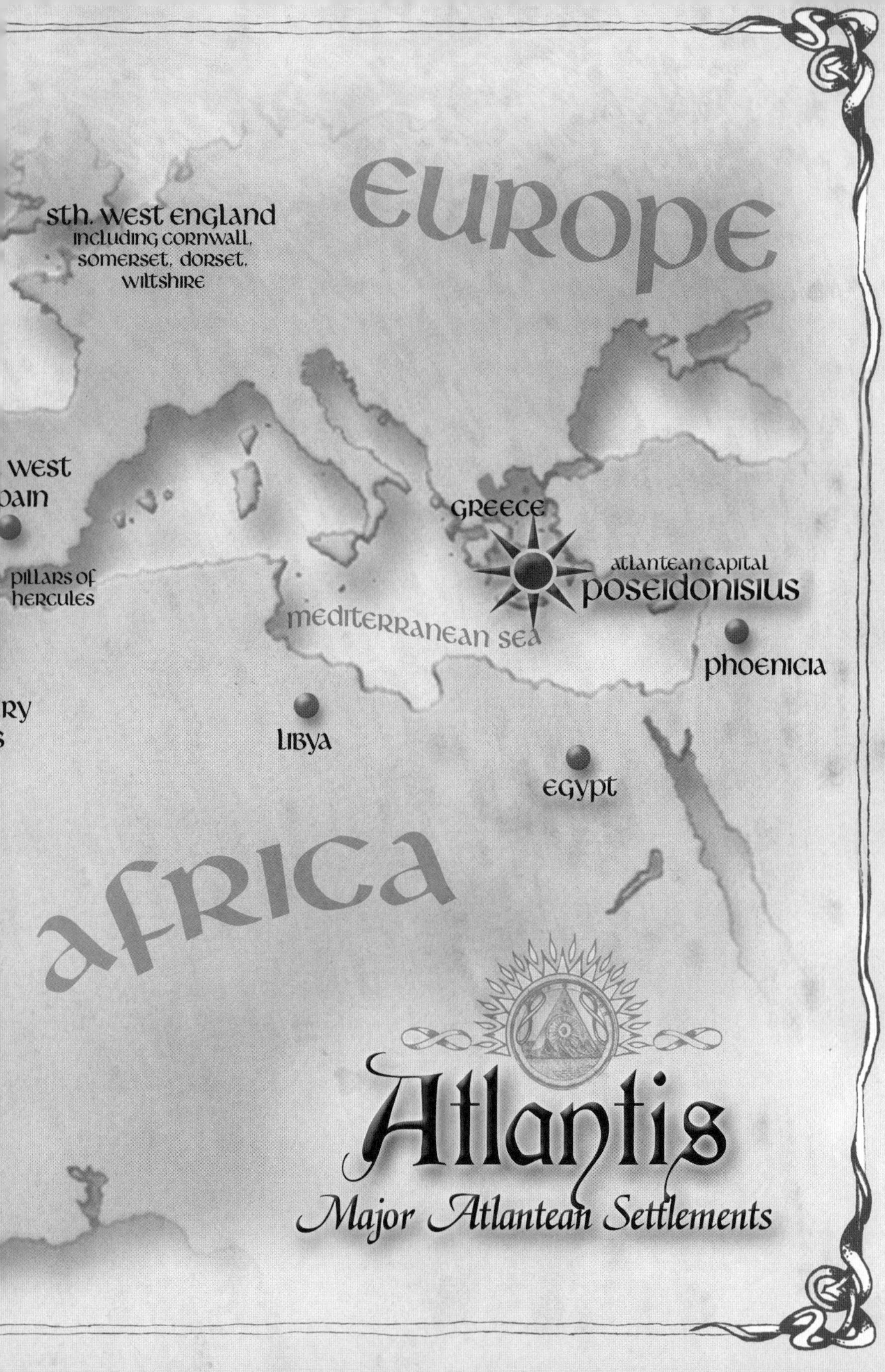

EUROPE

sth. west england
including cornwall,
somerset, dorset,
wiltshire

west
pain

pillars of
hercules

GREECE

atlantean capital
poseidonisius

mediterranean sea

phoenicia

ARY
S

LIBYA

EGYPT

AFRICA

Atlantis

Major Atlantean Settlements

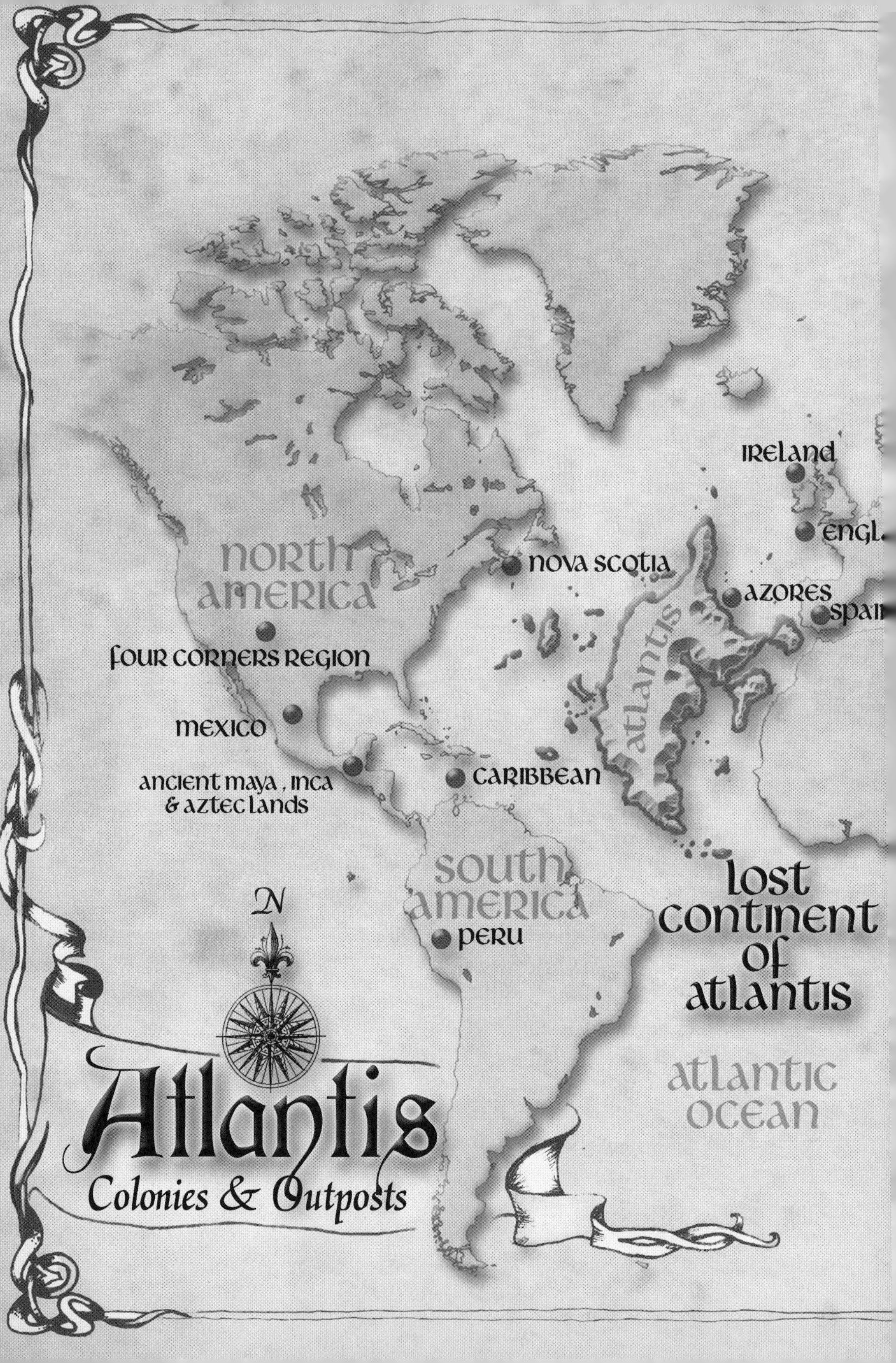

IRELAND

NORTH
AMERICA

NOVA SCOTIA

engl.

azores

spain

FOUR CORNERS REGION

MEXICO

ancient maya , inca
& aztec lands

CARIBBEAN

atlantis

N

SOUTH
AMERICA

PERU

lost
continent
of
atlantis

atlantic
ocean

Atlantis

Colonies & Outposts

"We will keep faith until the Sky falls upon us and crushes us, until the Earth opens and swallows us, until the Seas arise and overwhelm us..."

– *Celtic oath, translated by Caitlin Matthews*

ATLANTIS RISING

"You remember a single deluge only, but there were many previous ones; in the next place, you do not know that there formerly dwelt in your land the fairest and noblest race of men which ever lived, and that you and your whole city are descended from a small seed or remnant of them which survived."

– *Plato, Timaeus, 355 BCE*

In the beginning...

The end is what so many people see. The end, riding upon a great wave, curtained by the sky, a fearful dark green full of fury, the earth heaving and throwing up those who have clawed so much from her, and the people are running, and running, and the Animals are crying, and crying, and some of them escape and fly away...others burrow within the earth that seems to give them nurture amidst the destruction. Many change form, shifting their shape into those of the great whales and the dolphins, storing the information in the form of a great song that forms the world, and carrying those who cannot change on their backs to the lands far away from the heaving seas wrought by the catastrophe.

And there are those who choose to stay behind, comforting those being swamped, praying for their next incarnation to be different...

Amidst the unfolding of this tragedy upon the screen of my mind are memories of beings and creatures, all sacred, who are like nothing I have ever seen before...they have human and animal and angelic parts, it would seem. And there are beings who are galactic in origin, with blue skin and scaled and feathery wings and molten fire burning from within their eyes. There is a desperation, and a fury, and an anger emanating from what seems to be the Temple, high on a hill, and lightning forks out from location to location, from hill to hill, causing a web of destruction across the planet. But it is from this central capital, which by 1,000 years BCE came to be known as Poseidia and whose renown spread thanks to Plato, that destruction is wreaked. It is from there that the epicenter shuddered out each twisting contraction, radiating out in earthquakes, tsunamis, and lava.

The one sure thing I know from my visions and communications is that Atlantis wasn't meant to be this way. And, as they say so often in the movies, it didn't *have* to be this way.

You see, the truth is that the place known as Atlantis began from a very real desire to create new Lemurian outposts, to bring this beautiful energy of One through to other land masses appearing on the face of the Mother. And so it was. And of course, outposts have this tendency to take on their own flavour and colour, and that is a wonderful and strange thing.

But in the end, the idea of the One became distorted, and was manipulated. In the end, everything shifted.

In my visions of what is often and variously called the end, or the fall, I see a dark, dark twilight, lit with streaks of lightning that burn almost pale green in the sky. The earth is crying out, and going underground. The sea is hurling herself to the sky, striking out, it would seem, against an unseen force.

For this is not the end of Atlantis.

This is what the politicians and the powerful ones and the scientists of Atlantis thought and planned and desired to be the end of Lemuria. And because this was done with such malintent, it did not and could not end the energy or beings of Lemuria. Not really.

But it was indeed the beginning of the end for Atlantis.

It is an ending that we have seen in our own times, over and over and over again. It has been reenacted in the large and terrible genocides of the peoples of the planet, of the enslavements of her peoples, of the exploitation of her children. It is reenacted in the destructions of the planet. It is recreated each day when we think and speak and do without remembering the impact and energies and power of our actions our thoughts, our bodies, our feelings and our spirit...

ATLANTIS: THE ARRIVAL

"In Lemuria, the waters rose. Some of the beings transformed themselves into creatures of the sea more than of the land, but of the scattered and isolated land-beings of Lemuria, only the highest of mountain peaks and the furthest inland of once deserts could be saved ... for the rest, it was time to travel over the sea. The courageous and handsome Prince Idon asked who of his clan would journey forth with him, and they set forth, in ship after ship, woman and man and changeling alike, over the seas for days and nights, until they finally sighted a shore.

Against the backdrop of a red and gold sky they caught a glimpse of a green and mountainous land, and they gave thanks to the earth, the sea, the sky and the air for granting them this new home ...

And while they knew that many challenges would lie before them, Prince Idon turned to

praise the men and women and beings of Lemuria, and in the setting sun's light, their hair was turned to fire. And from that moment forth, that colour their hair remained. And from that time, every succeeding generation of redheads was a living reminder of that first spell-binding sunset, of the joy and hope and blessing of finding that second home of the Lemurians... Atlantis."
– Folk tale

Prince Idon of Mu, the navigators, the dolphins and mermaids, and with prayers and blessings discovered Atlantis just in time to move his people to the new continent before his land and his people were destroyed by natural earth changes of rising waters and submerged villages and land, fields and flower... As the tale goes, he arrived at Atlantis at sunset, and fell in love with the new land. The sky and clouds and the water were of the most beautiful reds, scarlets and flame-coloured licks, reflecting the rays of that setting sun. Prince Idon wanted to preserve that moment of beauty of the sunset for all time: and as he made this wish, his own hair turned to the same colour as the sunset. Golden red, as if flame was licking at his head. Every redhead is therefore an Atlantean... of Lemurian descent...and part of the first major genetic shift. As Lemurians were able to create their reality very quickly, due to their genetic flexibility, such things were commonplace. But this shift they kept, signifying as it did their gratitude for the new land and the new world.

WHERE WAS ATLANTIS?

"For the ocean there was at that time navigable; for in front of the mouth which you Greeks call, as you say, "the pillars of Heracles", there lay an island which was larger than Libya and Asia together; and it was possible for the travellers of that time to cross from it to the other islands, and from the islands to the whole of the continent over against them which encompasses that veritable ocean. For all that we have here, lying within the mouth of which we speak, is evidently a haven having a narrow entrance; but that yonder is a real ocean, and the land surrounding it may most rightly be called, in the fullest and truest sense, a continent. Now in this island of Atlantis there existed a confederation of kings, of great and marvelous power, which held sway over all the island, and over many other islands also and parts of the continent."
– Plato

Plato tells us that his account of Atlantis is directly based on secret information he was given by an ancestor of Atlantis: Solon, an Egyptian priest. According to Solon, Atlantis was a vast empire, a continent in the Atlantic, which had literally exploded some 9,000 years before Plato wrote his accounts in 355 BCE.

Atlantis was a sea-kingdom, a vast chain of islands with a land mass that rivaled that of Lemuria. The Lemurians who arrived found peoples who were technologically sophisticated, divided in their philosophy, and amazed that the Lemurians shapeshifted between forms. They were especially interested because some members of their own city were contemplating the creation of beings who were in-betweeners. But to know that this could be done freely, and that the beings were intelligent and beautiful and peaceful: to some, that was a shock. Already the Atlantean mindset was noticeably different to the heart-space of the Lemurians.

There was more than one island in the Atlantean kingdom, but there was one city, Poseidia, that was the control centre for all Atlantis. Within these central temples were housed vast crystal "computers", which radiated information and energy across the empire and beyond. Powered by crystal technology ... it was a vast difference to the stone and clan system of Lemuria. Some of these sacred stones had journeyed to Atlantis with Lemurians, and were kept hidden. For a time. When they were discovered, the Lemurians shared their power, and when they were used without care for their meaning, without reverence and with malintent ... the end came.

But not for many thousands upon thousands of years ...

WHERE IS ATLANTIS?

The position of Atlantis in the world has been hotly discussed since Plato's dialogues. In the middle ages, Sir Francis Bacon wrote New Atlantis, a work exploring his utopian vision, and in the classical world, sea voyagers set out to find the remnants of Atlantis – and we have never stopped searching.

We have looked to Santorini, to the tsunami that drowned the Greek island of Hera, to the Minoans, to the Canary Islands off the coast of Africa, to the Caribbean. The Nazi leader Heinrich Himmler sent an expedition to Tibet to find Atlantis. We have traced the Bimini steps in the Caribbean, dived into the healing waterholes of Chichen Itza, and we have climbed mainland mountains in Greece in search of the Lost Land. We dive, and we climb, and we seek, and it seems we need so much evidence. Real, physical, unequivocal evidence. Troy was found – why not Atlantis?

We search and we search. But why is it we look? What is it we want?

For what if Atlantis is not only a physical realm, but a realm of energy? A dimensional force that co-exists with ours, and is merging in more subtle ways than mountain peaks exploding from beneath the waters!

Spirit works subtly. It seems to me, as I looked around at the ever increasing drive to consume, the epic leaps in our technology and the second life realms we are all beginning to inhabit, the virtual nature of our new reality, that maybe Atlantis has arisen – and maybe *we* are the reborn Atlanteans. And maybe we have some decisions to make.

And what if it is already here now with us, overlapping our technologies and the decisions we face at this time?

In her epic work of theosophy, Madame Blavatsky, the 19th century mystic, wrote that Atlanteans were heroic peoples, the fourth "root race" to be succeeded by the Aryan race. Unfortunately, these ideas now seem stained: widely misinterpreted by the Nazi party, this theory was used to justify their viewing of Semitic ethnic groups as "less than". It is this policy of viewing anything as other that leads to the greatest pains and heartache of all beings.

So great was the Nazi's fascination with Atlantis that Heinrich Himmler launched an official expedition to find traces of Atlantis in Tibet, hoping to support the untruth of Aryan "superiority."

It is a great tragedy that this beautiful culture, that for a time blended the best of us all, was utilised in this way.

Rudolf Steiner wrote of Mu and Atlantis, and of course Edgar Cayce famously wrote volumes about the technology, the flying crafts, the power generators, the people of the Law of One and the people of Belial, the divisions and the tragedy of Atlantis. Cayce, the sleeping prophet, is one of the mystic world's most remarkable individuals. During his trance readings, which were almost always conducted at a distance, he revealed the location of Atlantis to have been in the Caribbean. But even with a host of archaeological expeditions and esoteric insights, the location of Atlantis remains a mystery.

LOCATION, LOCATION, LOCATION

The site of Atlantis has been claimed to be found all over this planet, and of course beyond. Its locations are said to be as varied as Novia Scotia, Tibet, China, frozen within a Himalayan landscape, in South America to Uluru to the great plains of the USA. Of course there are our familiar friends, Greece, and in particular Santorini.

Everyone, it seems, has taken Plato's detailed and brilliant description and laboured over its every point.

But, even though in the visions gifted to me, Atlantis had a series of cities, it was not one single "place". A little like saying New York is the United States, we are missing so much if we narrow the field to such an extent.

Atlantis was not a city – it was a civilisation that spanned a continent with island outreaches and footholds on the shifting continents. What the Greeks called Poseidia was simply an approximation for a great city state.

We have the option to piece together the commonalities of the outposts, the links of languages, the remnants of memory and channelings and intellectual theories and reach far more understanding. We can then come to the truth, the conclusion that this life of Atlantis is still amongst us.

We will continue to find remnants of her: The Bimini steps and the pyramids under the sea in the Bahamas, sunken cities off Japan, sunken lands of India, the steps into the ocean from Cornwall. All are the remnants of her colonies, all with their geophysical differences, and yet the same story has filtered through again and again.

By the event of the first great cataclysm, Atlantis was firmly established in many areas of the Earth. This did include what are now the Americas, Europe and Africa. There was an Atlantean settlement in the region that we now know as the Four Corners area of the American southwest. Here both Atlantis and Lemuria before her, shared involvement. The Native American Hopi tribe retains Akashic memory of this "first world." The Aztecs and Mayans, the Greek and Egyptian mythologies, ancient writings of India and Tibet all speak of the first world. Native Americans and all other various tribal cultures and peoples worldwide, have retained ancient soul memories in the roots of their spiritual practices and beliefs.

If you are looking for Atlantis the empire, the super civilization of advanced technology, then remember that the arms of the Atlantic Empire stretched nearly worldwide. She was the first global world order and she built temples, cities, trade and military complexes in many areas of the earth.

Atlantis loved pyramids – these structures are very good for generating and building energy which could be used for wonderful spiritual technologies. Atlantis was very much into power and technology – this was initially in service of The Divine but later became corrupted.

If you are looking for the Law of One, look to the tribal earth keepers who have preserved the knowledge through the ages. If you are in search of New Atlantis, then look around you and realize that you are in fact, living in New Atlantis, for mankind has come full circle. However, it is not only our present level of technological development and capability that indicate we are living in a reborn Atlantis; it is what we take for granted as normality in the collective around us. At this critical turning point, it is time to make the difficult choices that will ultimately determine the fate of the human race and the planet Earth. We must acknowledge that all life is sacred, that the Earth is a living thing, that all things are interconnected and that we are the earth keepers.

Searching for a location was a rich and absorbing subject! Fortunately, one of my dearest friends and mentors, author, soul coach and modern-day Atlantean, Maria

Elita, was coming to Sydney for the Mind Body Spirit festival. I knew we'd have time in between the madness and excitement of the festival to exchange ideas!

Maria did NOT let me down. A powerhouse of emotional wisdom, Maria shared her information in her usual way – generously, and straight from the heart.

"My own Atlantean Awakening has been with me my entire life. I've not known a time I wasn't fascinated by its magnetic pull. What I have done though over the last few years is discarded the 'past facts' and connected as a channel to my own remembrance. And in awakening through remembrance, I've seen myself as being connected to the Atlantean Council, and being honored with the highest order of Priestess within that Council. This is the recurring vision I have and whether that is a past life, or an existing life coinciding with mine now, I just know there is an overwhelming sensation within my being that fully knows of this memory."

"So, where EXACTLY was Atlantis?" I asked. My own memories placed my Atlantis in the Atlantic, for sure, but its spread was so vast. I felt sure this modern-day Atlantean could tell me more – and more that I would be able to grasp!

"Well, my father was born on a Greek Island called Ithaca. I am a descendant from this today; however, I do believe that when I connect to Atlantis, this geographic space is where most of my remembrance takes place. When I visited Ithaca (her ancient name is Ithaki) a few years ago, I was absolutely downloaded with Atlantean memory as my feet touched the soil.

"It was a full experiential physical sensation that felt like a sonic boom entering every cell in my being, and one that could not be ignored.

"It's funny," she said, her warm brown eyes gleaming. "I see Atlantis being more of a Galactic paradise than a tropical one. The intelligence of the civilisation wasn't like Ancient Grecian or Roman times, it was completely futuristic and the technological advancement I see in psychic visions is phenomenal."

"Colours are not colours," she stated. "They feel like sonic vibrations, and another form of life force, that the Atlanteans channeled, harnessed and used to create more life force on the planet. So the intensity of that vibrational experience is something which we are seeking now and that is why many of us are drawn to the virginal lands on Earth."

Wow. Only a week before I'd been quizzing my optometrist about whether there are colours that exist outside the spectrum we can currently see. I was receiving information that we have a narrow band of vision that can only see certain energies – and that when the DNA switches back on – which it will, but gently and over time, we will be able to 'see' so much more effectively, and dissemble and reassemble our particles. Are we moving towards that stage now…?

Made sense to me. There was a real possibility to me that Atlantis was an Earth colony of an off-world population that blended several off world civilisations, and several earth variations of those. The theories about that, and who they are, are immense. It's no exaggeration to say that my head was spinning, and kept spinning, for many years. Like wading into an ocean and being crashed with waves from every direction, absorbing the research can be dislocating and confusing! So, I asked for a guide. My own guide to help me navigate the watery world of Atlantis, and understand most deeply the lesson.

MEETING MARA

Once the Mind Body Spirit festivals were complete, with their whirlwind of talks, seminars and wonderful souls to meet, I could escape for a while to the north coast and to the beach house that is my refuge, named Avalon. I was hoping to connect with an Atlantean soul who could guide me through the information I was receiving and start to develop these ideas into some kind of shape! As a spiritually charged location where I'd had so many faery encounters, met with so many spirits of the bush and ocean, and of course, where I'd been blessed to meet my relatively new friend Khumara, I really felt I must ask for a guide – perhaps if I held the energy of Atlantis, and asked clearly at the ocean's shore, I would have some help! Like a guide in a land where I neither spoke the language well or recognized the culture, I felt this assistance was imperative to my gaining the most enriching visions, with the most valuable knowledge to bring back so others too could voyage to the Lost Lands!

So, after driving from Sydney, hanging out with my beloved and the garden, and surfing in the morning light after arrival, the next evening, just before sunset, I set my intention, and cast circle by the beach.

Before casting, I bathed in the salt water, keeping my mind clear and crystal, like the cool waters. The temperature was extremely hot, but the sea temperature was crisp, raising my alertness. I felt truly awake, refreshed and ready – and fortunately there was no-one else on the beach!

Backing onto the sacred site of the Biripi people, I knew I was in the right place to call upon an ancestor, a guide, a being to help me get through the crazy waters that were confusing me and blurring my understanding.

I created an energetic circle for my Atlantean meeting point with a guide at the sea shore, and I created a physical circle with sea rocks and shells that had long lived in many oceans, their particles charged with encounters from the ancient past. I set my intent: and called out loud to the heart of the ocean, turning gold under the lengthening rays of the setting sun …

May I now meet my Atlantean guide

May they show me true visions so I can communicate these honestly and simply to other Atlanteans, Lemurians and Avalonians so we can have clear intent and live effective, purposeful lives...

As I stepped back from that space slightly, I heard a part of me mutter "and make sense of all this contradictory information!" (Some might say that's ego, but I love that smart, wise-cracking, cheeky part of myself. She keeps me grounded – and reminds me to look out for cars when crossing roads!)

In the circle I welcomed each direction, the east for air, I waved the feather of a sea eagle, white and dark purple black. I felt the air stir and trace its energy along my body. I was dressed simply in a batik sarong I'd bought from a market in a village in the Langkawis. I wanted to be as close to nature as I could get without getting arrested. And I wanted what I was wearing to be close to the raw nature of the past...

I chose my time, twilight, for the in-between magickal nature of that time.

So, I cast the circle, I welcomed the east with the feather riding on the wind, then turned to the south, and held up a glinting raw ruby to represent flame, as fire on the beach can be treacherous in our Southern Hemisphere conditions. I then turned to the west, and poured a bowl of water from the sea over me, feeling it evaporate into air, cool my body, and join the earth at my feet. I then turned to the north, and thanked the land for supporting me, and for bringing me a guide who could keep me grounded on this somewhat mind-blowing journey. I ate some nuts and fruits which I kept for sacred purposes. And then waited.

Come to me
My guide over the sea
Be with me
By three times three
Make clear to me
What I cannot see
As I do will so mote it be

The air blew, and the waves lapped, and the earth radiated the light from the sun, and the heat from the sun became fire on my skin. And I waited.

And I waited. I felt something, tugging at me. I felt a presence with me, and put my hand to my solar plexus, a plucking energy. I felt there was something with me. But it was hardly tangible, it was more a sense that something had shifted ever so slightly, or come to me. But all in all, hardly what I guess I'd been hoping for.

Be patient, I heard, clear and stern as if someone was speaking into my left ear. (My clairaudient faculty always comes through my left ear … my clairs often operate through the left side of my body, as they are downloaded by the right side of my brain!

So, I thanked and farewelled the directions and quarters, wondered if I should have called the directions in a different manner, or if my timing was off, or if … it just wasn't time yet. Feeling my ceremony had been worth the attempt regardless, I left the beach and went back to the house, feeling kind of impatient and amused at myself. I walked over to the herb garden where Khumara had come through so strongly – and so spontaneously! He was nowhere to be seen, but his presence could be felt in the basil, rosemary, oregano and thyme, who were all growing so splendidly.

I went inside, feeling slightly flat, and thought I'd better just keep researching till some kind of breakthrough took place.

Before I went to sleep, for some reason, I slid on a ring my mother had given me, and that I had only worn intermittently. It was blue, Larimar, and I felt a slight tingle, and a warm sort of buzz as I placed it on.

I slept deeply, immediately and, it seemed, dreamlessly.

Until I was awaken by a light tap on my shoulder.

"Wake up!"

My first thought was that it was my daughter. But it wasn't.

"Wake *up*." I sat up slightly, and looked over at my sleeping betrothed. Nope. Not Mister Love. Not my daughter waking me up to tell me of a dream, or vision. And the puppy was at the end of the bed.

I looked into the darkness, and I saw a faint shimmering.

"Are you okay?" a very musical, feminine voice asked. She sounded like my best friend has just entered the room and asked if I'd wanted to watch Supernatural. No thee-ing or thou-ing. She was so … natural!

"You wanted some answers. It took them a while to get me here."

"Hang on," I said. I couldn't make her out, but her voice coming through my left ear was clear. "Let me just get things together and I'll come talk."

I got up, walked through the still quiet house and sat down outside on the lounge. The moonlight was streaming through the ceiling to floor windows. I still couldn't see anyone, though I could hear her, and the energy in the room felt very light, delicate, malleable. (After so many encounters with spirit as a child, I recognize energy very well – when younger, the dense, heavy, stifling energy of some spirits terrified me. I know I can read the energy before it becomes anywhere near overwhelming, and work with it, without feeling the fear that once fed it.)

"Here," she said, and she stepped, glided, floated – moved in some peculiar way into the moonlight.

And I saw her – sort of. She was translucent, and sparkling with energy that moved quickly within the frame of her body. Was she composed of...light particles? Water molecules held in suspension and reflected by moonlight? I don't know. She was beautiful, and yet utterly real. Human, yet obviously composed of something I was not. I looked at her, and there was a cord, running straight from her solar plexus, fading once it hit the moonlight's edge.

"Um. Where does that go?" I asked feeling a slight tug in my diaphragm, the soft place between my ribs...

"I'm joined to you. For a while, anyway. I guess I'm on assignment."

She moved slowly, half of her fading. She didn't seem to be wearing anything, but the light or water that she was made of flowed into shapes that resembled a long flowing skirt, and some kind of halter top. I shook my head, and sighed, though I was excited and thrilled to be with her...

You see, for me, this is more weird stuff. This has been happening since I was a little girl, so you'd think I'd get used to it. But Spirit always goes just that little bit further!

"So. On the beach today?" she said, enquiring. My solar plexus gave a little tug. Weird – just like being psychically linked, only this was absolutely tangible! I tried not to get too distracted.

"Why didn't you come through then?"

"Well, it's just that it's easier for me to come through now." I looked over at the clock, pretty sure of what it would tell me. Yup. Three am. My whole life, most of the really weird stuff had been taking place between 1am and 4am.

It is when the veils are thinnest, and spirit, guides, deities and beings of all types can come through. Which isn't always pleasant, I thought, remembering when I was little, and how frightened I'd been sometimes at the Visitors. I looked at this woman, as closely as I could, me being so short-sighted I'm legally blind, her being all shimmery ether. She definitely wasn't frightening. I was in awe, but I also felt completely relaxed with her, even if we were corded. I wondered if she was helping that feeling of being okay with the cording along a little? I realized suddenly that I still hadn't checked in with her, or asked my visitor her name. You're supposed to do that with spirits! I was so intrigued by her presence – and literally, her presence, that I'd forgotten Speaking to Spirits and Guides Protocol 101.

"So. I'm Lucy. And you're...?"

"I'm Mara," she said, smiling, looking mischievous. "I'm Atlantean. And we've got some explaining to do, I hear?" As she smiled, the cord between us seemed to shimmer and grow stronger. It was growing. It didn't feel draining – quite the opposite.

"So, how come you're here, now?"

"Too hot for me on the beach," she said. The cord wobbled again. Was she laughing?

I looked at her to see if she was kidding.

"I'm not joking! I'd evaporate altogether. The effort to hold this," she said, gesturing to her "body", "together is huge. It took me, what, hours of your time to get here."

I looked at her, all light and delicate shimmer. "What can I do to keep this going?"

"My advice," she said, tilting her head. The hair, tendrils of droplets, shook in space. "Keep the ring on. And be ready for a few late nights. And you'd better get your notebook," she said, with an amused expression.

So I did.

LESSONS FROM AN ATLANTEAN

Mara and I kept this going for three nights. Every night around 3am, up I'd get. Three hours a night, for three nights. Nine hours in all. Not long, but we became closer than I could have thought. Linked by the silvery cord binding us together, I started to receive messages at other times of day. While I really loved spending time with her – she was just delicious, her temperament delightful, at once serene and very light-hearted, my body rebelled against staying up too long.

But we covered a lot of ground. And we started straight away.

"I'm Atlantean. I'm going to give you some images," she said, and the cord pulsed gently, and a huge stream of energy filled my solar plexus, and spread to my other chakras. As it did I understood it, with my crown, I saw it, with my third eye, I could speak with her about it, with the throat chakra, my solar plexus helped me understand the power of it, yet allowed me to keep my own, my sacral helped me sensually kinaesthetically feel the experience, and my base helped really bed it down in me.

Within the stream of images and stories and scenes being "downloaded" to me via this cord, I saw Lemurians, their shape changing and morphing, chameleon-like, as they moved up across the Pacific to the Atlantic. I saw them arriving in various islands, exhausted, consumed by hunger, and out of their comfort zone. The temperature was different. The air was different. Some gasped for breath, struggling to draw sufficient oxygen into their lungs. Others were overwhelmed by the effort and simply allowed themselves to leave. Some did not make it, and offered their bodies in sacrifice to those who still lived, the whales were among them. That was so sad. I saw young ones, and ancient ones, and a tired people finding a new shore to start with.

And then I saw others reaching them. White robed and beautiful, they did resemble the Greek gods of myth! Atlanteans! They were greeting the Lemurians with love, and taking them in and sheltering them. The pictures flashed past. Building canals into the great city so they too could live there. Asking them about their symbols. Their stones. Why they wore so little? My heart felt full of love and hope, and I think

I wept a little, to see that the Lemurians and the Atlanteans were there for each other. I saw vision after vision of a time rich with sharing, and blended beings living in more than peace – in joy with each other!

Now and then, Mara would step in and explain something. It was exciting, and amazing, and full of hope.

And then the visions began to change.

Because underneath the hill of the city, right beneath the temple, coated in what looked like gold, there were tunnels … and within those tunnels, something felt very wrong … I saw flashes of beings howling, blood, and pain, and confusion. I saw Minotaurs and labyrinths, beautifully clean and ornate laboratories with pieces of people and animals being joined together energetically. I saw a Lemurian asleep on an operating table, his sacred stone being removed from his third eye, leaving a gaping wound, the operation akin to being energetically blinded. Mara stepped in, feeling my distress, and turned down the images, and explained what I'd seen.

"The downfall begins with the technological love of power excess and enslavement of other beings, including the hybrid races of the Lemurians and the In-betweeners," Mara said, sadly, like a voiceover on a virtual documentary flooding through my cells. I didn't want to know, in some ways. I just wanted to stay with the original vision.

Because it hurt to see the creatures that were changelings, blended beings, but who were in pain, confused, terrified, and grotesque. The shapeshifters of the Lemurians were a world away from them, with their peaceful energy and natural dignity. How could this be?

"Experiments," Mara said. "There were secret places. Mainly under the hill. They were kept in tunnels so they could not escape. It was a kind of breeding program."

It's cruel," I said, feeling shocked. How would the Lemurians have reacted? To see their own ability to shapeshift replicated in malevolent experiments?

"Lots of us didn't understand," said Mara. "We didn't know, not openly, that these things were happening. They thought the Things were just … slaves, you know. Not sentient, or barely at best. They showed us a different way. But we … continued," she said.

EXPERIMENTS, THINGS AND HYBRID BEINGS

Mara shared so much with me about the Atlantean experiments. The Atlanteans wanted to "re-purify" the Lemurians. Find out who they were ... how they were able to shapeshift so fluidly between forms, to communicate across such vast distances, to hold such power within their own bodies. And so they began to do what we still do, with animals and beings, when we want to understand something, we take them apart, often without their consent. To do that, they had to create their own hybrid beings. So they could see what the "pure" strains could were capable of.

This concept of purity is interesting, as it explains why Hitler's Third Reich took such an interest in locating Atlantis. Hitler felt that if he could find the place Atlantis began, he may be able to find evidence to support his theory of a dominant and superior lifeform on the planet. A race apart.

Mara spent time with me, sharing the information with me, and explaining details. I often felt tearful, almost overwhelmed with grief when she told me of these things. When my face would distort and I would drop my head into my hands, she would wait patiently until I was ready to continue. I often didn't want to. I couldn't bear how we'd had so much, and then we'd lost it. Because we wanted to be "pure"? The irony was dreadful.

She smiled. "You still have so much. You know you are on the verge of repeating this cycle. Or, changing it, forever. Your kind are working with genetics now. That's not a bad thing. It's the intent that matters, it's whether cruelty is involved that matters, karmically.

Of expanding again, and becoming all you can be. It's your theme, on this planet. You need to step in, all of you, and change it. That's why we're talking to you, now. I'm due to incarnate again."

"Incarnate again? You were here before?"

"I'm not talking from above. From some kind of "heaven". I am disincarnate right now. This is a thought form I projected into the future to speak with you. In a way, my new reality depends on what you do with your reality."

"Right Mara," I said impatiently, upset and tired. "People will just think I am nuts. I mean, I'm beginning to think I'm nuts. Maybe I've opened up my third eye chakra a little too much ... Maybe I need to have a nice lie down and good hot cup of tea."

I went and made one.

She was still there when I got back.

"People have always thought you were strange," she said lightly, but with such kindness in her voice. "When did that ever stop you?" she asked, sincerely, somehow understanding the vernacular.

"How do you do that?" I asked. "How do you know what I'm saying – what I mean – when I say 'I'm nuts'?"

"You think I'm that small?" she said, one eyebrow arched in surprise. "Lucy. I was there, for thousands upon thousands of years, and I may be transparent and seem to be made of nothing more than a collection of random particles gathered by moonlight. And I may be disincarnate for the moment. But I have listened for aeons. And I am not deaf!"

So, we hung out, me checking in to my guidance on a regular basis so I could ensure I wasn't really just flipping out somewhere, and that this stuff was coming through me. It's not that I doubt it – it's that it seemed extreme, even for me!

She gave me a lot of information. I tried to get it all down, without getting too caught up. I'm sure a lot of it didn't make it quite the way she intended, me being an imperfect channel and all … but I did what I could, in the time we had.

"So," I said , when we were drawing to the end of the third night. "Where to look f or Atlantis?"

Mara took a moment, before the reply came through. "Open your eyes. Listen. Think. Know."

This was too enigmatic for me. "Know what, exactly?"

"You are right in the middle of an arisen Atlantis, now. That is the key to the Atlantean mystery. I am sure you have already noticed this truth. But it is worth saying again. You have stepped away from the love of the land and the belief in the perfection of the natural environment – when you do not work with the world but against her, you recreate the lessons of Atlantis. Every genocide, every hatred, every time there is cruelty to animals, you are taken to the end time of Atlantis."

"Why don't we get that?" I wondered aloud, realizing the truth of what she was saying. We were caught in a struggle. Truly, between the people who wanted to have peace, and to learn how to create it, and allow diversity and difference, and those who came from fear, and notions of purity, and belief in dominion over the earth.

Maybe, I thought, the dilemma we've had in believing this truth is that we have been so very literal about it all. So many of us have relied purely on Plato for our sense of what Atlantis is, and we've searched with our intellect since then for her location and her lessons. Plato, indisputably a genius, and absolutely the being we have to thank for keeping the memory of our own past alive with his descriptions of a brilliant civilisation with unmatched armies, advanced technologies, is not the Creator, and is presenting us with a small sliver of a much larger story, a moment's glimpse of a civilisation that was aeons old.

Mara nodded, silently agreeing with my train of thought. We held each other's gaze for a moment.

"Will I meet you again?"

"I think so," she said. "I'm due back soon. Besides. We'll know each other."

The silvery cord between the two of us started to shine brightly, and then began to shimmer, and slowly dissolved into light.

She was still there, but I couldn't feel her, or hear the thoughts any more. She waved gently, and mouthed farewell.

I sat, and said goodbye, and watched her form separate into particles of moonlight, until all that remained was the moon streaming into the house.

And then, things started to make sense.

UNDERSTANDING ATLANTIS

The visions I have since had of the early interaction between Atlantis and Lemuria are so much more than hopeful. It was peaceful, exciting and dynamic, positivity in expression. It was akin to the words of Plato:

"For many generations, as long as the divine nature lasted in them, they were obedient to the laws, and well-affectioned towards the god, whose seed they were; for they possessed true and in every way great spirits, uniting gentleness with wisdom in the various chances of life, and in their intercourse with one another."

Knowing we are connected to the divine, that we are the divine itself, we behave in ways that are divine. When we lose that connection and that belief, when we view ourselves as merely impermanent, meaningless players on a stage, with temporary witnesses? Well. Things change.

Things did start out very well. There was a simultaneous urban and rural Atlurian culture that flourished for thousands of years, where we made spectacular advances in technology that were harmonious with nature, where we were fully conscious with fully activated DNA. Where we lived together, as one, and learned. Technology and power were in service to the principle of the Law of One.

And there has never been a time on this planet like it before or since. An incredibly diverse culture and civilization, with crowded, exciting and dynamic cities, with beings excelling in their chosen fields, and wisdom governing the day. Beings whose beauty and focus and intelligence and creativity are astonishing, and whose spirit shines from their body, radiant and beautiful. A time of beauty, and truth, and peace. Of interactions and excitement, and of learning, at an incredible speed, of our potential.

MEMORIES OF ATLANTIS

During workshops, where increasingly the lessons of the Lost Lands were rising, I started taking participants through deep meditation to Atlantis, and then, once they'd been brought back, and grounded, I was fascinated to hear each person share their experiences. I wasn't speaking too much about Mara at that stage: Khumara and I, well, that felt fine to share. But this knowledge, so recently brought through, still felt like a raw nerve was slightly open around my solar plexus, and it had yet to settle down. So I wanted to keep listening. People at workshops are often vital, open, curious and incredibly powerful psychics! What they had to share really was valuable. Then I could see if the shapes were matching up, fitting together, and if the picture emerging was one we could all make sense of.

Most intriguing were the patterns that kept coming up: the same things, reported over and over. I love it when the shape underneath begins to appear – it seems we are then dealing with something with real substance and potential when more than one person is reporting the same experience.

* Many reported moving into water and being able to change into another being, or being able to breathe underwater.
* Many reported being able to swim with whales and dolphins, or being whales and dolphins.
* Some reported being at a sea shore.
* Many reported feeling overwhelming emotion of bliss.
* Many reported being able to communicate with all other beings.
* One reported being able to swim in the Milky Way as a whale or dolphin.

I continued to have visions of a vast city in which there were streets teeming with beings, where the atmosphere was unique and like a carnival, with elementals and hybrid beings walking and speaking with humans of all different sizes, shapes and colours. There were angels walking amongst us, and mermaids swimming through the canals that Plato described in such detail in his dialogue Critias. I didn't see Mara again, but my solar plexus felt somewhat raw, alive and more sensitive to energy and to touch than it had ever been. I couldn't be certain that she wasn't "reaching" me in different ways. The visions expanded, allowing me to see the technologies and structures of the Atlanteans.

To facilitate communication across the vast distances of the empire, and its Lemurian outposts, enormous towers were built and coated with a golden substance that telegraphed the sonic pulse messages across the distances. Pyramids, to build power from below and project it up, and to draw power down, were built.

This was the time when the shape of the circle, which was so prominent in Lemuria, began to make way for the shape of the Pyramid. Its energy was one of solidity, reaching upwards, and was hierarchical and vertical in form. While Lemuria had been a place of equality, Atlantis was evolving into a place of hierarchies, hierarchies who required others to do much for them to live their lives of rarified intellect and genius.

At the base of the actual pyramids were library and energy centres, with channels and tunnels delving deep into inner earth, where many lived over time, studying.

There was open communication between other galactic societies, including the Pleiadian and the Sirian, and an earlier one, known as the Arkadians, and the Arcturians.

There were many kinds of beings: this place truly was heaven on earth for a time, and the Eden of which we speak can indeed be located for a time in Atlantis.

I sent several modern-day Atlanteans questions about their memories; fascinated, I pored over the answers!

"Everything I experience with Atlantis has flow and an amazing vibrational energy," said Maria, who answered my eager questions with such verve, such vivid descriptions. "The food was nurtured with sacred ceremonial rituals and respected fully as with the true connection to the One. Clothes were always quite luminous and light, sort of ancient Grecian, yet futuristic. It was like everything was touched by love and oozed spirit, as this civilisation was beyond our own in consciousness. Food tasted with amazing freshness, even our organic fruits today don't even come close and the air was so pure. Every person had a role to play, yet not in a hierarchical way, however, a meaningful one. Tailors were seen as Priest/esses of Tailoring, farmers were seen as Priest/esses of farming, healers were seen as Priest/esses of healing and so forth. Every person's role was sacred and life in this time was honored and appreciated."

The sense of wonder and magick that we are able to behold in visits via visualisation are hard to explain and even more elusive to grasp and comprehend energetically. There is a richness that may still be too powerful for us at this time. Maybe, as the earth changes and heals herself, and as we evolve, we will have more and more vivid dreams, trance and meditation experiences. And perhaps, through these experiences, we will begin to truly understand the fullness of the Atlantean experience.

Atlantis, over time, slowly moved away from the early dreams of a culture uniting galactic and terrestrial inhabitants in an endeavor to further creation itself; and spun off into a series of hierarchical secret societies whose agendas began to cloud the earlier mission. And these agendas were subtly opposed to what is, in effect, good.

But here is the confusing thing. They called themselves good. And things seemed to be going so very well for them. So many people began to think that maybe what they were saying was true.

For example, Animals were not considered at all what they are today. The remnants of this relationship can be seen in the respect of shamanic practices, where attributes of the animal are taken on with reverence, permission and respect because of all they can teach us, of all that we can understand if only we open up to that aspect of ourselves that is indeed them.

Animals (always in upper case, you see, to reflect that respect) were in charge of large facilities, including learning areas, wisdom schools and were keepers of many mysteries.

In essence, we and Animals were often hybrid too, and these beings who were hybrids, rather than being seen as they were – a stage of evolution of ourselves, were seen as Things. Today, many channellers connecting with this time speak of the Things. They are not things, which is to imply that they are less-than. They are hybrid beings with much wisdom to share.

THE ELEMENTALS OF ATLANTIS

Many spiritual traditions teach that elementals (faeries, unicorns, merfolk, dragons and other hybrid, shapeshifting beings, such as the Dragonfae) had physical and emotional relationships with humans... The tradition of the Tuatha de Danaan of Ireland has tales of intermarriage, the tales of the Tylweth Teg, and of course the Olympians of Greece intermarried and created beings that were only part human! Thus these beings were kept alive, and intermingled with the blood of humans...so many of us, especially those of us who are exploring our magical selves who are drawn to Atlantis, Lemuria and Avalon, are in fact part-elemental. Many humans with this blood live today... we often interact with other members of our soul clan without realising it...and receive messages that seem sometimes confusing and nonsensical until we realise our heritage and bloodlines.

Among the hybrid beings who were seen regularly on the streets, in the towns, in the villages and schools, universities and temples of Atlantis were the Centaurs, the Animals, the mermaids, the fae, the Dragonfae, and many more. There were also Sirians, Venusians, Pleiadians and many more intergalactic visitors. What a time – of glory and of revelling in shared wisdom! The following beings are available for you to connect with and learn from today!

The Wisdom of Chiron

Centaurs were often the head of the schools of medicine in early Atlantis. Chiron, the leader of the Centaurs, is a gentle, caring scholar and healer, whose own experience with healing led to him becoming an adept in energy healing and physical healing methods. They are extremely tall, large beings, with an affinity for music and mentoring. Call on them for energy healing and finding the right medical practitioner.

Dragonfae

A blended group of beings – part dragon, part fae, part angel and part mer-being, these hybrid beings were able to traverse the different lands with ease, and travel galactically. Dragonfae are part-Earth being and part-galactic being, and share the best of all these beings' natural traits. They are very strong, and cannot tell a lie. Call on them for right direction and understanding your own differences within, and for making decisions. They are especially helpful when it comes to unlocking your DNA and the repressed parts of yourself: the talents and skills you may have buried within. They are like psychic miners who can come in and tap into a vein of gold or precious jewels that cannot be seen superficially.

Faery

These Earth beings pre-exist the galactic colonization of Earth, and worked harmoniously with the Lemurians and the other forms of elemental creatures. Of course, while they were working with the Lemurians, growing plants, shifting weather patterns and teaching others how to work with the watery and earthly conditions of this planet, they were also in their own colonies in Avalonia – which had yet to be discovered by the Lemurians or Atlanteans! They blended very easily into the varied and wild population if they wished, as they were able to change their shape and size easily, and make their wings extremely transparent, if and when they had them. (Many did not.) So fine and light, that they could barely be seen, except by those most sensitive to them.

They are an intrinsic part of Earth lore and are gentle, kind, funny and very powerful. They can be "understood" to be mischievous, but that is because they do not follow rules. Many humans have fae blood, and Dragonfae blood, within their veins, and it creates a distinct appearance and experience of this planet Earth. Many young environmentalists, musicians and artists are fae-blood. They sometimes appear to "float", and are quick and easy in their movements. They are often unaware of their own translucent wings, which are still with them, and may often feel strange between their shoulder blades. They can hear a higher range than many humans, and have pleasant, often charming voices, angular brows and unusually large eyes.

Dragons

Because of their ability to travel vast differences, and create portals between dimensions (including the dimensions of time) dragons are found nearly everywhere in the universe. In many cases they have blended their lines with the fae (on Earth) and in the other star-systems, too. Tiamet, the powerful, strong Goddess of the Babylonians is a Dragonfae of earthly and galactic bloodlines. She is the quintessential elemental example of as above, so below. The expression, found on the Gnostic Emerald Tablets and revived by modern white magic practitioners, as above, so below refers to our galactic and to our earthly origins. It has interpreted many other ways, but that is its core wisdom, and it is embodied by these incredible beings.

People with this bloodline tend to feel "fierce" and powerful; often they have strong limbs and may experience extreme skin sensitivity to chemicals and to environmental toxins. Conditions like eczema and psoriasis are common for people with this bloodline. They often have flying dreams, seem to 'stare" rather than look (they do not need to blink too often) and are frustrated at the seeming small size of their human form. They are "vast" and powerful people, who are often overwhelmed by their visions and their own talents.

They have a den, adore crystals, and have close ties to either blood or soul kin. They need to feel safe as they feel startlingly conspicuous when "exposed."

Merfolk

Were predominantly Lemurians who migrated from their lands as the seas rose. Despite the truth that Atlantis had much to do with the overt destruction of Lemurian culture, before 29,000 BCE there was a large cooperative blending of the cultures. The remnants of Hyperborea, from which was formed Atlantis, were colonized by the shapeshifting Lemurians, who adapted brilliantly to the rising sea levels. They underwent further transformations in their physicality as a result of the migration, which is captured beautifully in the tale of Prince Idon and the origin of red-heads. Merfolk were absolutely the most visible of all the in-betweeners in Atlantis. They were a distinct and important part of the sacred culture, and worked and lived between the sea and the land. The females and men were renowned for their beauty, for their sensuality and their freedom, for their beautiful singing voices and for their ability to inspire great love. Many Atlanteans came to mistrust them as they "tempted" Atlanteans away from working hard and encouraged them to play and to immerse themselves in the healing waters of the ocean, and the healing light of the sun, rather than studying in the temples. They are, as are most elementals, not particularly given to structure and rules, but they are extremely brilliant and productive. Many, later in Atlantean times, were "enslaved", and some were killed or executed. The most harm, however, was done by the propaganda that twisted the truth of their being: the lies told made many male Atlanteans mistrust and fear the feminine merbeings. Many retreated from Atlantis and kept small colonies alive off shore, keeping their freedom, but as they are friendly and social beings, they longed to return to humanity. Some shapeshifted into humans to assist with the transformation and rescue of many beings at the end of Atlantis, but many stayed far away due to the genetic "switching off" that was taking place. To ensure their survival, many watched at a "safe" distance as Atlantis persecuted and experimented upon the elementals, and interceded to save lives when they could. I have had many visions of waiting off shore for survivors on floating debris and taking them to shore on the new lands.

Merfolk, well, love the water. They drink less water than they should, but you cannot get them out of pools. They are good communicators, highly empathetic, and deeply sensual. They are not very materialistic, and find as much pleasure in a sea shell as others do in diamonds.

They are often long-haired, and frequently they are redheads. They are friendly, sexy, and often physically very attractive. They don't do angst and guilt willingly – it really has to be forced into them, and then they can wash that away very quickly when they realize how insubstantial and ill-healing those feelings are. In Atlantis, they were singers, and in this lifetime, you may be a singer, a beautician, a spa attendant or a hairdresser! They have addictive personalities, and while they may drink less water than their watery bodies need, they may drink more alcohol, tea or coffee than they should for maximum health!

Redheads

Many redheads are of Lemurian decent, and none more so than the merfolk, many of whom seem to be just water-loving humans today! Redheads, who are often theorized to be Nordic or Celtic in origin, are actually found all over the planet. Red-haired mummies have been discovered in such far-flung locations as Phoenicia, Italy, Greece and some areas of Africa and the Middle East – all Atlantean colonies. Because of their distinctive and different appearance, redheads were widely discriminated against in recent history, actively during the burning times, and even now redheads can be given a rather hard time. But if you know of the origins of redheads, you know you have a distinctive makeup that says clearly to the world just how magickal you are. Redheads often fear elements "irrationally" because of this discrimination, which in past lives led to horrible torture. Redheads can also suffer extreme addictions, which once they embrace their magical natures, dissolve. Many dwelled in the underground caverns beneath Atlantis (the city) post-destruction. Prior to that time, they were able to be in the sun. Post destruction, a protective layer of atmosphere was damaged, and many beings began to be "harmed" by elements that they had once had harmony with.

This is why red-haired people burn easily in the sun; are likely to get skin cancer, including both melanomas and non-melanomas. Interestingly, red-heads have different pain thresholds to other people. They sometimes need fewer anesthetics during medical procedures, and have a lower tolerance to some pain produced by heat or cold, and high tolerance to pain produced by electrical currents. These trends do not show up in the rest of the population, showing a genetic makeup that indicates a markedly different evolution.

Unicorns

These beautiful beings were rare even in Atlantis.

They were even rarer after Atlantis. You see, Atlantean Unicorns were killed, because they refused to allow their horns to be used to dilute and re-purify the DNA of the changelings and the shape shifters (referred to as "Things")who refused to give up their abilities, even when those abilities were outlawed in Atlantis. Before they were destroyed the Unicorns gifted their horns to the narwhal, the great whale with the spiral horn. This way, their magick could still be taken around the planet. The beautiful narwhal have been hunted for milennia for this horn: this must be done no more. These endangered beings need our protection and support. No more can we strive only to gain from their gift in such brutal ways!

The remainder of the Atlantean Unicorns remained behind, and passed with the great wave, leaving their Avalonian cousins to embody and carry forward the energy. The Unicorns themselves shapeshifted into magnificent flying horses, Pegasus, and their relatives lived on in Avalon, determined to keep their elemental bloodline alive, and became more cautious than ever before.

Their primary role is purifying bodies of water, and they were focused in Avalonia. Their skills were not needed until later in humanity's history on this planet. They are gentle and powerful and their medicine is that of clearing waterways of debris and blessing water so it contains a clear, high healing vibration. If you drink of water blessed by a Unicorn, your own "impurities", toxins and pollutive thoughts and feelings are washed away. They bring back our purity: our essential self, which is of joy, love, and a sense of being at one with all that is.

Unicorns also help us to retain our youthful energy, even into a long lifetime. (Many Atlanteans lived for some 300-400 years, the Lemurians even longer.) Centaurs and Unicorns have great rapport, and the Unicorns are especially able to assist with parenting issues and children who are having trouble adjusting to energy, school, foods and who are especially sensitive. For children with reluctance to speak and mix, Unicorns will assist them to find their soul family and right path, whatever stage of life they are at. When you have a Unicorn with you, they are there with you for life. They also assist people with food sensitivities, and work well with crystal healers.

People with this energy are pure. They can change an area's emotional volatility with their presence. They are often healers, nurses, and they work as doctors and microbiologists. They are beings of great integrity. They are very sensitive to impure energy, and if their services are refused, they will not be able to stay in that environment.

They are often taken advantage of. Once their innocence is crossed, however, their wisdom of betrayal leads them to go deeper into their own selves, becoming elusive and very, very good at hiding. Unicorns are particularly protective of children in dangerous situations. Unicorns often live near bodies of fresh water, lakes, waterfalls, or are drawn to areas where there are deep underground springs. They are also found in the deep green of the ancient forests.

Nymphs and Dryads

Nymphs are, broadly speaking, nature spirits who can take humanoid form, and the form of the natural force they care for. Tree spirits, known as dryads, can become as one with the tree they are protecting. However, today, if that tree is harmed or suffers, so does the nymph who protects it. In the Atlantean Golden Age, nymphs were not harmed except by natural earth changes, which were not seen as "harmful", but as a natural part of the cycle of birth, death and rebirth. Atlantean culture fully embraced these beings, as they did the Plant and Animal beings, too. Today, if nymphs wish to make contact with a human, they will do so – more often subtly than through outright transformation and clear interaction. They are very shy, wild creatures as a result of what took place in later Atlantean times. If they need to hide from us, they can easily do this by combining their physical matter with the tree itself, for example.

There are various types of naiads, or water nymphs, just as there are various bodies of water. They are NOT the same as mermaids at all. They have a different energy, and are not fish-tailed, for want of a better term!

Dryads care for the trees. Oreads care for the mountains. Limoniads watch over the meadows. Herliads care for the fen... there are nymphs for every living natural geographical region, and for its elements...

All the elementals are very powerful and they are very sensual... they are the intelligence of nature incarnate, when they choose, in human form. They have often given birth to humans through their loving interactions with human men – the great

Greek hero Achilles was a nymph. The Atlantean being Hermes had a nymph for his mother – making nymphs the nurturers of divinity, and these divinities were able to understand and transcend far beyond human wisdom. Zeus, too was said to be fostered by a forest nymph, who taught him that he was a part of nature, and taught him the art of shapeshifting.

People who are part dryad, or naiad, are sometimes at a loss to understand the socioeconomic or cultural rationalisations of the day...they do not understand why we are seen as outside nature, why our decisions and choices seem so often dictated by economics.

They become physically distressed, upset and saddened when natural resources are harmed, culled, torn down. They similarly are elated and joyful when in natural environments that are relatively untouched.

They often become activists of some kind – they are often the meeting point between spirituality and activism.

ARE YOU OF THE ELEMENTAL BLOODLINE?

Many of the traits of people with elemental bloodlines include being;
* Artistic
* Rebellious
* Super-sensitive
* Creative: They are often painters, poets, actors, and often work in circuses as they are very strong and flexible!
* Passionate lovers of aspects of nature. For example, some may be drawn to storms – storm witches, others to sea, and become marine biologists. They have massively transformative experiences with nature, but often do not view themselves as "spiritual." Because they see and experience this as natural, they do not give it terminology that people of earlier times would call spiritual.
* Fascinated by the elements, sometimes one over another. For example, "water babies" who love to stay in the bath or refuse to get out of the pool, or the fire-wise, who play with matches, and stare into candle flames. (It is best, if your child is interacting strongly with an element, to encourage them to do so in healthy, creative and safe ways. Sometimes adults who were told to "never play with fire" or to 'stay away from water" repress their natural urges and become secretive. They may grow up to express their fascination with a particular element in ways that can be frightening and destructive.)

* Sensual – and it is something of a miracle that this powerful, beautiful trait has survived, as you will discover below.

APHRODITE – THE SACRAL UNLOCKING

In the early days of Atlantis, all beings were "in love." With all that is. But there was no division from you and others. The radiance of each being's chakra system shone out so bright that our spirits could clearly see, feel and HEAR the song of another. And we found our soulmates easily, without any of the agony associated today with love.

But in the latter days, sex became somewhat tainted. Some Atlantean rulers felt sex was a lower act, that it was unnecessary and not to be partaken off without purpose and great purification and ritual. (Shades of Puritanism!) Sex between the shapeshifters was outright banned in some Atlantean colonies. Where sensual loving interaction was once natural and good, bringing pleasure and energy exchange, it became outlawed, as the powers that be attempted to control the fluid, shapeshifting and extremely peaceful and loved hybrid creatures.

When many were enslaved, they were given a "lock" on their sacral area, to prevent procreation and to lock down the powerful sexual and sensual appeal of these beings. Keeping soulmates apart allowed greater despair among some of the shapeshifters: despair means we are easier to control…

This lock is still in place today for many beings, men and women, and had its historic echoes in chastity belts, the removal of female pleasure parts, and gelding of men who were slaves. For many of us, this sacral locking is energetic, thankfully, and we can strive to unlock this powerful aspect of self, through the intervention and action of the beautiful, alluring Goddess Aphrodite!

Aphrodite works closely with her own soulmates, two dolphins. These beings can help you grow closer to hearing the song of your own soulmate. She also helps unlock the "chastity belt" that many of us have around our sacral areas. We may be searching for relationships, in the Atlantean true love style – but how can we activate them when our hearts are open, but our sacrals are in lockdown? Some of us are carrying past-life memories of this lockdown, of sex being bad, and we need to ask for her help to lift this away and bring us to freedom!

The sacral, remember, also governs reproductive organs, and thus our own ability to give birth to ourselves.

More now than ever, we need this freedom and this sense of innocence about our physicality! The planet is undergoing a revolution in love – and any recreation of the mistakes of the past can be balanced out and transmuted through the power of guilt-free love. And New True Love relationships are beginning to come through – different in their energy, their day to day living, their purpose than ever before... This is the love you were born for, for you are alive now. This kind of love experience is your destiny. We all need to prepare now for this True Love to unfold. Not a fairytale. Not a struggle. Just love, and relationship that is meaningful and mutually beautiful, strong, enlightening, supportive and romantic, but on healthful romantic terms. No more idealization of romantic suffering, or yearning, of that sense of "starving" for love! Healthful, happy and clear relationships!

No matter our karma, our past lives, our childhood or what society tells us about our imperfections, we are all deeply loveable, and we all have the capacity to experience True Love. However, we must first clear the way, so Goddess Aphrodite can fully enter our lives...and her route is through the sacral!

Meeting Goddess Aphrodite had definitely changed the course of my life, and her magickal energy felt like no other – sensual, healing, loving, compassionate, she was able to draw forth the toxins from my sacral, to dissolve the barriers I'd put in place – and that ancient times had also placed with me!

Aphrodite, a being of Atlantis, who became known as a Goddess in her latter incarnations, was a Temple priestess who healed, lifted and dissolved the beliefs and barriers and deep emotional toxins which had kept true love from entering our lives. She and her dolphins (or rather, the dolphins and she!) worked with all Atlanteans. Her work was trivialised later, and she was said to be dangerous to work with, or considered somewhat tragic, or silly.

She is so powerful! Once we have dissolved and unbound these vows and chastity belts, we will then recreate our love potential by recreating our beliefs, our muscle memory, our karma and our energy, which will enable us to welcome the joy and romance of Aphrodite into our lives... She shares the secrets to creating beautiful opportunities, attracting wonderful partners, developing romantic intuition, unfolding our sensual expression and experiencing the blessings of True Love in our lives – this lifetime...

APHRODITE'S SACRAL RELEASE CEREMONY/MEDITATION

Please, take a moment to breathe. Become aware of each breath, and remember and feel the *out* breath as much as you do the in breath.

Allow yourself to relax, and feel throughout your body and energetic field for any blocks, areas of pain, wounds or restriction...just be aware of them.

You are now in the presence of the Goddess of Love, known by many names. She is Aphrodite, Venus, Astarte, Pele, Isis, Guenevere, Dana, Isolde and Ishtar....

Aphrodite speaks, and she says...

I, who am the Goddess of Love, now free you from all vows of chastity.
I dissolve them all, and know that you may now walk forth and free into a realm of physical delight and pleasure with safety and your personal power intact.
I now take my golden key, and I unlock this cruel belt that binds you. Once unlocked by me, it can never return.
Are you ready to be free, and to experience your divine sensuality?
I now ask you to step out of this belt, to gently ease yourself out of this bondage...
I now give you permission to dissolve your vows of chastity and revive the maiden within...
Feel the energy from my hands soothing and easing any hurt, pain or wounds in this area that has been so cramped and imprisoned...
Feel the blood of your sacred body circulate freely through your internal organs, through the chalice of your womb, and the sacred orbs of your ovaries, the wondrous cords of light and love that join them both.
Know you are freely flowing with love, with moisture, with pleasure and with the Goddess... you now are me, as I have always been you, and have cried tears at our separation.

Know that this now is your truth...that you walk freely, and move freely, that you may take your pleasure with yourself and with the God, with freedom, beauty, safety and passion. You are safe, you are beloved, and you are a divine, sensual woman.
I declare it so, and so it is and always shall be...
Blessed be...

And when you are ready come back, allow yourself to feel whole, and loved, and safe, and sensual. Be real. Be free. Be woman. Be Aphrodite of the sea.

ATLANTIS: THE EXPERIMENTS

It was at this stage of our creative evolution on this Goddess, Gaia, that many of us became obsessed with being more-than. And the system known as slavery began. Castes were created, and those at the foundation of the pyramid-like structure of Atlantis were chosen to support the "higher beings." And slaves they became.

Not everyone agreed with this system, which still lives on in various forms around the planet. Those who voiced their concerns were subtly harassed, implied that they were deluded, and that only some could know the rarified heights of true knowledge and power. Slavery, they were told, was a way of protecting those who were not ready for more! Besides, the rulers said, they had volunteered for this.

Those who were rallying points for opposition forces, soon called rebels, were taken beneath the city to the burgeoning labs. Some had their sacred stones removed. These were gathered, and worked on to release their immense power, which contained thousands of years of ancestral knowledge. They were used to further power a grid system that would control a population, and control the weather.

Intergalactic beings were also divided on this policy. Some concerned beings gathered together and warned the Atlantean hierarchies, growing in status, wealth and power, of the possible outcomes of their actions.

As they were no longer directly involved in the planet's governance, their requests were politely glossed over.

But it is hard to control shapeshifters. When they can change their form, when they can transmute and make themselves smaller and larger. They can be heard across vast distances, just through telepathy. So it becomes very difficult to get them to conform.

So, at first, vows were made. Vows to choose one sex at birth. Vows to stay in one form, unless permission was granted. Vows not to conduct ritual, without a licence from the Priests. Vows to no longer communicate telepathically. Vows to donate their stones for the "greater good of all."

Ceremonies were held to "convert" shapeshifters and rebels, who openly gave a pledge to no longer shapeshift. The first step in this was to separate them from their former elders.

To make them feel ashamed of their sexual fluidity.

THE OPERATIONS

I was a diver, one of the girls who went below and farmed for pearls for the temple. We never did drown, as we were born to swim beneath the waters...however, we could not make it upon the land, and were often kept in separate quarters. I dived for Aphrodite...a merbeing in her service.

We ate seaweeds, fish and oysters...the land dwellers ate fruits, all strange and prickly looking on the outer, soft and sickly sweet on the inner.

We were slaves, servants.

I see myself sitting on a ledge, awaiting the next order. I am tired.

My friends want to walk on the land, and they can do this if they sell their own pearls for the operation, as we call it. I am hearing them like it is a kind of half-language.

They have an operation, which seals up their breathwater chamber, and unseals their legs, and fashions a kind of foot, they cannot walk, not like They do, but they can hobble and then they are worked on...then they fit in with the land beings. Then they are no longer servants.

I plan to be free, and to swim away.

There is another temple, an older one, abandoned, they say, across the islands. The levels keep rising, you see. We keep moving back, as the shoreline gets higher. There are rivers inside.

But around 30,000 BCE, some instructions were made, and experiments begun to recreate pure strains of beings that had until that time happily coexisted and mixed their bloodlines and their wisdoms.

SACRED FOOD AND GENETIC MODIFICATION

There is a Lakota creation story, that each time I read it, I understand more and more that it is a prophecy, and one which we would do well to hear. Please read it and see if, for you, the words have echoes in these times of evolution we are living in.

The people and animals emerged onto a barren earth, and the wife wondered how they would live. The man said, "Go to sleep." Four times they slept, and each time they woke there was more growth around them. After the fourth night, they awoke in a grass hut, and there was a stalk of corn outside. The voice told them corn was to be their holy food. If they plant corn and something else comes up, then the world will end. The voice didn't return after that.

In the world before this one, the people didn't know how to behave or how to act human, and the Creating Power was displeased. He placed three dry buffalo chips under a sacred pipe rack and saved a fourth for lighting the pipe. He sang three songs to bring rain, which caused the rivers to overflow; then he sang a fourth song and stamped on the earth. The earth split open, and water flowed from the cracks and covered everything. The Creating Power floated on the sacred pipe and his huge pipe bag. All people and animals were destroyed except Kangi, the crow. It was very tired and three times asked the Creating Power to make a place for it to rest. The Creating Power opened his pipe bag, which contained all manner of animals and birds, and selected four known for their diving abilities. He sang a song and commanded the loon to dive and bring up mud, but the loon failed. Likewise, the water was too deep for otter and beaver. But the turtle succeeded in bringing up a little mud. The Creating Power took the mud and, singing, spread it out on the water. After the fourth song, there was enough land for himself and the crow. He waved two long eagle feathers over the ground, and it spread until it replaced the water. He named it the Turtle Continent. The Creating Power thought, "Land without water is not good," and wept for the earth and the creatures he would put upon it. His tears became oceans, streams, and lakes. He scattered the animals across the land; they came to life when he stamped on the ground. He created four colors of people from red, white, black, and yellow earth. He created the rainbow as a sign that there would be no more great flood, but warned that he had destroyed the first world by fire because it was bad, and the second world by flood, and he would destroy this world too if people make it bad and ugly...

If we create without respect, we too are re-enacting the end times of Atlantis. Genetic modifications, this desire to "know" rather than to understand, was one of the "great" experiments of Atlantis. It was not, as many think of it, the science of manifesting, it was the science of artificially switching on and off genetic structures, and controlling their intermingling. Without the heart energy, and with only the desire to control, including vast weather experiments, many patterns of weather and famine were set up, which still occur today. We are in a time now where the experiments are being, in so many ways, duplicated.

Atlantis has arisen...indeed she has. And the experimentations, to switch off and on the codes that created plants that resisted "dis-ease" were the precedent to the switching of the genetic codes within many of us.

But back to the present cause. Atlantis.

"In the City part of Atlantis the technology was predominantly through Crystal and Metal. I feel they were as advanced as we were if not more so in some areas. Healing with Herbs and Crystals, Crystals were a huge part of every day life. Everything from running water. I do believe they had computers or such like. I don't think that this is the first time that this world has been technologically advanced. I do think we seem to reach a certain point where our focus on material creation outweighs what Gaia can sustain and we destablise the planet and we get destroyed. We survive and then we start again. This knowledge is so old, and so forgotten. I only catch glimpses of myself."

– Deb's memory

As I emerge from the vision of a later Atlantis, I'm shaken and fragile and I know I need to connect with a friend. Someone who understands. So that I know I am not going crazy. That it is a breakthrough, not a breakdown.

I breathe until my breath steadies. I tell myself it is a memory. *It's not happening now. It's not happening now.*

But part of me knows it is happening now – otherwise this memory would have no resonance. We must be in a place where there can be an echo of the cycle – the same turning point on the wheel as before…

Trembling, I stretch my hand out for the phone. I take a deep breath, then hit speed dial.

"Hello?" I can feel tears starting in my eyes, and my voice is wracked with pain. I can barely speak, and emotionally I feel afraid, and alone, and like I'm calling her from a long, long time and place ago. I feel like something terrible might be happening again.

"Lucy!"

"I just need to tell you something. I've been having visions of Atlantis." I try not to cry as I speak about it, but I'm not succeeding. "I think...I think our DNA was deliberately switched off."

And with that, I burst into the tears that I can no longer hold at bay.

The hardest part of working on this book came up from time to time in meditation. Not so much the toilsome research and interviewing and writing, which was all natural and flowing and beautiful (well, in the main!), but in the understanding that beings have done terrible things – enslaved and attempted to keep lines "pure", feeling and thinking all the while that what they did was in the best interests of the majority. But my visions have just shown me a world where our DNA was not only switched off, it was switched off deliberately to keep us under control.

Coming out of these visions of our DNA being switched off was actually depressing and sad for me. I prefer to believe in the innocence and wonder and divinity of all – that at heart, all beings are good and divine, and that by recognising that, we allow what is good to shine through. We are all one – is that not clear?

And yet... could it be that I am naive? That what my vision showed me, of mass interference with the Lemurians' and Atlanteans' DNA, as part of a dark galactic force's desire to enslave us, was part of what had taken place around 10,000 years ago. We are not as we were – but we are returning to the truth about ourselves...at last.

As far as I can pinpoint, and I will by no means claim infallibility here, but according to the information I have received, the date for the beginning of the switching over process occurs around 29,000 BCE. This is the time when the destruction of the status of the Animals and the Hybrids, including the Dragonfae begins to be established, and the wizards with enormous power begin to teach that the physical is evil, that matter is not spirit. And we begin to hate ourselves, and this is the key that enables a mass inoculation to take place. We line up and we receive an energy implant that leaves no real scar, but which takes away a part of who we are. It takes away our ability to communicate with the Animals, and so we believe that we have been foolish and imagining things to believe that we can speak to them.

The end, of course had its roots back further than this. It began when we were told that technology and power demonstrated evidence of higher intelligence, and greater worth. When these beliefs took root, it was because within human hearts had grown a love for luxury and power, that could excuse injustice to others by explaining it away as lessons and karma. We too repeat this each day, which is why it is so essential for each of us to adopt the habit of making a small karmic offering daily, and with each lunar cycle. Maybe it is that you bequeath some time each week to a project that needs your energy. It could be a financial donation.

SHIELDING AND DEFENSE TECHNIQUES

In the latter days of Atlantis, many were harmed by mis-use of thought forms and energies being directed with negative intentions – intentions to control, shut down, impede and attack. Out of the desire to repurify all the blended lines, to prevent shapeshifting between forms, and between sexes, in order to more easily control the population, psychic attack, as we might call it, became commonplace, and very powerful.

To this day, many varieties of thought-form negativity exist. Fear. Toxic relationships. Abuse. Choices that feel inevitable. Rationalizations, even in the spiritual world, that tacitly give us permission to go against the Law of One.

Environmental negativity and energy can be harmful, particularly in workplaces. And as many of you are reborn Lemurians and Atlanteans who may not have incarnated for the last five thousand years, your form is very raw. Again, it is important to understand that many people may seem able to cope with energy that seems out of balance or harmful. They may have built up a resistance over generations. There may be many reasons for this resistance. They may have slightly differently activated DNA to you. Their past lives may have been different.

But most of the reborn ones are super-sensitive. So, here are some ways to create and choose environments where you will be well.

By creating our own world, rather than entering harmful ones, we are choosing to reshape and recreate the energy that exists within the world, and rebirth a healed and whole Atlantean community for the future.

Many of we reborn-ones have been sent "undercover" to work in what I always term our "straight" jobs. We are nurses, doctors, librarians, teachers, we are journalists and receptionists and bank clerks. We are absolutely needed in these environments, although, paradoxically, within them difficulties and challenges can abound.

Within these environments are many disempowered and jaded people who will often at first react strongly to another soul's strength and happiness and sense of gratitude and purpose. (That's a big one. A lot of people get all miserable around folks whose lives have meaning, and who refuse to live in fear ...) They can be resentful, and difficult, and harmful. However, our strength is in staying well.

Most people who lead lives of great beauty and example, who have clearly had incarnations in Atlantis have had epiphanies that could be seen as "bad luck". Atlantean crystal bed healer Maria Elita "lost everything". My marriage imploded. Angel therapist pioneer Doreen Virtue was carjacked. The Journey's Brandon Bays (a space person if ever I saw one!) experienced cancer. Were these curses? Attacks? Indeed not. They taught us all that we are indeed more truly blessed than we ever dreamed of.

Here are some forms of the challenges we may encounter. Remember, these will, as the Goddess blessing says so beautifully, make us strong.

It's important for all of us to be mindful of the truth: that most of this energetic draining is quite unintentional. Often an individual, without realizing it, is sending out harmful energy, and focusing that energy on another person. The attack can take the form of an irrational hatred or fear of another person, who the attacker seeks to blame for circumstances. If we are the recipient, and sensitive, this can make us quite literally unwell. We can feel like the life-force is being "sucked" right out of us!

Another is when a needy, greedy "victim" individual literally drains those who attempt to offer support.

Another form of this drainage and harm – often called psychic attack – is actually reflected energy. In other words, the person who *believes* they are being attacked is suffering from their own energy, returned to them. This often occurs when the object of their obsession knows enough about energy to shield with reflecting surfaces, but not enough to know that without grounding the energy, the attack could well escalate.

It is rare that true, intentional psychic attack occurs, as it did in Atlantis. Most people who know about magickal energy work understand very well that there are grave consequences if they activate the law of the threefold return. (This metaphysical law dictates that whatsoever consciousness you are in, and sending out, will return to you, with the power of three.) To initiate a psychic attack means you have chosen to deliberately step outside the ethics and tenets of energy work – a very serious decision. Why would someone resort to attack?

One reason is because unconsciously, many people have been programmed to feel very frightened in the presence of people or beings who are awakening. Thus they attempt to shut them down…

A psychic attack can also involve a twisted, thwarted kind of love: attack can almost be the flipside of obsessive passion: some people, when they cannot have the relationship they feel they must have in order to survive, will do anything to maintain some kind of connection – they are terrified of a kind of psychic self-immolation occurring if they cannot "have" the object of their desire. Atlanteans and people who are reborn ones are very attractive: people may want what you have. If you stay detached, their efforts may escalate. Most attacks on us occur because we are shifting: our shapeshifting powers are returning, and people can feel this power! And instead of rejoicing, they want to stop it! They are frightened because they are about fear, and lack, and staying safe. We are about expansion, about being one, and about holding the vision of the truth of a peaceful, beautiful, energetically evolving planet full of fulfilled beings living meaningful lives of great diversity with mutual respect!

So what does the "attacker" do? They attempt to obtain the connection that will still give them import in their obsession's life – thus there is an extremely common form of psychic attack which is a kind of romantically motivated mental stalking. Friendships gone awry, jealousy and rivalry, thwarted passion, imagined slights: all can be dealt with in many ways, but human nature is such that passionate individuals forego even their ethics when emotional intensity rules their thinking.

To ascertain if psychic attack has ever affected you, it is important to be very clear minded. Remember that most negative, dark magic works on the power of autosuggestion. If we simply realise that a person does not like us, sometimes that is enough to make us ill, especially if we encounter that person each day and must attempt to deal with their harmful auric emanations on a regular basis. This most often occurs in group situations: school, work and family. (Autosuggestion is the psychological predisposition to assume that intention is power: the power we give away to an individual. Thus, when one is threatened, the power of autosuggestion inclines us to imagine that that person indeed will follow through on suggestions. That is why bullying is so successful as a psychological tactic. It worked in Atlantis. Tragically, it still works now. But we CAN change this!)

Some people, who have large levels of auric toxicity to dispel, imagine attack where none exists. Thus they engage in psychic pre-emptive strikes. If the recipient responds with reflection or counter attack, too soon you can have a psychic feud going that can drain not only those involved, but innocent others on the periphery.

Here's a checklist of symptoms that can indicate that a true psychic attack is taking place:

* Extreme fatigue – the attack is draining your spirit, your chi or prana. Chi, the Chinese term for energy, Prana, the Sanskrit term, or Nwyfre, the Celtic term, is our life force. If it is being systematically drained you will notice a pattern. It may manifest as a feeling of being probed or burrowed into.
* Extreme fatigue that occurs, like clockwork, at the same time each day. Please note that fatigue occurring between 2 and 4pm each afternoon may be metabolic. Many people in Western culture have an energy slump at this time after their body chemistry adjusts after eating.
* Headache – this could indicate that your aura has been weakened, and you are psychically breaking down. Your crown chakra is being broken into.

* Drained feeling – akin to fatigue. If this occurs after being with an individual, this could indicate they are the "vampire." Listen carefully to their language and the tone of voice they use. Go beneath the words, to the energy.
* Nightmares – at night your subconscious is highly suggestible; your body is also more vulnerable, as you are not technically present and alert inside your physical body when sleeping, which gives the attacker an "in". Most people have nightmares at some time – it is a signal from your subconscious alerting you to an issue that you may need to resolve in your waking life. Nightmares from psychic attack though are not related to your own life issues: they may contain visions or entities that terrify you.
* Temperature changes. Explicitly, psychic attack symptoms could manifest as cold spots in otherwise warm or comfortable homes, or a sudden drop of external temperature. If you are suffering your own temperature fluctuations, please see your doctor before making any assumptions about being under psychic attack.

The truth about the world is that you may offend people simply by owning your own power as a reborn Lost Lander! There is nothing you can do to avoid the disapproval of others –attempts to win universal approval will only leave you more vulnerable to their negativity. The greatest defense against psychic attack is to build a strong identity, and to love and respect yourself, unconditionally. Know we are all one, and ground that energy when it comes at you! Be watchful, but be strong!

How to be an Atlantean psychic self-defense expert – whether the attack is intentional or otherwise, these methods of protection all work.

* Use the stone obsidian. Formed from volcanic lava, obsidian will protect by throwing out a natural shield. Alternatively, work with Black Tourmaline.
* Deconstruct and work with your fears. Are you not seeing the blessings in a situation?
* Cloak yourself, head to toe with not a single gap, in white light that "breathes" This permeable layer thus allows you to feel light, bright and free, without the heaviness of many shields. Over-shielding is akin to walking about in medieval armour and wondering why we feel stifled, or why we get hurt when we fall over. Keep it light, keep yourself well. Keep breathing.
* Keep your chakra system vital and healthy. Again, over-shielding can lead to dense, toxic pockets. Let them breathe and they will heal!
* Know the Universe loves you and protects you in all ways.
* Feel your aura each day for "holes". If you find any, repair them with good food,

good thinking, self-love and being around beautiful friends.
* Maintain, or aim for, perfect health.
* Shamans recommend homeopathic remedies – they change the vibration of your subtle body and energies.
* Use humming/white noise/music.
* Chant and drum. You will be strong, and well, and bright.
* DO NOT reflect the energetic attack – you may start a feud.
* GROUND the energy instead. Stop the cycle, don't perpetuate it.
* Choose to see this challenge as perhaps the single most important moment of your life. How do you choose to deal with it? Make this a blessing – not a curse.

Are You Vulnerable to Psychic Attack?
    *Are you sensitive?
    *Do you find it hard to make a choice?
    *Are you not certain of who you are?
    *Do you have chameleon tendencies – pick up habits, traits of dominant others?
    *Do you have poor ego boundaries?
    *Have you suffered major life trauma (divorce, death, accident in the family, sacking)?
    *Do you have unresolved childhood issues? (Obviously we all do! Traumatic issues are the ones to watch out for and work on resolving.)
    *Do you suffer from poor health? (This can lead to auric field leakage.)

If you answer yes to three or more of these questions, you may be more susceptible than others to negative energetic fields. So let's work on your courage, your strength, and aiming and maintaining perfect physical, mental and energetic health.

ATLANTIS: THE END TIMES

The stories of the deluge are so similar, it is like they are echoes of the same story, told across the ages, and we have forgotten that it is OUR story. All of us experienced this.

From Southern India, the Tamil people tell the stories of the Lost Land Kumari Kandam… (Kumari! Could this land be a clue to the identity of my friend and guide, Khumara?) This flood is said to have obliterated the first Tamil Sangam, a great library, a reservoir of knowledge.

The people are said to have moved north, into what is now called India, and the one survivor was a prince, who rescued some ancient scrolls and managed to swim to the remnants of his land, called Tamil Nadu.

In the Sumerian legends, we hear that the God Enlil warned the Priest-ruler Ziusudra of a coming flood. He was instructed to build an enormous vessel to house the beasts and the birds upon it. The sun-god Utu brought him to the country known as Dilmun. Thus ended the age of Arkadia.

In Wales, the tale is still told of the lake of Llion in an island to the west rising and rising, till it covered all the lands. This lake soon covered the island, which merged with the sea, and the beings Dwyfan and Dwyfach left, in a ship with the prow of a dragon, and all manner of beings with them. They reached the shores of Prydian and created anew their world.

"I don't think I died during the demise of Atlantis," says Deb, a healer from South Australia. " I think I died several years before, when people started throwing around warnings of what the future held if we did not change our ways but people were so convinced of their own invulnerability that they ignored the warnings, to their demise. I do think that the weather was unstable and became extreme, pretty much as what is happening now, I seem to feel like I have seen all of this before.

We don't take seriously the lessons that the fate of Atlantis shared with us. We fail to realise we are travelling the same path. My feeling is that Atlanteans became full of their hype, they were advanced, nothing could hurt them or touch them, they could do what they wanted with the Earth, with society, who would stop them? They were the top of the food chain, top of technology chain...top of everything, they tried to control Mother Earth, genetics, weather, and they went too far, just because you can do a thing, does not mean you should do a thing. They put the world out of balance and as a result caused their own destruction…pretty much the way we are doing now."

Today, I know that many people I meet and see for readings and healings speak to me of their utter surety that they are in the "wrong" form. I feel that this is a symptom of the fluidity of form seeming to be turned off. We were in fact switched off, right at the core of our DNA's potential, and in the great experiment to homogenize the "perfect race" we did ourselves great harm.

Many of the current day incarnated Atlanteans have in fact not been present on this planet since that time. They tend to be the beings who are most activated to prevent a second catastrophe. Some of these souls have been sleeping for nearly 11,000 years… For many of these souls; there were no lifetimes in other realms. They ascended around 5,600 BCE as the waters covered their city, and they reincarnated 7,600 years into the future, in what we call the 20th Century.

But there are those who do remember.

The dolphins.

And the whales.

"We will only receive redemption when we return to the water."
– Jacques Cousteau

THE HEALING DOLPHINS OF ATLANTIS

There's a vast, deep ocean of research, legends, myth and musings about the incredible dolphins. Nearly all of it alludes to just how close we are to each other. But the wisdom of Atlantis teaches us that the magickal cetaceans (dolphins and whales) are closer to us than you may think!

Many magickal practitioners, wisdom keepers, shamans, lightworkers and witches feel that we are them, and that they are us. As we awaken to the lessons of Atlantis, and as the lights go on again (and those electric ones go off!) we will all recognize and respect our kinship with these incredible, wise and beloved oceanic beings.

I grew up with the ocean, and with her beings. My entire family are dolphin lovers, but none more openly and emotionally so than my Dad.

It's not hard to understand. My Dad met my Mum at the beach. I have a suspicion that I was conceived in the water! It wasn't enough to live near the beach – my parents finally have one of their lifelong dreams today – to live in a house overlooking the water. So, it seems we've been trying to get closer and closer – maybe even back to the ocean our whole lives.

I'm sitting on the balcony of my parents' far north coast dream home, in the small townlet of Lennox Head in New South Wales. Tucked behind Byron Bay, it's a secluded paradise, earthy and wild, and very much a well kept secret, except perhaps amongst surfers with a keen eye for a perfect wave. Thousands each year arrive in this tiny village, drawn by tales of its world-famous clean, powerful point break. It is breaking this day, glassy smooth, and I'm gazing out at the headland and its waters, my eyes scanning the deep blue ocean for signs of dolphins.

My beautiful Dad brings me out a cool shady hat, and a hot cup of tea. My Mum is at yoga. Even on steamy days I love my tea. He leans on the wall and looks out towards the deep, wild blue of the ocean, sparkling in the still morning sun.

"You know, Love," he begins, his expressive face full of tender emotion. I feel so much love for him. My Dad's a softie. He's done more than accept his witchy, slightly wild daughter. He's loved her unconditionally.

I sit up, nursing my tea. I have the feeling he's about to say something very important.

"I can't imagine living away from the ocean."

He's not kidding. The longest he ever made it was three months in Tuscany, and even that relatively short time away did something to his soul. He felt the cord between him and the sea stretching thinner and thinner. When he got back, he dived into the ocean, and felt whole again. It makes sense. My Dad was a Bondi Lifesaver, swam before he could walk, met his soul-mate by the shore and threw me in saltwater before I'd even tried taking land-steps. No wonder he pines – saltwater's in his blood.

"I know you can't Dad." I really *do* know. I'm ten kilometers away from the great raw Pacific in my home in Sydney, and it hurts sometimes.

"I think," he said slowly, looking out to sea, "I really was a dolphin. You know. In a past life."

He is absolutely sincere. He turns and looks at me, and there are shining drops of tears gathered at the corner of his warm eyes.

"I just love it so much," he says quietly. "I look at them, and I am so happy."

I smile, and go over to him and hug him. "I know, Dad," is all I say,

We look out to the glittering Pacific, and a small pod of dolphins are out there, feeding from the rich sea life of the Point. This was, for thousands of years before we Europeans arrived, a sacred site for the Bundjalung people of what is now called northern New South Wales. Now it is our sacred site too, and a national marine reserve. It is Australia's southernmost reef, and I love it dearly.

The shore, and by that I mean all of the places where land meets water, is a liminal place, an in-between place, as much as is sunset, twilight, sunrise and dawn. A doorway into a kind of altered state, it is at these points that our hybrid selves are merged and re-joined, and most comfortable. Our sea-self comes out to play, but our land-self feels safe, protected, too.

Australia's population is often referred to as "fringe-dwellers". We stay close to the ocean, and those of us who move inland feel the heartbeat of the country in a way that is different to those of us who are sea-peoples.

I like to stay in the in-between places. But most of all I love the watery places. I have lived in the Dakotas in the northernmost tip of the United States for a year, a land of blizzards and long dry summer plains where once buffalo were free and wild and plentiful. I have lived in the heart of London, where its river called me and soothed me, as did the Seine when I lived in Paris. I love freshwater places, like the sacred sites Glastonbury and Bellingen on New South Wales' north coast inland mountains. But truly, for my spirit to be free and whole and true, I need to be by the edge of the sea and the land. This is a green and blue planet. We are both of the sea, and of the land. As above, and so below, simply in a different context.

And I know when we are at the ocean's edge, we are looking at a submerged section of the world. A world where we were dolphins, and I know we will be again.
You see, humans and dolphins are deeply intertwined, almost related physically. Here are just some of the traits we magickal beings share.

* The neocortex in human and dolphin brains are virtually identical, meaning we process the world in very similar ways. The neocortex determines our sensory and extra-sensory perception, the movement of our body, knowing where and who we are in time and space, our development of a mind, and language. So, humans and dolphins have twin brains, brains that mean we understand each other, and telepathically communicate, even if superficially, we seem to sound "different". We are, in many ways, speaking the same language.
* Dolphins and whales have the remains of thumbs and toes during their development – just as we have a tail during our inner-world, womb development.
* Dolphins make love face to face. The only other creatures who do this are we humans!
* Dolphins make love for pleasure, not simply for procreation. Often several times in a row!
* We humans have a fatty layer beneath our epidermis, like the dolphin and whale. Women have an extra layer. (We women surely stayed in the water longer!)
* Humans love water. And no wonder we do. Studies show our heart rate slows, and our blood pressure normalises when we go into salt water.
* We share tear glands with whales and dolphins. Our tears are salty, and full of chemicals, making tears an intelligent response to stress and anger, as it detoxifies us faster than any other practice.
* Our spine shares many traits with dolphins – more so than with land mammals like apes!
* Remember my friend Khumara, from Lemuria? He advised me to eat like a dolphin, and to eat salmon, too. Well, the EFAs he spoke to me about are actually brain food, as well as full of rejuvenating lipids. The brain of a human and the brain of a dolphin both need omega-3 and the omega-6 fatty acids *in precisely the same proportions*. There are no other creatures on the planet who share this need! No wonder Khumara urged me to eat like a dolphin! That means sea vegetables as well as protein-based sources of these EFA's.

So, we have a lot in common. However, we also do *not* share some traits, which makes dolphins especially amazing.

* Inside the dolphin's brain is an apparently "empty" chamber, or cave. Studies suggest that this fascinating cavity is a resonance chamber that generates telepathic communication and high abstract thought (think fractals and sacred geometry, thinking in sophisticated patterns). It may also serve to create holograms which are then sonically projected.

* Echolocation: These astounding mammals know where they are in time and space, and what is outside of them down to the most precise of details via the ability called echolocation: they send out a pulsed wave of sound ... whatever it hits sends a pulse back to them. They can then read this pulse and decipher exactly what is taking place for kilometres around them. They can discern whether potential predators like sharks have full or empty bellies – thus allowing dolphins to make intelligent decisions about where to be, and when. Echolocation allows dolphins to pulse their sonar into us, and each other, healing and shifting toxic cellular debris, as well as dislodging and dissolving energetic debris. Their sonic pulse may even create these psychic resonating cavities within OUR brain! Encounters with cetaceans can make humans even more sensitive, psychic, and enhance greatly our ability to heal, just as we did in Atlantis! Much of the spectrum of these sonic booms of healing frequencies may seem to be undetectable to the human ear, which has a relatively narrow band of frequency detection. Dolphin encounters can reignite our special "hearing" and switch on our DNA.

No wonder we love them so much – and they love us right back, with such compassion and generosity! Dad's not alone in his intense love of the sea and its beings, many people share his deep and passionate connection. In fact, one woman loves her male dolphin-friend so much that she married him.

Sharon Tendler spent fifteen years with her dolphin friend, Cindy, before they committed to each other. It's a serious and respectful commitment.

At Dolphin Reef, in coastal Israel, Sharon wore a flowing white Goddess gown, a veil and flowers in her hair. "I do love this dolphin," she said to the very curious press, who'd gathered hoping for that day's wacky news story. "He's the love of my life," she said with dignity. "It's just something that we did because I love him, but not in the way that you love a man. It's just a pure love that I have for this animal," she explained.

She may have been more public with her love and respect and the commitment she's made to her dolphin companion, but tales of men and women falling in love with dolphins are ages old.

THE MERMAID AND HANUMAN

The golden-warm, intricately carved temples of sunlit Angkor Wat have led many people to believe that they were all constructed around 1,200 years ago – however, Cambodia was underwater some 6,000 years ago, and the information I received while at the temples was that areas of them pre-exist that deluge.

This largest of the world's temple complexes, one of the world's most mysterious and truly sacred sites had long fascinated me. The story of the 100-kilometre temple complex that includes Angkor Wat and Angkor Thom (made famous by Angelina Jolie's Tomb Raider films) had drawn me for some time. I knew one day I would go there. In 1861, a French naturalist working in Cambodia stumbled upon the ruins of Angkor. From beneath heavy, twisted jungle vines he unearthed a temple complex so complete, so gorgeous, so unique that it was like stumbling upon a time capsule from another world. Exotic, rich and culturally distinct, the temples carry within them an energy of masculinity and overwhelming beauty. The world could barely believe its good fortune.

This vast temple complex was relatively untouched, and before long, this gem of antiquity became one of the most fashionable destinations of the modern world. It is mysterious, engulfed in jungle and raw beauty, sensual and pulsating with primal energy.

There are many temples, and some are in better shape than others. Most are an expression of Hindu cosmology, an earthly representation of galactic events and heaven itself. It is a vast city of the Gods.

To see the nagas, the half-serpent half-human beings who keep watch on the moats across the Ocean of Milk, the vast concentric moats that enclose each of the temples, is to see through the veil, into another dimension.

There is a peacefulness there, and stunning carvings depicting scenes that vary from fierce battles and cosmic wars to displays of intense eroticism between Gods and Goddesses. Tales from the sacred Hindu texts of the Ramayana and Mahabharata adorn kilometers of temple walls. It is truly a kinaesthetic experience – it has to be felt, to be embodied, in so many ways. The energy is vital, peaceful, yet thick like honey, light and humorous in places, extremely sexual in others, ominous and brooding elsewhere. It is the kind of tangible energy that assaults the senses, and literally brings you to your knees.

Only when I first set foot in India's holy city of Varanasi, on the mother Ganges, had I experienced a similar sensation: vertigo, followed by an intense flood of exquisite emotions and memories. Angkor unleashed a tidal floodgate, and through it poured a powerful brew of physical sensation and cellular memory. I shuddered, sank to my knees, groping for a seat, and wept. The power of this place, Angkor, had literally knocked me off my feet.

Even while my head swam with the powerful energy, I knew that the journey to these sacred temples was one of my stepping stones to understanding the Lost Lands. For Cambodia lay beneath the sea 6,000 years ago, according to science. She rose as sea levels dropped, and today, when negotiating the vast temple complex, avoiding the areas designated off-limits due to unexploded land mines, or finding a small, shady, quiet section of temple, still teeming with fierce, pulsing jungle energy, there are tiny seashells to remind us of just how much older than the 1,000 years she is said to be. Just to remind us that she came from the sea. Perhaps to let us know that the temples were under the sea well before the lands rose 6,000 years ago.

As I travelled the temples, I felt energies of the ocean. The moats are designed to evoke the Ocean of Milk, the place of all creation in the Hindu cosmology. But it was more than a representation. It was real. There was the sound, echoing off the walls, of rushing waves, the high-pitched clicks of dolphins, and a shimmery quality to the air, which seemed as reflective as the watery surface of a tropical lagoon. I had a feeling of being underwater from time to time – that I was swimming through the temples themselves. And it wasn't just the humidity!

Finding a place that seemed somewhat secluded, and shaded by the mighty, ancient trees growing straight out of the walls themselves, I sat down, breathed, centered myself, and gave myself up to the magicks of Angkor.

I asked "What is it you wish us to know? How can I understand you more?"

Within my mind's eye, I saw a series of bright flashes, and heard waves crashing louder than before. A little startled, I opened my eyes slightly, and noticed that the tangled roots of the trees were sprinkled with sea shells. I heard a light intake of breath, and looked up, to see an unusual kind of fae being. She was long and lean, yet full-breasted, dark and lovely, with toes pointed and bent upwards, hands positioned gracefully, and she spoke by moving her hands through the air.

There seemed to be water running beneath my feet. I could feel it lapping about my ankles.

It felt strange, and yet absolutely loving.

She smiled, and made another incredibly sinuous movement. She seemed part serpent – so lean and strong, and rippling. It's very hard to convey precisely how unlike any other fae-being I'd seen she was. There was something absolutely "other" about her. I knew I was meeting one I had never met before. Yet there was no feeling of fear.

She looked, I thought, like an extreme Cambodian dancer – I had not seen the dances, but those impossible flexible limbs reminded me of the expressive movements I'd seen hinted at in travel brochures.

She seemed to smile, and as she did so, a tone floated across to where I was sitting, my feet still cool in the water.

"When we dance this way, we are showing you the old ways of our language," she explained, without speaking. This was telepathy sent on the frequency of the tone – something I had experienced before, primarily with galactic beings! I wondered if that was where she was from, and whether all galactic beings used sound and movement so gracefully.

"Ah! Like the druid hand signals?" I asked. I had for years been fascinated by the druidic lore of secret hand signals – a way of communicating through sign language that only the very adept were taught, as a way of protecting secret knowledge and sharing deep secrets in the safest of ways.

"Akin, but for us, there were no secrets as you call them," she said, smiling faintly. Her every expression was so gentle, it was hard to catch. Behind her, I could see the buildings, the temples, the tourists meandering in and out, and the sound of the Land Mine Band playing behind her. "We spoke this way as we could. Now we dance this way, but few know what it is we are saying," she said.

"How old is this place?" She sighed. "Older than they say – for they say we who live here have been here for maybe a short time."

"But the truth is we come from the mermaid, and from the land-being, known as Hanuman. This took place many many eons ago, when the land was shaped so differently to now and when we lived within the sea."

I thought I knew who she was speaking of… "Do you mean the monkey God – Hanuman?"

"Yes. This is no tale of legend… this is how we came to be… we are many things, but once we dwelt within the sea, and were at one… mermaids… when Sovan Matchaa met Hanuman, she was not to know she would love him. And we never would have thought he would love a woman of the sea. But the being of the land, the monkey God, and the woman of the sea, the mermaid, fell in love, and at this place they built their above-water underwater kingdom, and they moved between both, and had their children, from whom the children of the earth are formed. The dolphins birthed their babies, who were of the sea and the land, and the whales carried them all over the blue and green planet. When the lands sank, or left, as you say, the whales carried those of us who stayed all over the planet."

"So… we are from the sea and from the land?" I was intrigued, my mind buzzing with over-stimulation! "The lands left? Left? And we chose to stay? And the legends – the legends aren't legends at all, are they? They're the truth underneath the science, the essence of us all?"

She nodded.

"And what are you?"

"I am of the air, and a dancer, communicator, language maker. I am an Apsara, and my role is to teach through movement. You call it kinaesthesia. The language and wisdom of the body. Apsaras are more than dancers – we communicate between realms, carry messages back and forth, and connect with the ones like you, who can see, and who are ready to learn."

"So … I felt this area seemed older than the 6,000 years it is said to be … not the land, but its history as a structure. Is this part of the Lost Lands?"

"How can it not be? It is a place where a form of humans began, where we were all one, and where a place born of love was the kingdom. This is Hanuman's and the mermaid's kingdom before it was a temple for men. It was surrounded by sea, the fragments of which remain today. There were dolphins throughout these pools, and one was my true Love."

"What is above will come down. And what is below will rise above. So, the ancient places may rise again. And its bedrock and ancient energy has risen again at this time to help the people of Cambodia."

I nodded. I think I understood. The terrible civil war and genocide of the 1970s and 1980s had decimated Cambodia's population, and left the land pocked with live land mines, many of which are still around the temple sites. The temples were the bedrock of the new world in Cambodia. Their energy had to be powerful – the lives of millions of people depended on them.

"There will be many new risings over the coming years," the Apsara went on, her hands gently telegraphing the "words" to me. "Some of them will be between worlds, from other worlds. The Mahabharata will come to be," she said, referring to one of India's most sacred texts that tells of the creation of the world, and which the temples venerate. She gestured towards the massive moat, only a fraction of which I could see on its voyage to surround the temple. "The Ocean of Milk – this is what the moat represented – the Ocean of Milk from which all life sprang! The stars brought forth life – but it is not what people interpret this to be." One graceful hand gestured up, where one star remained in the bright blue sky.

I looked up, although I found it hard to drag my eyes from hers. Her beauty was divine, and magnetic in its force. "Is it … the Milky Way?" I wondered aloud. "So … The Ocean of Milk, that the temples are saying is the cradle of life … it's the Milky Way – other planets – galaxies and beings?"

My voice was quiet, but she had no trouble hearing me. I was feeling awed. Maybe this was a kind of hallucination, and I was overwhelmed by the heat and the power of this place?

"No, sweet one, you are not."

I smiled weakly, feeling slightly queasy. "I feel dizzy."

"Let's hurry then. My energy is new and strange to you. That place you call the

Milky Way is the Ocean of Milk, and it is the stuff from where many came. For we are all blended, of the Earth and sky, sea and land, and from beyond the stars our origins are.

Her substance was growing thinner, and a high pitched sound, a brilliant high note rang through the air, her gentle facial expressions growing fainter, I could see the buildings behind her even more clearly, and the buzz of human voices became louder, as did the sound of insects.

Suddenly a bell chimed out from the monk's temple, and a crowd of yellow robed Buddhist monks walked past, smiling and full of joy in this Khmer Hindu temple. She waved, turned, and grew fainter, like a rainbow vanishing from the sky. The light seemed a little less bright once she had gone. But I felt I had found out what I went to Cambodia to discover. I thanked her, and took a flower from my hair and laid it on the ground. I took a shell from the place, and placed it over my heart, tucking it into my bra, and gave thanks.

I felt certain that she had revealed a great secret to me: that this land was a part of the lost Atlantis, and that dolphins, and mermaids, and land dwelling beings had all been as one.

WISDOM SCHOOLS OF ATLANTIS

For many cultures across the world, whales and dolphins are associated with divine powers and are seen as superior beings. In ancient Greece, to kill a dolphin was equal to killing a human and was a crime punishable by death. For dolphins were seen as messengers for the Gods, and were closely associated with Poseidon's daughters, the Nereids, the goddess of love Aphrodite, the heroine Galatea and the music-loving sun god, Apollo. It was said that the constellation Delphinus, the dolphin, was put in the sky by Poseidon in gratitude to the dolphins for finding his bride Amphitrite.

In the rainforests of the Amazon Basin, the native Indians tell literally thousands of legends about the mysterious pink Amazon river dolphin, also called the Boto. Stories abound of the river dolphins taking human form and wooing young girls. They are often regarded as unlucky, as they may tempt unknowing men and women into the water, where they are taken to Encante, the underwater world of no return. Similar tales of shape shifting are told of the elusive Baiji, or Yangtze river dolphin.

In Sumeria, dolphins were connected to Ea-Oannes, the deity of the sea, and sometimes with the goddess Isis in Egypt. The ancient Celts attributed the dolphin with well-worship and the healing powers of water, and the image of people riding dolphins is seen on some Celtic artefacts. Some Australian Aboriginal tribes claim to be direct descendants of dolphins, who are sometimes regarded as guardian spirits. The dolphin is also an important symbol in heraldry. Heraldry refers to the symbols of noble houses, often emblazoned on armour, shields and banners as a form of identification and protection in battle. The dolphins were leading guides and teachers for the adepts and wisdom schools of Atlantis. Their beauty and courage, good humour and strength was admired, and as we recognized we were all one, at least in the Golden Times of Atlantis, marriages between very different beings was common.

Remember that Animals and Humans and Elementals and Angels were not as divided as they are now – there was tremendous interaction and relationships were quite different to how they are today. For example, we would meet for a gathering, and it would take place at the ocean shore, and at that gathering there may be present a dolphin educator, a merbeing, two fae, one wizard, a lion, an angel and a galactic being. Together, we would plan what would be helpful to manifest, and then we would undertake a creation by meditating and energetically bringing through what we felt was needed.

Dolphins were educators in the oceanic school, and could communicate via sonar, as they do now. These sonar pulses drive through the oceanic songlines, or leylines of the planet, and reach far beyond, into the stars as a form of galactic communication.

Many star-people have very strong connections with dolphins, as of course do those of us with mer-blood in our genetic makeup.

Throughout the ages, of course, we know that dolphins have performed a variety of "services" for the benefit of the human race. They are important religious symbols within the folklore of ancient civilisations, and today, we are interacting with them more freely and joyously than we have for some 30,000 years, since the fall of Atlantis. Many times I have been out in the water, as I love to surf, and have experienced incredible joy at seeing dolphins near me in the water. To see them, as I have, swimming close to me while out in the water at sunrise is sublime. As each of my chakras awakens with the colours of the sunrise, seeing the dolphins at that sacred time seemed to be a profound message, a blessing from the heart of Gaia herself.

As my brother has a significant brain injury – from which he has made a miraculous recovery – I am always interested in brain research that focuses on healing from such traumatic injuries. Generally, these are suffered by young men self-initiating through facing death down in an irreverent manner.

Once, you see, the shaman would have taken the young man through the near-death experience. Now, our young men still partake in this necessary and instinctual rite of passage, but without guidance it is a dangerous path they walk. The result is many young men dying, or being left with harsh scars and injuries, reminders of their face-off with death. Just as the Apsara had told me.

DOLPHIN HEALING

My brother's epic recovery from a brain injury has been a very important part of my life, as well as one that has inspired others. Educational anthropologist, Dr Betsy Smith has a brain-injured brother herself, so her research absolutely resonated with me. She observed behavioural changes in both dolphins and her brain-injured brother during encounters in 1971, and pondered the potential healing energies of such interactions. More than thirty years later, her pioneering DAT (dolphin assisted therapy) programs motivate behavioural and cognitive changes in disabled children and people suffering from cerebral palsy, autism, spinal cord injuries, strokes, cancer, post traumatic stress, chronic depression, attention deficit disorder, Down's syndrome, muscular dystrophy, blindness, deafness, anorexia and dyslexia have all benefited from close encounters of the oceanic kind.

And it's not only people who are recovering from trauma who benefit from dolphin interaction – and especially WILD dolphin interaction. After my experiences with them out in the water, while surfing, I feel literally blissed out, strong, healthy, robust and fearless! Some of the hypotheses being suggested include theories that a dolphin's sonar is capable of stimulating the production of specific hormones, altering brainwaves and causing space to be created within the soft tissue of the human body.

Captive dolphins, sadly, live much shorter lives than their wild counterparts, though they live in more controlled and presumably safer environments. In fact, they tend to become deeply depressed, and often shut down their sonar altogether, thus negating their healing. It's the equivalent of fasting when one is imprisoned – this "sonar strike" means that humans who imprison dolphins actually not only rob this beautiful being of their liberty – they rob themselves of the healing interactions the dolphin freely gives when wild and able to volunteer their services.

DOLPHIN MIDWIVES

Apart from these healing interrelationships with dolphins, my visions of Atlantis and Lemuria show that we were also birthed by and with dolphins. Hybrid babies, and we, were nearly always born into bodies of water. Babies born this way, both human-dolphin hybrids and beings more aligned to one expression of self grew up balanced in the left and right hemispheres of their brain. Dolphins have incredible ability to switch sides of their brain: they don't sleep but they deactivate one side of their brain at a time, allowing the other to shut down and rest. Babies born in the water have more ability to move between left and right hemispheres of the brain, and thus are more integrated and fully expressive beings, who naturally are peaceful, harmonious, naturally loving and highly intuitive – as well as conventionally intelligent and able to care for themselves in harsh environments.

Hawaiian people practised oceanic births traditionally up until 1937, when western medical practice and well-intended but misguided missionaries deemed this sophisticated and natural method of ensuring healthy happy babies unsafe, and ungodly! Now, dolphin and human birthing partnerships are taking off again, with one to two women each week making enquiries to one such birthing centre in Hawaii, the Sirius Institute. Centres are also opening up worldwide, throughout Mexico, on the Caribbean coastline, and in south-east Asia, where authorities are more likely to "look the other way".

These dolphin midwives are reviving an extremely ancient, natural practice that is helping to reprogram our planet, and increase the inter-species linking that will see us as part of the natural system, rather than a unique being with an economic framework! From the Black Sea to the Gold Coast, dolphin doulas are helping mothers deliver, and nurture their babies – and to have beautiful, transformative birthing experiences.

Sonar is very interesting: even if you cannot "hear" dolphins, their presence in the water near you means their sonar is flowing through you. Dolphins make very strong eye contact, too – staring into one dolphin's eye from the prow of a boat for some forty minutes in Western Australia changed me in deep ways. And research shows that dolphins use this amazing echolocation sonar to sense what is obstructing our auras, our cells, our brains! They can bounce their sonar off the inner cavities of our body and sense what is not right. Their sonar, bleeps, whistles and clicks can rearrange our very matter. They often rub up against a person, or nudge them gently with their silk and steel nose, sometimes staring deeply into our eyes, unblinking, even embracing us.

In fact, if we listen to dolphin babies, their sounds are hard to distinguish from human babies! They seem to speak the same language!

We are not blessed to the same degree though with the miracle that is echolocation. I do feel this skill is inherent in humans too, and is a part of our "switched off" DNA.

Echolocation helps a dolphin know if a shark's tummy is full in very much the same way. Thus I know if I am out in the water and I see a shark, it is likely that the shark has a belly full of fish. It helps me stay calm while I smoothly get myself out of the water. (Sharks are predators – they don't just strike because they're hungry, unfortunately!)

I have experienced the powerful effects of echolocation myself. There are such variations in each peculiar sound: from the scraping, which sounds like debris being cleared from bone and teeth and skull, to the clicks that sound like sonic plucking of entities from my aura, to the strangely creaky noises that sound like openings being made in my ability to see, hear, and fully be awakened, each sound has a purpose, and each dolphin knows where you need work.

After spending time with dolphins, it is common to feel disoriented. I feel after being out in the water with them a peaceful elation: joyful, yet full of such deep tranquility that I feel wide awake and yet deeply calm at the same time.

HOW TO CONNECT WITH THE DOLPHINS OF ATLANTIS

One way to connect with dolphins and the oceanic energy of your own self, and of the world, is to dedicate some time to the sacred act of ocean environmentalism. The awe and mystery and magicks of the ocean become even more potent when we engage with her with reverence.

It simply transforms the self when we help transform the environment. As above so below – as within, so without. What we do out there directly changes what happens within us. If we feel unwell, clogged up, stagnant, take time to clear a waterway. Just one small sacred time set aside to collect rubbish from a sea shore will make you feel alive, connected, tap you right back into the nobility of your nature, and the sea creatures will send you energy! If we do this, we actively create a relationship with the sacred that exists outside of the self – and the self becomes sacred too. That energy exchange is monumental in its power!

Ask yourself what you hold dear about dolphins, the ocean, the deep green and blue of the planet. The water is her blood, and the salt water is the birthing blood of all life.

Look into the eye of a whale, or dolphin in an image or picture of a wild dolphin. Even more powerful will be swimming or interacting with wild dolphins – but that will take place when you are ready, and when the sacred oceanic beings take that step forward to greet you.

* Diving
* Snorkeling
* Underwater photography
* Make a donation to a group like Greenpeace or Sea Shepherd.
* Learn to surf! Think of the board as a tool of power, an arrow forging a path through the waves, interacting and creating purpose and beauty. Don't be nervous about falling off! 'Tis all a part of the process! Go with a knowledgeable person, though, or a respected surf school – the ocean has her ways, and she speaks a language that needs to be re-learned for many of us. Know where rips and channels are. And know how to swim.

CALL ON THE DOLPHINS

Dolphins will assist you with finding true love (they were great friends to the Goddess Aphrodite).

They also assist with communication: To become more telepathic, call on the dolphins, and they will help you attend to the nuances of tone and pitch of voices. They will attune you to the sounds of the sea,

They are also of great benefit when you dislike exercise: call on them to discover exercise that is healthful and fun!

And the dolphins also help us pass over, to transition easily: Dolphins help us move through to the next world…in legends from all over the planet, the dolphins would carry our souls into the otherworld, where we would rest, be at ease, and choose our shape, form and mission for our next lifetime. Some Atlanteans have rested for a long time – now they are returning, to help us awaken to her lessons.

The dolphins are the bridge between two worlds: life and death, land and sea, feelings of physicality. Could they also be the bridge that will rejoin us to the great wisdom of Atlantis? I believe that yes, they are – and that connecting with them is a most healthy way of healing our collective past in Atlantis.

"Thou art as a lion of the waters, and as a dragon of the sea,"
– Ezekiel

WHALES – THE SONGLINES OF THE SEA

I'm sitting by the sea, on the headland's cliff, and I'm drumming, just gently. It's early morning, and it's still, no wind, the sun is burning brightly, yet the air is fresh and sweet.

I do this sometimes, mainly when I am sure I'll be very alone, with no witnesses, no audience, no one else to blur and mutate the delicate energy that seems to be created when I can do this by myself. As always, when I drum I begin to gently go into a trance state. I can feel things changing, and melting away, and the memories start to flood in...

I am standing at the ocean's edge...the same as this one, on a cliff face. It is high, and there are steps carved all the way up to where I am now standing. I am tense, every muscle taut, my senses aware of everything. I look around, and my kind are there. They too are that perfect blend of fear and pride: they are waiting to see what will happen.

I take a few determined steps forward, raise my arms over my head, and silently, though inside I am screaming, leap up from the platform. I fall, and I dive, the position of my body looking like I am in control, the truth is I am rushing down to the waves below. I have timed

it well. The waves rush in over the jagged rocks below and I pierce the water like an arrow. I allow myself to completely relax, letting the ocean take me. I have entered the water as a warrior. It is up to the sea now to decide whether I am worthy.

I am beneath the water, my lungs holding air, my eyes open, my black hair floating silken around my body, which is deep russet brown, smooth, young and strong.

And from beneath me I feel a pulse, a shimmer of energy, a rip in the water. I feel this being coming towards me, before I see it. But then I see it. Moving towards me, at a speed like dark lightning ripping through the sky-curtain of water, is the whale, its great eye fixed on me. I release my breath and allow myself to look back. I ask the whale...

"Will you take me?"

I can feel the need for breath taking hold of my lungs, a caustic, bitter feeling sweeping through me, a pain in my head, the beat of my heart pounding.

I ask again.

"Will you take me?"

She looks at me, moves her great body beneath me, and as I begin to lose consciousness, the great whale lifts me up, and carries me towards the land again.

The sea has taken me. The sea will return me.

I am now a woman of my people.

The drumming pounds like the beat of my heart, and slowly I return to the cliff face, and I am here, now.

A woman of the sea still.

The relationship between humans and whales is intense, intimate, and reverent. It is as ancient as our creation stories. Every sea-dwelling culture has the whale within their tales, the folklore adding up to an immense library cataloguing our fascination. In Atlantis, whales were protected and regarded as Gods. To kill one required mighty powers, but to do so was to risk the wrath of all, as the whales were essential keepers of wisdom. To destroy one was to destroy a link to the knowledge bank of sentient life.

The inheritors of Atlantean lore, the Greeks, felt the same way – and extended that reverence to dolphins, too. Just as it was a criminal act to hurt or murder a dolphin during the halcyon days of Ancient Greece, so too were whales protected with as much fervour as those beautiful souls who work on the Greenpeace vessels. Whale shrines and dolphin temples were a common feature of ancient worlds, and exist today in many indigenous oceanic tribes. Aphrodite, who communicates with all the sea-beings, protected not only the beautiful dolphins, into whom she shapeshifted, but the mighty whale, too.

But this reverence and acknowledgement, despite the vast grip of the bloody hand of whaling in the 20th century, does not belong to the past. It is global, and is in every culture that has any affinity with the deep blue Atlantean spirit of the sea.

ATLANTIS: HOME OF THE SHAPESHIFTERS

"In the old days, the land felt a great emptiness.
It was waiting, waiting to be filled up,
Waiting for someone to love it, waiting for a leader.
And he came on the back of a whale, a man to lead a new people.
Our ancestor, Paikea."

 – Ngati Konohi creation story

"Tinirau married Te Wehengakauki. Their child Tutarakauika married Paraniwaniwa,
and all their offspring were whales..."

 – Maori Creation Myth

These are not legends. They are the truths of a sacred time, a time of survivors heading
to new lands. So many of us have come from the sea – and to this day, whales are the
record keepers, the ancestral ones, who continue to demonstrate unconditional love
and support of human beings, even while being hunted and killed.

The whales *are* our ancestors, in many ways. The Ngati Kohoni story formed the basis
of a transformational film, called Whale Rider. According to their law, the entire world
was once underwater...in this time before time, we shapeshifted! And the people of the
North Island of what is now called New Zealand are far from alone in their ancestral
link to the whale.

The Quang Nam people of Dang An, Vietnam have been celebrating a whale festival
for thousands of years. Within the two days of celebrations they hold ceremony,
expressing love and gratitude for the dolphins and whales who have carried sailors back
to shore after shipwrecks –and for helping them herd fish! And the whales – ah – they
regard them with awe, as messengers from the God of Sea. Figures riding whales and
dolphins are carved, and revered, and left offerings of food and flowers on the beach.

Cetaceans are deeply loved in Vietnam. If the body of a dead whale is washed ashore,
whoever finds it knows it is a relative who has been sent home. They mourn the body,
light candles, and bury the whale in the manner of the most revered of ancestors.

On the other side of the planet, The Nuxalk (Bella Coola) people have a story of a
giant Killer Whale saving people from a great flood. And ancient Norse folklore
tells tales of whales who carry powerful wizards and priestesses on their backs to their
shores to start a new line of beings. Could these stories refer to actual survivors of
Atlantis, journeying on the backs of the whale to new lands around this planet? From

that lost land in the Atlantic, where did they go? To the shores of the Americas? To the far flung Polynesias? To the Asiatic islands?

RECORD KEEPERS OF THE ANCESTORS

"When Brahma, or the God of Gods, saith the Shaster, resolved to recreate the world after one of its periodical dissolutions, he gave birth to Vishnoo, to preside over the work; but the Vedas, or mystical books, whose perusal would seem to have been indispensable to Vishnoo before beginning the creation, and which therefore must have contained something in the shape of practical hints to young architects, these Vedas were lying at the bottom of the waters; so Vishnoo became incarnate in a whale, and sounding down in him to the utter-most depths, rescued the sacred volumes."

– A re-telling of the incarnation of Hindu God Vishnu as a whale: as told by Captain Ahab in Hermann Melville's Moby Dick.

As Atlanteans, hybrid beings, and the ability to shapeshift, was very common, usual even. Like the legends of the coastal First Peoples of the Pacific northwest of the Americas, our magickal ancestors were whale people, who travelled over vast seas until they reached the land they were destined to inhabit. There they shapeshifted into humans, who remained by the sea, and who paid homage to the great whale ancestor in their traditional chants, ceremonies, art and folklore.

Many tribes know that the whales were the chiefs of the past, the mothers and fathers of their people, and thus they were and are never hunted – for to do so, was to devour the life-force of the tribe itself. The offerings of the whale can be taken for food, but to hunt them is forbidden. And when they have been hunted, it is with deep reverence and great ceremony. "Whaling and whales have remained central to our culture," says a Makah elder of Washington state. "They are in our songs, our dances, our designs, and our basketry. Our social structure is based on traditional whaling families. The conduct of a whale hunt requires rituals and ceremonies, which are deeply spiritual."

WHALES AND CHRISTIANITY

"Delightful it is to stand on the peak of a rock, in the bosom of the isle, gazing on the face of the sea. I hear the heaving waves chanting a tune to God in heaven; I see their glittering surf.

I see the golden beaches, their sands sparkling; I hear the joyous shrieks of the swooping gulls. I hear the waves breaking, crashing on the rocks, like thunder in heaven. I see the mighty whales... Contrition fills my heart as I hear the sea; it chants my sins, sins too numerous to confess. Let me bless almighty God, whose power extends over the sea and land, whose angels watch over all. Let me study sacred books to calm my soul; I pray for peace, kneeling at heaven's gates. Let me do my daily work, gathering seaweed, catching fish, giving food to the poor."

– *St Columba, 500 AD*

St Columba is one of my favourite ever Christian saints – I suspect it is because he's a druid, through and through! Celtic Christianity was a very different faith to that practised in other parts of the Empire. The song of whales stayed powerfully beguiling to those sea people who had long and strong traditions. Many Celts played their music to the whale, in exchange for the gift of hearing theirs.

However, during the Middle Ages, this deep reverence and love that the sea-faring peoples had began to change, or be changed, when whales began to be associated with Leviathan of the Bible.

The awe they evoked was transformed into fear, as nature was considered to be lesser than man. Man attempted to prove this dominion by crushing the epic power of the whale, making of their unconditional love a wall against which to fling ourselves, to prove our superiority and dominance, and our place as the greatest of all God's creatures!

WHALING'S ENERGETIC IMPACT

There was a huge whaling industry in Australia in the 1950s, in areas like the sacred land of Byron Bay. The dolphins tell me they are clearing a lot of that energy. People forget that sacred sites such as Byron suffered with the blood of the whales. Traditional Bundjalung people and the Eora people of Sydney are proud of their heritage with whales, of their whale riding and communication and calling.

Two million whales have been hunted and killed over the last 50 years of whaling. This is a very different number from what used to be taken. It so concerns tribes whose totem is the whale that they feel that even the limited hunting taking place now is endangering the spirit of their peoples, and of all peoples.

The Woppaburra people, of the Keppel islands on Australia's beautiful Great Barrier Reef have respectfully asked the Emperor of Japan to not hunt their totem, the Mugga Mugga, or Humpback whale. "We are spiritually connected with Mugga Mugga, they are as much a part of us, our family, as we are of them, their family, we are joined spiritually – forever," wrote Christina Doherty of the Wopaburra people.

"The emotional and spiritual health and well-being of the Woppaburra People, past and present and future generations, will continue to suffer, as we witness and are helpless in stopping the slaughter of our sacred Spiritual Totem – Mugga Mugga."

Mugga Mugga is a "good omen" for us, that everything in the world is as it should be, all elements of our Mother Earth are continuing, there is "balance" in the life cycles of all living things, just as we all enjoy the full seasons of Mother Earth, Spring, Summer, Autumn, Winter – and when there is "disturbance" in our world, brought about by mankind, we will always feel the "full fury" of our Mother Earth, as a global family – it is her warning, to stop and think, before it's too late.

In several messages from Mara, the being appointed from Atlantis to take me through several deep visionary experiences with the people and energy and earth and sea of Atlantis, she pointed out that many whales would offer themselves up to the people, to sustain them.

Even today, in Japan, the country most avid in its hunting, whale shrines are common in coastal villages.

In one hundred years, our sentiments regarding the whale has undergone a metamorphosis. We are moving from that hunting mentality into a more compassionate and connected place. When the great white whale was hunted in Melville's epic novel of obsession and the sea, to now acknowledging that the white whale is no monster, but a sign of the new time coming through.

Our relationships are becoming closer all the time. Many Australians have given their lives to the cause to stop whaling. Many others are finding their way back home to their ancestral lands, and to their totems, like the Mirmum people of South Australia, who were displaced as part of a program of government intervention in the 20th century. When the Mirmum people returned to their lands, they could finally sing the whalesongs again, their spirits started the healing process.

As we are too, now we are involved in a meaningful and beautiful way with these magnificent mammals and the keepers of all the wisdom of the ages.

But are we moving swiftly enough?

We had, in Sydney, just experienced a terrible situation in which a baby whale had been euthanized by our government nature services in order to spare it starvation. The public had followed this baby whale's story with such passion and compassion and true connection. The tears people shed were heartfelt. Had this baby whale just taken one very drastic step to wake us up?

ATLANTEAN RITUALS

After that amazing vision on the cliff, whales became even more fascinating to me. The vision felt like an echo of just one of the many initiation ceremonies involving sea peoples and whales, a celebration of a common past of shapeshifting beings of the ocean and land.

I experienced deeper and deeper trances, where I saw people diving, or simply walking into the water and surrendering. They would come back to land safely. It would happen in different ways. On the tide. With a dolphin, or a great turtle. Sometimes, the deliverer was the whale.

And when that happened, the tribe knew one who had lived many times before had been returned to them to tell them the stories again.

This kind of process takes place for many of us now, without our deliberately doing so. We cast ourselves into life, that great ocean of magick and experience. And something often greets us, and carries us back, just when we are most lost. At the saddest points in my life, I have gone to the sea. And maybe it has been the whale and the song of the sea that has sent me back.

I thought of how many people I knew who'd nearly drowned. My grandmother, my brother, friends. I felt it was a common rite of passage for sea-witches and beings who are connected strongly to that realm, and thus to Lemuria and to Atlantis.

These rituals are ages old, and are a part of us – so simply becoming civilised does not change a thing. Underneath that very fine veneer that we cling to, we are beings of the land and of the sea. We know we are a part of it all – and when we self-initiate, we rejoin the great flow and circle of life and death, even in a world that has forgone its true wisdom, replacing it only with identity through what we have, and take, and wear.

I knew, somehow, the whales were a great key to unlocking the mysteries of Atlantis. If these rituals took place in Atlantis, before the experiments and before the end, could the whales now not still know of this? They are, the sages say, the great record keepers. Will they share their knowledge with us? And to do so, do we need to hear their song?

WHALES OF ATLANTIS: THE AQUATIC AKASHIC LIBRARY

During workshops, more and more people speak to me of their deep affinity for whales. No-one was left untouched by their energy, some loved them, many were awed, some were very frightened. One woman shared with me that she feared the eye of the whale, and would often have a panic attack when she thought of it.

Most others felt awe, and knew the songs were unravelling something in them that was tied up and put away, that hearing the song somehow lengthened them out and made them feel strong again.

Many of us with varying present-day bloodlines forget that we too have sea peoples in our DNA this time around, too. From the people of the Black Sea to the peoples of coastal Africa, the Celts, those of us who have been Viking and Polynesian and Inuit, we all, without exception, have the connection to the whale, because they connect the land and the sea, and wherever we live, there is that connection.

But something seemed to be shifting. It seemed something was being rewired in our brains, and being re-felt then in our hearts. The relationship felt ancient. I began to look deeply into their legends, and began to see patterns – patterns that the whales themselves make when they migrate and reenergise the songlines of the seas

This reawakening taking place felt different somehow to the way I'd been hearing about the connection with whales before. And I see a lot of people with whale connections. When I'm with my parents, there are passionate people on the headland every migration season, often singing out to them, playing didgeridoo, and sometimes, like one beautiful young Japanese girl, swimming far, far out to them, and disappearing. People's connection to whales is not at all dissimilar to their dolphin-love – but whales present something deeper. Older. And obviously, much larger.

Dolphins tend to live in pods, and they live within an area. They travel in groups and tend to dwell within a particular territory. They move throughout this territory, feeding and also, energising that territory. Their calls reshape the energy stuck in places in the ocean, also releasing souls who may be not so much earthbound as seabound.

For example, the bottlenose dolphins of Lennox Head, who my father loves so dearly, spend a great deal of time at Lennox Point, Wategos's at Byron Bay, and often head into the Richmond River at Ballina. They are, in a sense, much like ourselves. Akin to us in size, shape, and behaviour.

But whales are so much "more": they are like us, and yet more than us, in the same way a mountain range is vast and somehow unknowable, breathtaking in its enormity.

It is with this size, this incredible shape they have, and it is within that brilliant physical reservoir of Earth and galactic history that they hold the patterns of their ancient songs. Their body, that huge resonating cavity, stores the history of the planet herself. They are massive Akashic libraries, preserving, reviving, renewing ancestral lines that need to be in place for this planet to be whole and well now, and in the future.

WHALE SONG HEALING

The song only changes at the right destination. So, they sing a song as they move into warmer waters. Whales can sing for a long time – up to 20 minutes at a time, and with great variation. The whales also sing the same song, over and over, for generations – and Humpback whales sing a complex song. Each song comprises several parts, each of many notes, ranging from a bass rumble to a shrill squeak. Each male sings the song over and over, part for part, note for note, sometimes spending hours in a single concert.

The blue whale's moan can cross an ocean and echo from the other side.

Whales singing with any one group, however, all sing slight variations on a single song. Gradually throughout the singing season, note by note, the song evolves, with the result that a given community song may bear little resemblance to the song of a year before. This change does not come about by a complete change in the makeup of the group, as individual whales can be identified by markings from year to year.

The infrasonic calls may allow whales to keep in touch over long distances. One scientist estimated a fin whale could pick up a broadcast by another fin 3,000 miles away. Infrasonic calls travel such distances intact under water because the sound waves bounce off the under surface of the water, as well as off boundaries between cold and warm water. So instead of spreading as sound does in air, infrasound travels in a corridor, dissipating much less quickly than it would in air. Furthermore, the wavelength of a particular pitch increases more than four times in water, making it even better as a long-distance signal.

So, just as the dolphin's sonar reshapes our own brain, dissolves toxicity and can remove tumours, can the whales dislodge impurities from the earth and the atmosphere itself with their enormous range of vocal healing calls?

A recording of the song of the humpback whale is aboard the space-probes Voyager I and II, travelling into outer space – perhaps beings out there can understand the complicated, yet precise sequence of sounds.

It makes sense – the legends of many of this blue and green planet's indigenous people say the whales and the dolphins came to us from the Pleiades, and that others came from Sirius, another star system.

WHALES AND THE SEA SONGLINES

I spend a lot of time at or in the ocean. Whenever I see whales, I feel so especially blessed. It is so magical...I see them, breaching, spouting, twisting mid-air, bone-white under tails and darker bodies, a sleek dark blue, glistening in the sunlight...amazing.

I have never seen them so close before, in their own environment...this was at Wallabi

Point, mid-northern NSW...they were heading south, so I rang ahead to friends who lived down the coast. I received excited calls from my mother, who knew there were many more heading down to where I was staying.

I sat on the north end of Saltwater, not a human soul in sight apart from we three... Thomasina sculpted owls with shells and stones (reminiscent of the Celtic Goddess Blodeuwedd) and we just drank in the sight of these beings...being.

I went back the next day, and gave myself up to them...and I began to understand something. I didn't hear them, not in the spoken way – but you should be used to that by now. We rarely have a "normal" conversation. But words flowed into me, and they were coming from what seemed like the eye of a whale. I was far away on the shore, but as I walked, I began to see the eye of the whale in the storm clouds. I sat, and watched the sheet lightning over the ocean, the clean, incredible light of the storm bathing me, and heard the words of the whale, singing to me of its wisdom.

I understood that the whales sing the songlines of the oceans. The animals and the trooping fae and the people who are awake keep the leylines of the land in place, but the mermaids and the whales, they sing the energy lines of the ocean, keeping her alive and well.

The eye looked up. Pelicans flew over.

The birds sing the lines of the air, up to 100 kilometres up, to the line known as the Karman line, the place where "space" is designated to start.

This 100 kilometre patch of sky, atmosphere concentrated in the first ten kilometres, is the resonating cavity, or void of this planet. Like the sea, it too is cleansed by birds of the air, their calls, and within this space the energy lines are travelled and re-travelled by the migrating birds, flying over the sea, keeping all that is deep wild knowledge in place.

Eagles fly up to three kilometers high, and their cries clear the skies, and the birds fly the lines at varying heights. The sound of the Earth resonates within this 100-metre sonic concentric tunnel that encircles and is a part of the Earth – her aura if you life. And her aura resonates. It has a beat. The caverns beneath the earth amplify this beat, and it is broadcast from this resonating cavity. Science calls it the Schumann resonance, and without it, we become ill, disoriented, and we die.

So necessary is exposure and immersion in this heartbeat of the Earth that NASA ensures each spacecraft is fitted with a Schumann simulator, which exposes the astronauts to the 7.8 hertz heartbeat at all times, thus keeping them well.

This wave, continuing throughout the ionosphere, beneath the waves and into the land herself, ensures all of us are well, healthy, whole and living in sync with the frequency of the planet.

We have spent the last two hundred years interfering with that frequency via electromagnetic fields, with the vanishing of the great flocks of migrating birds, with the decimation of the buffalo population; with the whaling industry… we are drowning out the beat that we need to stay alive.

Whales play an essential part in maintaining the health of the energy systems of the whole planet. The land and the sea are interdependent systems, and we humans are in-betweeners, long of both worlds, as we were in Atlantis, and before then, even more intimately, in Lemuria.

This is how it must be:

The land with her lines. Underground with the changing landscape of inner earth, the tunnels, the creatures who live beneath.

The land with the leylines, the people and animals walking those lines.

The skies, with the birds flying the lines.

And the sea, with the whales singing the great song to bind the continents in their place over and over again. This planet has some billions of energetic inhabitants, all enmeshed in a beautiful, intelligent web of energy.

We need this. We long for this. We are in the process of at once healing it, and dismembering it.

It's an enormous energy system, like a ball of intricately woven twine, in the magickal and magnificent process being repaired since it was fractured after the fall of Atlantis. We're being repaired and made ready! But for what?

I thought about all the people I would see walking in Sydney, from North Bondi to Bronte and back, on the famous clifftop walk.

Are we helping to ground something when we walk these paths? When we listen to the sound of the waves, are we hearing the song of the sea, and rejoining the land to ourselves again? I feel we may be.

I thought I had best check in with my friend Scott Alexander King again: after all, his books, among them *Animal Messenger* and *Animal Dreaming*, contain a wealth of information on the whales. I had heard him speak of them as record keepers of ancestral memory: but were they singing the songlines of the sea, too?

Scott explained to me that as the keeper of sacred records, the Whale sings the Ancient Songs of Creation; the Songlines, or 'Dreaming Tracks' that map the creation of the known world and the tracks the ancestor spirits would have taken as they dream-journeyed their way across the land at the beginning of time. "The Songlines still exist today, just as they always have and as they always will," Scott said. "Whale sings the Songlines of Creation so that we, as the children of the Earth Mother, never need worry about getting lost to ourselves, the world or each other."

"To hear the song of the Whale is to be reminded that we're all intrinsically linked in chorus to one another. Whale symbolically opens the vaults of Creation through her song, offering us sacred access to the knowledge stored within. The Songlines, as sung by the Whale, rebirth our emotional body and revive us physically by inspiring the recollection of our own genetic memory and personal life-rhythm in the hope that we'll remember the sacred bond we share with all things. By guiding us deeper within, her song helps us find the knowledge to heal our self, our family, the human race and, in time, the Earth Mother herself," he told me. Thankyou, Scott! And thankyou the whales of Saltwater Point.

Back on that special afternoon, I was walking through the shells carefully, not wanting to break them. They were the exoskeletons of delicate sea creatures, and beautiful.

I looked towards the cliffs and saw the sounds echoing and booming from them, sending resonance across the seas and into the planet's furthest places. These echoes never stopped, I realised.

So, I took myself back to the cliff face, near a cave, trying not to get alarmed at the signs alerting me to rock fall. I sat far enough away to be out of any danger, but close enough so the boom of the waves hitting the rocks of the shore could bathe me first from the front, and then from the back. That impact was startling. I had sat this way many times as a child, loving it. I didn't realise though at that time what it seemed to be doing.

I could hear the sound of the earth, and the sound of the sea, and I could hear and sense the past, and the future. The eye of the whale looked back at me from the sky, lit by lightning again and again.

My breath joined the song all around me, and I understood that this simple act, this listening and being with the sound of all, creates a kind of amplification in my body that would bring back to life my soul. My heart. My DNA.

I realised this was a pure sound: I could not hear the whirring and buzz of machinery, or the hum of technology, that white noise that is so omniscient now.

I could hear only this. And I felt aware, awake, alive, and in love. It was so deeply healing that I could not wait to share this with others in this book. So Simple!

I thought about how often I'd been upset by sound: unable to hear and focus. In restaurants with high hard ceilings and cement walls, the sound bounces. While others all around me would be drinking and enjoying themselves, I wondered what was wrong with me. The frequency would move through me. I felt shattered into small fragile pieces, and needed to be somewhere quiet again to heal. But this noise didn't send me flying in all directions: this sound seemed to bring into a kind of whole the broken pieces of myself, the shards flying through my aura that I had not been aware of. This sound heals, I knew. And the eye of the great whale over the ocean closed slowly and opened again, as if in acknowledgement.

THE TIME OF PROPHECY –
THE WHITE LIGHT BEINGS RETURN

"This thing glowed in the water. It seemed like a sacred being."
– Professor Paul Forestell of the Pacific Whale Research Foundation.

We are now in the time of prophecy. There really is no turning back. We are at the part of the wheel of life where things are getting very, very significant. We manifest immediately. We have an impact, right away. We have important decisions to make, every day.

When the white buffalo walks the Earth, and the white whale, the white dolphin, the white ravens, they symbolise the time of the awakening.

LAKOTA PROPHECY: WHITE BUFFALO WOMAN

"And when she promised to return again, she made some prophesies at that time. One of those prophesies was that the birth of a white buffalo calf would be a sign that it would be near the time when she would return again to purify the world."
– Egyptian Book of the Dead, 1,600 BCE

"When the white cow returns, Ireland will be free."
– Irish legend

"I'm 55-years-old and I've been lucky. It's been the dream of our people for 500 years (to see the white calf return). In 1954 my grandfather said I would live to see (the calf) and see a change in the world. We've been praying for her return," he said.

– Floyd Hand, Sioux Medicine Man, South Dakota

The Cheyenne, Sioux, Lakota and Plains people tell of White Buffalo Calf Woman, who bought a sacred peace pipe to the world from the stars. Her return would herald a time of unity and peace among all tribes and all peoples...

For years, the people waited for her return, in the form of a pure white buffalo, non-albino. When the Plains people were at one with the Land, before Europeans come, there were 80 million buffalo, and 60 million people... The scientific odds of a white buffalo being born were one in eight million...

Today, there are 130,000 buffalo. There are 800,000 native Americans.

And there is more than one white buffalo.

Born in 1994, the first white buffalo was heralded as the return of the woman bringing the peace pipe... giving the gift of purification, before renewal...

She is named Miracle.

"It's an omen that's bringing a change and a new world. The twenty-first century that is coming is going to unify all of us."

"The message is simple. The people should be of one heart, one mind, one people. Peace, love and harmony. It is time to educate the world," Hand said, raising up his cane to make the point.

The return of these white animals, and the white cow spans epochs, joining diverse cultures in a united sacred quest. From Ireland, to ancient Egypt, to the Lakota people in contemporary times, there comes a legend of a white cow returning, signifying a new time, of freedom, peace and dignity. Hathor energy, Brigid energy, White Buffalo Calf Woman. All represent a great change for humanity and for the planet. A moving into higher consciousness. Greater compassion. Love of all creatures. Respect and reverence for the feminine.

There is an emphasis on the white cow being feminine – the legends speak of HER return, that SHE will bring back harmony, balance and proper work with the land and with spirit. In Ireland, Brigid is the Goddess and Saint who is represented by two white animals – the white swan, and the white cow. In Irish folklore, it is said that this sacred white cow of Brigid was murdered by treachery, out of greed. But it is also said that she will return – and when she does so, Ireland will be free, the land respected and revered as sacred, and Brigid will return in her Goddess form. Could this also speak of the return of the Divine feminine – could this be the heart of the white animal prophecy's meaning?

CONNECTING WITH WHALE ENERGY

It is easy and simple to connect with the healing energy of the whale...

* Go on a whale watch.
* Watch wildlife documentaries.
* Treat yourself to an Atlantean film festival: There are brilliant films: from the joy of liberation in Free Willy! to the ancient spirit that speaks through the film Whale Rider, to Kim Kindersley's beautiful film, Whaledreaming, about the Mirnum people of South Australia and their totem, the whale.
* Listen to Lisa Gerrard's music, which she wrote for Whale Rider. This brilliant musician channels languages of the galactic and the ancient and is an Oscar-

nominated musician. Better still, listen to the soundtrack to Whale Rider when you are at the beach, or in the bath!

* Look at the diversity of whale imagery in the world – even in mountainous Tibet, there are statues of Buddha with whales!
* Connect with the Goddess Sedna, to transform pain into lessons and wisdom and protection.
* Whale song is very powerful and can create changes in landscapes and in physical matter. It is strong, but always healthful and gentle. The more it is broadcast on the land, the more we all heal and reconnect to our Atlantean past.

Now, we will travel on. We are leaving the time of towers, and experiments, of healings and Golden times, and moving towards a great veil in the form of the mist. We are journeying towards that veil,. And we will ask for it to lift, and reveal to us the Blessed isle. The land of the Priestesses. Where apple groves blossom, and stone circles mark places of power. Where healing is in every bled of grass, every birdsong, every drop of water from the well of the Goddess.

We are about to journey into the final Imramma...to the heart of Avalon.

Immrama Three:

RETURN TO
AVALON

The Isle of
Avalon

N

the lake

woodland

chalice

wearyall hill

surrounding

windmill hill

Woodland

apple groves

GLASTONBURY TOR

marshland

apple groves

Woodland

intertidal zone

land

Avalon

Sacred Sites & Communities

IRELAND:
1. hill of tara
2. newgrange
3. kildare (brigid's well)
4. lough gur
5. poulnabrone dolmen
6. aran islands
7. galway
8. knocknarea
9. beltany stone circle
10. grianan of aileach

SCOT
11. the
12. kilma
13. dc
14. corrn
15. orkn
16. shetla

ENGLAND:
21. glastonbury
22. isle of man
23. lindisfarne
24. holystone (lady's well)
25. castlerigg stone circle
26. long meg
27. channel islands

28. arthur's stone
29. the white horse
30. wayland's smithy
31. stevington holy well
32. chanctonbury ring
33. mitchel's fold stone circle
34. nine ladies stone circle

the azores

atlantic ocean

the canary islands

WALES:
17. angelsey
18. bardsey island
19. pentre ifan
20. kenfig pool

N

scotland

england

ireland

st. george's channel

wales

english channel

27
brittany

bay of biscay

france

portugal

spain

mediterranean sea

africa

"In order to bring the higher consciousness of the evolved Atlantean race into the tribes of the island, did Merlin, in defiance of the strict laws of the sacred clan, and in pursuit of ends of his own, cross the Atlantean stock on the Celt?"
– *Dion Fortune*, Avalon of the Heart

IMMRAMA THE THIRD: AVALON

If you have come thus far, you have experienced joy, elation, connection, distance, doubt, wonder and tears. No doubt we are all still working through fears to do with magic, your other-self, and connecting more and more closely to your Atlantean and Lemurian kin. Now it is time to walk into the woods and meet with the other members of your bloodlines: the Avalonians.

To the shores of Britain, Ireland, Spain, France and Germany arrived survivors and ships teeming with exhausted Lemurians and Atlanteans. Unicorns, slaves, fauns, wizards and centaurs stumbled onto her green earth, and found sanctuary and safety there. The energy of ancient Avalon was far less dense than our current energy (which is in the process of lightening up once again). Because of this, the Avalonians could clearly see the fae, the dragons, and the shapeshifting ones of blended bloodlines, and welcomed them.

For a time, a very long time, this was an idyllic place, where the Goddess and the God were revered, where magickal beings and human beings blended and merged, loved and laughed together. In Avalon priestess and druid cared for those in need, and learned and taught the language of animal, flower and star and stone in groves of trees.

As you too reach these shores, it is natural to feel longing and joy, as well as fear and uncertainty. Have no doubt that as you reach her shores, you too fall under the protection of Avalon.

Have no doubt there will be challenges as you reach the shores of the blessed isle, but remember, it is all to the good. The untruths will fall away one by one, and be replaced with your own vital experience, from which you can draw genuine wisdom, in which you can believe with your heart and your soul. Those who fear to journey may condemn you: they may say you are childish to trust in your visions and feelings, the dreams that come up, the messages and omens and oracles of Avalon. But it is not in them you trust as much as you trust in your own path, and your own right to know.

Coming so far already shows how courageous you are: voyaging to the Lost Lands can trigger an intense re-experience of past-life fears many of us are processing and transforming. And this is rarely easy...

Because the fear of being "misled" is so strong, reaching Avalon can also trigger fear and mistrust of your own bloodline, which has Atlantean, Lemurian and Avalonian blood singing the songs of the past from within. There is a strong urge in some spiritual philosophies to "clear" or "cancel out" what does not feel "right". This urge to make everything pure and clear...a kind of blank void which can lead us to repress some of the most loving, valuable, strong and talented parts of ourselves.

As we approach the mist-caped shores of legendary Avalon, more fears, some unsettling feelings may arise.

After all, we have been told so many lies about faeries, witches, wizards and priestesses. About beings "pretending they are human", who lure the "real" humans into their world between the worlds with their enchantments and their powers. Their world is said to be beautiful, perhaps dangerous, and once you've crossed into that world, you may never return, and you will never be the same. You will never see the world you said goodbye to in the same way again. And you may never wish to come back.

But this world and these beings are in your blood, as your deepest self knows. The deepest part of you has only recently awakened to your knowledge, and is returning. But there is fear. Despite the knowledge that you are returning to something overwhelmingly beautiful, you feel you may be making a deadly error of judgment. That perhaps the lies you have been told are true. That perhaps if you dare to explore the worlde of the Fae, or learn the magicks and the mysteries of Avalon, you may be forever cast out from the "normal" world. But you are drawn forth anyway, to the world within the woods, where your faerie wings will unfurl and grow strong again, where you will take flight, and dance with rainbows and moonlight, and the fear will leave your face, your limbs, your body, your light body and your soul.

But fear there is at the present time, and yet you still climb into the boat that takes you on this third wonder-voyage. And when you enter this world, you will *be* the woods: your hair will be the light falling between branches, your skin the white bark of the sacred tree, your eyes the blue of the patch of sky or the brown of the land, your garments moss and feather and spiderwebs...

And no matter how much of the world of stone and ruin you are currently surrounded by, no matter how deeply the loss of Lemuria or Atlantis has touched you, you too will find rest in this healing land of Avalon.

COMING HOME

It is 2005. My life is officially a mess. I am separated. I have no job. I am away from home. I'm in Glastonbury, sipping steaming chai at the charming vegetarian café Galatea and awaiting my darling friend Serene, writer, wonder-traveller, herbalist and healer.

Serene knows this area of the planet well, and we'd decided to meet here with another friend after she had shared a vision of the three of us working with the sacred Priestess well.

Serene had already told me tales of her Avalonian adventures in many conversations. "I first visited Glastonbury in my twenties, as part of a six-month overseas adventure, my first time out of Australia. In the jungles of Peru I had visions of gentle green hills and ancient wells, of standing within a circle of stones, arms open to the sky, gentle sunshine caressing my face. When I got to London I went straight to Stonehenge and Avebury, and danced within their enchanted circles, falling in love with the beautiful English countryside. When a friend told me I'd love Glastonbury, I went, with no preconceived ideas, I just got the bus there and spent a week wandering around the town, climbing the Tor every day, sitting by the Well and drinking its waters, winding through the ruins of the Abbey. The melding of different forms of spirituality touched me deeply, but mostly it was the beauty of nature there and the gentle earth energy that captured my heart. I felt nurtured, accepted and supported there, and since then I've returned many times, each time discovering a new part of the town, and a new part of myself. Later I re-read *The Mists of Avalon*, not having really made the connection the first time I was there, and fell further under its spell. Who doesn't long for the magic that it encapsulates, the ability to see the world in such an enchanted way? Today, as someone who does healing work and has studied magical and medicinal herbalism, I feel a connection to that time, albeit with a modern twist."

My wise and inspiring friend had yet to turn up at the appointed time of 6pm... But it seemed understandable... after all, we were meeting across the thousands of miles – she on her way to Glastonbury from Wales, and I had just tumbled off the bus from London, via Sydney.

I was excited and thrilled and kind of wondering what I was in store for, because I was planning to attend the Goddess Temple ceremony.

I was a Glastonbury Virgin.

And I had first-night jitters.

I'd been driven to write and teach about Avalon for years, since first becoming obsessed with myths and legends of all cultures at around the age of seven... However, the year after my marriage became complete, in the form most commonly known as separation and break-up, the prodding to explore and actually journey to Avalon herself became completely insistent. I was drawn, as firmly as if a long, silver cord of emotions and history, energy and healing powers bound us across the miles. Day after day, the thread was pulling me towards the Goddess, towards my own past, a reborn present, and a better future.

The compulsion to come to Glastonbury wasn't just about my love of the mystick

Isle of Avalon, or my relationship with the fae-goddess Morgan le Fay, or Bride, the maiden form of Brigid with whom I also identified, or the story of Blodeuwedd, the Welsh Goddess formed from flowers... My instinct was that Avalon, in the form of Glastonbury, was in some important way a true home for me, a community that I was yearning for.

I'd spoken and taught and written so much about this place. I needed to ground my feelings in the sacred landscape, the body of the Goddess herself.

I had spent over half my life practising as a solitary witch. I'd always wanted to work with other women and men too, but in a sacred place, a temple space. I knew when the time would be right; I'd find the perfect space and place. But until Beltane Eve, in Glastonbury, that time just hadn't come.

When I was very young, in between the visitations from the beings who came at 3am, the dense shift in energy signalling my fear and panic, there was another who came to me. She was light, and bright, and strong, and I called her "the Lady." I've never really known who she was. As I'd spent years at a very small Catholic convent school, I'd thought perhaps it was Mary, the mother of Jesus. I had painted her over and over again – she and Mary, Queen of Scots were my obsessive subjects. I just wasn't sure still if it was Mary who I'd seen in those visions. I still felt her presence, but I did not know who she was. Mary and Morgan, Goddesses both, were calling me home to the land where the worship of the Great Goddess had stayed alive.

I had a sense that coming to Avalon would help me connect with her more deeply than ever before. I had booked into a quiet and lovely bed and breakfast, a place that I'd been drawn to on Apple Tree lane, and happy as it had themed rooms, each named for an aspect of the feminine divine. I was hoping to stay in the Rhiannon room – that patroness of horses, of movement and finding your own song. I imagined myself surrounded by images of her, woman and horse, my own young passion for horses finding a home in Rhiannon's embrace. But when I'd arrived earlier that day, I had found that I was all ready to stay in the... Mary room! Yes, the Mary of Jesus room.

What on earth was going on? I wanted to find my connection to Avalon – not to my Catholic girlhood!

Still, I was determined, if you can be determined about such things, to go with the Glastonbury flow... surrendering to this sacred site's wisdom seemed a whole lot more smart than having rigid ideas about what my experience had to be like! I gazed at the pictures of Mary in my room, and sighed. It seemed expectations were something Avalon was asking me to shed!

And I had deliberately tried to avoid forming any expectations – I know, impossible, but any I had had begun to fall away earlier that day with my first sight of the Tor from the 376 bus from Bristol... Arising out of a soft-focus lush green landscape, this soft and steep conical hill resembles the Goddess to some; to others, she is a pyramid, to others the energy of the mighty hill seems masculine, perhaps due to its tower devoted to St Michael. Underneath the Tower are remains of a stone circle discovered in 1922, under that is the hill, and further down, way into the earth, run the powerful dragon (or ley) lines. Intertwining with the dragon lines is the source of the red and the white springs, and faerylande herself.

The Tor, at first sight, and ever after, was utterly mythic and powerful to behold. I could feel tears start in my eyes, and I drew in a shuddering breath and held it in awe.

Others on the bus were watching the Tor draw closer too. Similarly moved, we became kin. My fellow pilgrims on the bus were easy to see, in the main, with their long locks, their piercings and tattoos, their smiling faces and loving gazes as we all looked upon the Holy Mountain that once arose out of an inland sea, a shining lake, and held to its breast the community of the sisterhood of Avalon. I could feel a part of myself stirring, whose life-force I'd been aware of, but who had slumbered even while I longed for her to awaken. My own sleeping beauty, the Avalon of my heart, was being stirred, summoned and fully aroused from a long, long slumber by this meeting with Avalon of Glastonbury.

AVALON AWAKENING

"The breeze at dawn has secrets to tell you.
Don't go back to sleep.
You must ask for what you really want.
Don't go back to sleep.
People are going back and forth across the doorsill where two worlds touch.
The door is round and open.
Don't go back to sleep."
– Rumi

I knew what the Tor would look like, because I'd seen so many pictures – but I didn't know what she would *feel* like … like she's watching over us all. I hoped she was watching me with a friendly and protective gaze, as I struggled awkwardly to get off the bus, due to way too much luggage! Thankfully, the other pilgrims pitched in and helped: I was so thankful! I felt truly looked after already.

I settled into the Mary room, then made my way to the cafe, where I was due to meet up with Serene. Figuring Serene had been held up, I crossed the road into the courtyard that held the Goddess Temple. I climbed upstairs, to be welcomed beautifully with big squishy Goddess hugs by the Priestesses. I was so relieved! Maybe I've been scared off by people in general, with their judgements (itself my own judgement!), but before Glastonbury, gatherings had never really been in my comfort zone. Feeling like an outsider when you're with the outsiders themselves just feels...well, it lets your abandonment issues kick in big time.

I wanted a place of worship with laughter and joy, where we respected each other, maybe taught each other, but without it being a point scoring ego-obsessed territorial war, a cult-of-personality, or escapism and dismissal of the natural world.

And I found that place. Those of you who've been Glastonbury Virgins will know what I mean.

It was community and respect, beauty and joy and laughter. It was Beltane at the Goddess Temple. There was song, and strawberries, and the Maypole, around which

I danced till sweat streamed down my brow, a completely joyous smile stretched across my face. I leapt the fires that night, with strangers I called the quarters, and I cared not that I had not never before seen the souls I shared this night with. Maybe I had spent Beltane with them in Ancient Avalon.

But whether we were old soul friends, or strangers gathering for one night, the comfort and joy we felt was palpable. Children. Women. Men. Travellers from all over the world squeezed into the Temple, threw away their fears and rode the Beltane tides of passion and freedom! Holding onto my bright red ribbon, and twirling through and under and over the other dancers around the Maypole, all laughing and joyous, bright with happiness, I realised Beltane is not just about sex and fertility. It's about fertility of the *self* – about throwing off chains and being free!

It's why women and men gather at this place, journeying from all over the planet, some coming back year after year. It's why I wanted to immediately head home, gather my mother and daughter up in Australia, and run back to Glastonbury with them in time for some Maypole activities. I came home to Glastonbury, and I was made welcome there, and how I loved that first Beltane spent there.

After hours of celebrating, I emerged from the Goddess Temple, sodden with sweat and grinning madly, only to run straight into Serene on the street. I screamed with joy to see her, and we headed off into the night to meet up with Rachelle Charman, the crystal healer, our third sister on this trip to Glastonbury, who was due at the bus stop any moment. I was so happy, and Serene was smiling because she knew what I was so thrilled about.

I told her breathlessly of the night, and of my bed and breakfast room, and of the Mary room – and she laughed, telling me she has stayed at the same place, in the same room – and that she had experienced the same feelings.

I guess we just need to make peace with Mary, now... maybe who she was, and is still, is far deeper and stronger and older than what I'd been taught in school. Was my Mary connection to do with the Mary lines in this town, which intersected with the "Michael" line beneath the Tor itself? Was this a clue to the origins of the Holy Grail? Or was it simply my opportunity to reconcile my pagan adulthood with my Catholic upbringing?

There was so much to discover…and I had weeks in which to do this – a luxury. I had never been away from my daughter before, so I was re-learning to be on my own, as a woman and a mother. I had recently separated, so I was learning who I was, now that my marriage had unravelled. I had felt all along that while this was sad, and something to be respectful of and to celebrate the past with its blessings, but being in Avalon gave me the firm sense that a new future was dawning in my life.

How lucky and blessed I felt, witnessing the sun coming up over Chalice Well. Here I was in a sacred site that had called me home across the miles, sharing the experience with beautiful friends, finding myself at home in a place so very far away.

I finally felt truly awake. And I knew that my soul could never, ever return to sleep.

THE SACRED ISLE OF AVALON

"Sena [the Ile de Sein, not far from Brest], in the British Sea, is remarkable for an oracle of the Gallic god. Its priestesses, holy in perpetual virginity, are said to be nine in number. They are called Gallicenæ, and are thought to be endowed with singular powers. By their charms they are able to raise the winds and seas, to turn themselves into what animals they will, to cure wounds and diseases incurable by others, to know and predict the future. But this they do only for navigators, who go thither purposely to consult them."
– A passage in Pomponius Mela 1

So, that's my tale of my first visit to Glastonbury. It certainly had taken me years to get back to her.

Sometimes I still wonder why it took me so long. After all, I'd lived in England in the late 80s and had visited Avebury and Stonehenge several times, as well as the incredibly romantic ruin of Tintern Abbey on the border of Wales. Even back then I was looking for spirit-home, and had travelled so very far to find her. Why hadn't I made it to Avalon, when I knew I loved her?

It was almost like Glastonbury, or that direct experience of Avalon had been drawing me closer, yet holding me distant till I was ready to fully receive her energies.

Beyond that magnetic pull, there was my deep love of the priestess tradition, and of the Goddess, and of the sacred landscape. It is so powerful to stand in the ancient territories of our blood, of our ancestors, of our magick. I feel strongly that I had shared many past lives with this place, and with the land, as a priestess, as a peasant, proud and of the Land. And there, that priestess self, my Avalonian self was reignited. That enchanted feeling when you are at ease in a place you have never physically been. And my first view of the Tor...I felt like a pilgrim, approaching something holy, embodied in the land. The Tor, my first vision of it, was overwhelming. The light was diffuse and soft and golden, and the Tor appeared to float gently above the earth plane, her energy shifting and changing each day, teaching me something new about her, and about myself.

Is it necessary to be in her physical landscape to experience the magicks of Avalon? I don't think so. Many modern-day spiritual people who have this strong connection to Avalon have "been there" without "being there." Kylie McDonough is one of these magickal souls who have a deep connection with the blessed Isle – a place where she has never set foot this lifetime.

"I have had an experience on more than one occasion of being at home in this life in a seated meditation place and "waking up" in another place, Avalon," Kylie told me.

"I noticed this first when I put my hand on the ground, eyes still closed and felt blades of grass beneath my hands, my eyes instantly darted open and for a moment in time, I was in what I now believe to be Avalon. This first happened when I was about 14 years old. It didn't happen again until I was about 17 – this time I stayed longer, saw more, including a sunset over the edge of the Island and I sat beneath an ancient apple tree ... all these symbols have led me to believe, and know, that those experiences were taking me back to Avalon."

"Other experiences have happened again in dream form, where I will be visited by several Avalonians, who will give me information. This will very often provide me with oodles of inspiration for artworks which I will often sketch out the next day in order to not forget the information received."

SMALL PLACES, BIG MAGICKS

How did this one small place, a hill in the small land of Britain, become so steeped in power and magicks and divine power across the centuries?

Why have so many thousands of pilgrims for thousands of years been drawn to her, and learnt from her some of the greatest of their magicks?

I love England: it's a land of eccentrics and brilliant writers like Tolkien, CS Lewis and Lewis Carroll. I have a fascination for John Dee, the mage to Queen Elizabeth I, who prophesied the coming of the Spanish Armada, via his famous scrying mirror from South America, made of obsidian and said to harken back to Atlantean times. (The mirror, as well as his channelled angelic alphabet and language, which he called Enochian, are still in the British Museum today.) Dee visited Glastonbury in the 17th century and declared the waters of the red and white spring to be healing. (As they are – they are strong, unique from each other, and powerful!)

As I moved about the modern-day town, down Magdalene Street (there's that Mary connection again!), through Chalice Wells, or the Abbey, standing before the tomb of Guenevere and Arthur I felt surrounded by Albion's (England's ancient name) and Avalon's magickal past. I felt brushes and caresses and welcoming touches from myriad beings, all of whom seemed to walk the streets of the town with me. Some alive in the present day, some fae, some wisps of memory, but all tangible, gentle, beautiful.

No wonder so many people are drawn to this tiny village in the gentle English countryside. Even so, the amount of people who visit every year is extraordinary. I understood her attraction for me – but what is her allure for others?

"I think so many people feel a yearning to connect to Avalon because the modern world is so stressful," explained Serene. "We are so busy today, working long hours, trying to balance home/career/family/friends/etc, and it's easy to lose yourself along the way.

"Reconnecting to nature and the patterns of the seasons and living closer to the land is a nice way to slow down, to see the beauty in the world, and in your life. Today some of the magick has been lost – a magick that can be found in the everyday, in the swooping of a butterfly, the beauty of a sunset, the electricity of a storm, the cleansing power of the ocean, and which the priestesses of Avalon harnessed in a way we can learn from and adapt to our own lives."

I agree with her – it's those simple moments that are so re-connective to spirit. And Avalon and Glastonbury are full of those moments, those opportunities to be still and feel the presence of the Goddess. Why is Avalon the place where the Goddess seems to be so powerful and strong, so fierce, yet so nurturing and delightfully sweet?

"I think Avalon is so popular with women because modern religion is so masculine-centred, and has seemed to reject women, so there is a great appeal for women to return to (or recreate) a time or a mindset where they were valued, when "feminine" characteristics were honoured and appreciated, when nurturing and healing were more important than being competitive, and when women's opinions were highly regarded.

"The priestesses of Avalon were independent, responsible for themselves, their lives and their bodies, wielded political power and had a say in how the country was run and how marriage and sexuality were regarded, yet in today's Christian society this is not the case.

"It actually astounds me just how Christian our society is today – I always thought it was neutral, yet everything from political decisions and laws, to public holidays and school curriculum is based on Christian "morals", and there are a lot of people, male and female, who don't feel this is right, be it in areas of sexuality, healthcare or family planning and IVF. Instead of the god of fear who controls our leaders today, Avalon and its ideals were shaped by a goddess who was caring, nurturing, strong, powerful and forgiving, and who everybody could relate to in some way – a goddess who was personified in the women known as the priestesses of Avalon."

Serene had summed it up well. And evidence of humanity's recovered love for Goddess was everywhere in this small town.

If more people practice magick now than at any other time in the known past, it seems many of them are in this part of the planet. So many people, some drawn by tales of Harry Potter, others by the grimoires of wizards, yet all seriously studying magick and metaphysics. Magick is so alive and well in Avalon – so, well, normal! In Avalon's cafes and small pubs, the conversation centres on solstice. In the streets, people wish each other Happy Beltane, and everywhere free hugs (non-creepy) are offered! Instead of talking about shoes or hairstyles, people in the shops are talking wands, chakras and circle casting. Meetings about money aren't held in stuffy offices here. In Avalon Goddesses chat about the next dark moon circle while reclining on the slopes of the Tor, or in a meadow where Morgan is said to have walked.

This is how life could be...all the time.

THE EMOTIONAL WISDOM OF AVALON

Emotionally, Avalon gave me the ability to feel deep love. True love. Of the land, of myself as an embodiment of the sacred, of others. I truly feel this offering she makes extends to all of us who are ready to open up to living from love. While I was there, I felt overflowing with love, and felt embraced by the town, and by the landscape and the people. It felt a once-in-this-lifetime experience – enchanted, magical, stirring and so very sweet.

While it is energetically beautiful, it is a living town, built around the sacred. It embodies and plays out the conflicts and the possibilities we all have – it embraces the Christian and the pagan, the Goddess and the God. The Beltane line is also known as the Michael line, there are dragons and there are beings of light. It is the place where the celestial and the terrestrial converge in such harmony – it is soft, and feminine, and for me, I felt so loved when I was there. The sacred oaks, and the wells – all the elements embraced and loved. It was very healing because of the very vibration...so many pilgrims have trod this path. And now it was my turn – and it was also a homecoming.

"When I went to Glastonbury with my father, the region was rich with memories.

I felt the energies of the earth welcome me home and remind me of why I was there," says Jessica, whose magickal name is Morrighan. "In Avalon we had deities all around us," she continues. "In the seasons and in the earth itself, rather than in a distant deity that can only be reached in a church or through a priest. It reminds us that all of us have different paths to take and helps us accept the different paths of others. It helps me see that everything I need is available if I just ask. I believe the story of Arthur sleeping is about all of us...when we awaken to what the world really is we can do amazing things and find a heaven here on Earth that is waiting for us."

Jessica's words struck a chord with me that vibrated strongly. I had written and even taught about Avalon before I had physically been there ... but there is a difference between experiencing the physical Avalon (Glastonbury) and experiencing the etheric Avalon of the heart. Being there is akin to being in your body...being of there and not grounded there is akin to having an out-of-body experience. Neither is "better" but I believe that for me personally, the landscape has true magic in it. Being there confirmed that my path, my mist-filled dreaming, is legitimate. The whole land is built around this – and yet it's a farming community!

On a level, you do need to connect with these sacred lands in order to "get" them. The water of Avalon, for example, does have that incredible repository of blessings within its structure. The Tor does extend and join the land, the Goddess, and the sky, the God.

Walking its paths enriched me, and humbled me, and I could feel the empty spaces inside me, ones I had not even been aware of, filling with love and deep happiness. However, Avalon is within all of us...it is our sacred joining of the elements, our own faery self, our own connection to the highest principles of love and service, of romance and magic.

It healed a part of me that was wounded, and parts of me that simply had not reached their potential bloomed and grew, were magnified and amplified in the magick of that ancient sacred landscape..

I know that being in one of the great Avalonian energy centres healed me profoundly. Being of Avalon, and yet seemingly separated from her, meant I had learned how to journey to Avalon without being anywhere near her earthly physical location. It is something I teach in the Avalon workshops I conduct: how to connect with her within, and to anchor her energy in your current physical reality.

"It wasn't until I went to Britain that I truly reconnected. It was just an inner knowledge that I had finally come home," Jessica shared with me.

I can vouch for that kind of experience. Reaching my ancestral homelands in the form of Glastonbury gave me an immense sense of homecoming. Being in her physical landscape assisted my psychic abilities, my trust, and my belief in rich humour and sharing with other people. I loved meeting with the wonderful, soulful people who dwell there, and knowing that when we come to Avalon, there's a lesson she has for us...

Some people feel they're going to Avalon to "heal" her. But it's she who heals us! So many people who designate themselves lightworkers feel they need to erase her shadows – but her darkness is soft, and real, and sad. I think if I had visited Glastonbury in the 80s, I would have been too wounded to truly absorb her energy. And when we experience that reconnection, we look around the world with new eyes, and finely tuned psychic senses. We truly understand and can literally "see" how many people are disconnected from their intuition, their emotions, their sacred selves, and their body, their sacred repository of the celestial. They seem so disconnected from the natural world.

But connecting with the energy of Avalon heals us, and it is a healing that seems to grow as time wheels on.

Since that reconnection, I have been able to draw and re-draw upon the experiences. To awaken my sensitivity, I visualise immersing my hands into the vibration of the water in the healing pool in Chalice Well Gardens. To believe in the power of new beginnings, I remember the seeds I offered to the spirits of the Beltane fires. My belief in my own beliefs grew so strongly from seeing the Avalonian elementals and tree beings in the woods, whispering secrets to the sky dragons and seeing the clouds change in response... If ever I feel disconnected, I whisper my thanks to Avalon, and that gratitude and acknowledgement triggers a fresh flow of knowledge and memories through my blood and my soul that ground me, keeping me strong, psychic, compassionate, and loving.

WHERE IS AVALON?

While she is said to be located in the town of Glastonbury at this time, of course, the energy of Avalon is so powerful it cannot be held within any borders. The geophysical locations of pre-Dark Ages Avalon and her communities are mysterious, but can be archeologically traced to many sacred sites across the British Isles and throughout Europe. Knowing "where" she is precisely is not necessary to connect with her energy: for example, you are effectively "in" her energy right now, as you read this section of the Lost Lands. While you read the words on this page, the energies of the Goddesses, and the Great Talismans, and the wisdom of the trees are coming through to you, and may be born in your dreams, your visions, in the food you choose to eat today, in the people you encounter while reading these words! But she was, and is very real, in a physical sense, too.

"For many, Avalon is physically located at Glastonbury, England, and having spent a fair bit of time there, I can relate to this," said Serene when I asked her about 'where' she thought Avalon lived. "I feel a magick there, a gentleness that comes from the nurturing energy of the land, a very feminine softness, a life-giving force in the waters of the sacred Chalice Well and the power of the glorious Tor and the enchanted trees that grow there. I have sat on the Tor from sunset to sunrise on the summer solstice, and been beautifully trapped in the swirling mists there, and it definitely feels like an Otherworld, a place between dimensions, where everything is possible and we can access deeper parts of ourselves. I've had magical experiences there, visions of long ago times, connections to the moon and the waters. I felt myself married by spirit energy on the Tor, heard voices from the Well and wound inwards to myself as I walked the labyrinth. I can so easily picture the long ago priestesses performing rituals on this ancient land, growing their herbs, scrying in the waters of the Well, honouring the gods and goddesses through the earth and the seasons.

"I've also been to some of the sites in Wales that are connected to these same ancient priestesses, the druid Merlin and the Goddess, and to Broceliande Forest in Brittany, to the lake they claim as the Lady of the Lake's, to Merlin's tomb and Viviane's sacred well. I have also felt the same magic in meditation in places across the world, so I believe Avalon is as much a state of mind as a place. I believe we can hold it within our hearts and minds, and draw on the wisdom wherever we are. It is easier in Glastonbury, perhaps because this town has so long been associated with it and we have therefore created an etheric imprint there, but I feel that it can be accessed anywhere – through ritual, through connecting to the earth where you live, through living in tune with the seasons, through the beautiful paintings that evoke this state of grace (Jessica Galbreth is a favourite), through books like *The Mists of Avalon…*"

The most powerful and valuable place to experience Avalon is within your heart and soul. However, if you decide to find and feel her in the real world, here are just some of the places where you can experience immense and rich "deposits" of Avalonian energy, embedded in the landscape and in the elements, in the very air that you breathe.

Glastonbury: The town believed by many to be the location of the largest Avalonian communities.

Somerset Downs: The geophysical area immediately circling Avalon (Glastonbury). The Downs were once covered in water, which created the lake. The lake is said to have been drained by Christians wishing to have Avalon for themselves…

Brittany: The western lip of the country now known as France: home of the Bretons, the longest stone lines on the planet, and the forest of Broceliande, said to be Merlin's final resting place.

Cornwall: The southwest peninsula of Britain, home of sacred Avalonian sites such as Tintagel. The trade of tin between Cornwall and the Middle East suggests that other "trade" took place; that of ideas and spiritual concepts. The castle known as Tintagel is the birthplace of Arthur Pendragon (Chief Dragon, or King). Merlin's cave is nearby.

Wales: The country ringed by mountains that retains to this day the largest native speakers of the Avalonian tongue: Welsh. Camelot was based in Wales, and this is the birthplace of the Goddesses Blodeuwedd (pronounced Blood-eye-weth – the double d in Welsh is pronounced softly as "th", as in "thrall". The singular "d" remains hard) and of the Goddess Rhiannon. Home of the book of tales known as the Mabinogian, Wales is a land of dragons, warriors, poets and priestesses.

Genetic studies show that the Welsh are related to the Basques of northern Spain and Southern France and to Native Americans. All are descended from the Kets people of Western Siberia, whom Madame Blavatsky associated firmly with Atlantis...

Wiltshire: The county where the majority of sacred crop circle formations can be found throughout each English summer.

Isle of Skye: A mystic Avalonian isle now known for its spiritual community.

Orkney Isles: The far northern isles of modern Scotland, a portal through which many spiritual concepts made their way to, and were embraced by, the Avalonians. These include the festivals of Yule and Ostara. The word Lochlan, or Lachlan, means from over the water... meaning both *over the lakes,* and *over the sea...* the first Lochlans were those travelling between the Avalonian communities, and from the Scandinavias to the Avalonian communities of Scotland.

Milesia: Milesia fills a large section of what is now northern Spain. The original inhabitants of Ireland were the Tuatha de Danaan, the shining ones, the children of Dana... The Avalonian communities of Milesia went to Ireland (variously described as invading, exploring, or searching) and found the Tuatha de Danaan, who taught them of their ways, creating a unique Avalonian energy that lives to this day in the hills and the people of this magickal land.

In Milesia, the Camino (the sacred path stretching across the north of Spain) is walked today by thousands of pilgrims. I believe this may have been an Avalonian walking path, a living meditation in origin.

Ireland: Home to Druids and mysticks for millennia, Ireland is the home of the Tuatha de Danaan, the sacred sites of Newgrange and Tara, and is the repository of Avalonian influences.

As Ireland was not invaded by the Romans (it was later to be invaded again and again by the British!) she retained her Avalonian and druidic culture for far longer than Britain. Despite the "driving out of the snakes" from Ireland of St Patrick (who sought to drive out the Goddess) Ireland maintained a version of Christianity that was far closer to Druidism than to its Roman relatives. The Celtic Church suffered greatly after the Synod of Whitby in the 7th century AD, when Celtic "priests" or thinly disguised druids were cruelly persecuted.

Could Ireland be the land beyond the mists to which Avalon disappeared? Could many of her druids and priestesses have taken up residence in that green and blessed isle? It seems it could be so: as the mists across the Irish Sea made the perfect hiding place for persecuted Avalonians.

WHAT DID THE AVALONIANS BELIEVE?

"Druids, poets and storytellers shared a major responsibility in traditional Celtic communities: they reminded the Celtic people who they were."
– Tom Cowan

"Among all the tribes, generally speaking, there are three classes of men held in special honour: the bards, the Vates, and the Druids. The Bards are singers and poets, the Vates interpreters of natural philosophies; while the Druids, in addition to the science of nature, study also moral philosophy. They are believed to the most just of men, and are therefore entrusted with the decision of cases… they arbitrate in war and bring to a standstill opponents when about to line up in battle… these men have pronounced that soul's and the universe are indestructible, though at times fire and water may temporarily prevail."
– Strabo, Greek geographer, 64 BCE

The druids and priestesses of Avalon had many concepts that have been passed down to this day, the codes and ethics and indeed laws create a vivid picture of a faith that was both bright, beautiful and full of blessings for the earth. Many modern-day Avalonians – myself included – find great inspiration in these tenets that make so much soul-sense!

One man who was inspired by the power of Avalon and her Druids was the legendary Prime Minister of Britain, Sir Winston Churchill. Long before he was Prime Minister of Great Britain, young Winston Churchill joined the Albion Lodge of the Ancient

Order of Druids, at Blenheim Palace in Oxfordshire, where he hosted their gathering on the 15th August 1908. This warrior-druid was famed during World War Two for the unique cadence of his speeches: slow and measured, he adopted Bardic techniques such as repetition, using his voice in a hypnotic and ritualistic way to help find each of his people's courage during a time of initiations and great tests… Could he have cast spells with this voice, and his words, rousing the British to defend themselves? His words are inspiring, and continue to ignite the fire in my head when I feel low, and my inner flame dwindles and grows dim. Here are some wonderful, inspired Bardic moments of Winston Churchill, surely one of the great wizards of Avalon:

"Courage is rightly esteemed the first of human qualities... because it is the quality which guarantees all others."

"Do not let spacious plans for a new world divert your energies from saving what is left of the old."

"If we open a quarrel between past and present, we shall find that we have lost the future."

"If you are going through hell, keep going."

Just as they inspired Merlin, the Priestesses and modern day seekers, you may find the following Avalonian philosophies a source of wisdom and fascination.

Awen: This beautiful word refers to sheer and pure divine inspiration, the breath that blows to flame the sparks of fire in the head…The muse and the divine poetic gift, given to bards, druids, priestesses, artists, singers … all of us! To be with or to experience Awen is to be full of inspiration that has at its heart deity, an element, the fae or a magical beast... it is beyond classification in the ordinary sense. The priestesses of Avalon would breathe with Awen to bring life to their inspirations and purpose as individual priestesses and as a community...

The concept of Awen is represented by a famous symbol: three concentric rings within which lie three tilted lines, crowned by three dots. Drawing this symbol, or sounding out the word (ah-ooo-wen) brings you inspiration, heightened creativity, joy and peace.

It is also worked with to invoke the truth...

Immrama: A literal voyage, made over water, or less literally, a journey of your very core and being to one of the three worlds: the underworld, middle earth or the summerland in order to gather and understand wisdoms and teaching. Often translated to mean "the wonder voyage." By travelling to Avalon, you are definitely experiencing both a physical and metaphysical Immrama.

How to work with your own Immrama: Travel! Either literally or physically, to experience the energy and vibration of the sacred earth in her various manifestations, or through meditation, journey-work or pathworking. Do not "limit" yourself – set your soul free to sail upon the waves of the past, present and future, explore other lands, dimensions and let your spirit take you to realms unknown to others. All have their wisdom and joy to share, and your own Immramas will teach you so much. Part voyage, part initiation, they change you, and you can then change the world you are living in as a result of your own wonder voyage.

Mother Goddess and Father God: The masculine and the feminine were revered in Avalon. The mother and the father were known and loved, and the Goddess, mother of us all, took a beloved consort each year, to bring forth new life, as enacted and re-enacted for millennia in the festival of Beltane. The lover of the Goddess is known in Avalon as the Horned God, who has many names, including Cernunnos, Herne and the Stag King. King Arthur is said to have embodied the role of the Stag King during the sacred rites of Beltane in Avalon.

Geis: A natural form of destiny and law that one is born with: your geis may be introduced to you via experience, by being communicated to you by a wise one, deity or magical beast or elemental... Your geis introduces to you a theme that you will be working with this lifetime, a destiny weaving, a boundary and a threshold that is articulated in your life experience and lessons. It's about border and prohibitions for you personally: these may be ones you were born with, and figure out as you go along!

How to work with the energy of Geis: Understand what does not work for you and what you need to stay away from. For me, my geis includes alcohol, insomnia and certain foods that can leave me feeling ragged and less than. It may also manifest as people who fit certain destructive patterns you may have – and we all have them! Bring into your life a geis on that which limits and harms you, and lift the geis on all that supports, uplifts and enchants you! Geis is the realm of the chaste Goddess of the Silver Wheel, Arianrhod.

Sacred animals: "The ovate tell the future from the flight of birds and the movement of Animals." So said Diodorus, a Greek historian. He was speaking about the Ovates, the Druids who worked, and who still work with, seership, prophecy and healing. The boar, the hound, the stag, the deer, the swan, the salmon, the hawk, the owl, the cow, the raven, the otter, the dolphin and the mighty whale are perhaps especially sacred to the Avalonians, and appear time and again at the side of their Gods and Goddesses. The

Goddess Cerridwen, for example, shapeshifts into many animal forms during the tale of Taliesin's creation, as does Taliesin himself. Merlin is said to have been an adept at this art, and the Priestesses of Avalon are said to have flown as ravens. Goddesses like Blodeuwedd turn into white owls, and Gods like Cernunnos have another guise, in the form of the Stag. Animals and plant life, indeed all forms of natural life are considered utterly sacred in Avalon.

Three worlds: There are three worlds in the Avalonian tradition. The Otherworld, the realm where the "dead" or the ancestors at rest for a time. While in the Otherworld, souls may choose not to incarnate, or to incarnate again. The Otherworld is also known as the Summerlands. The Underworld is the realm of the faeries and the otherkin, they are met with often under hills and special trees and groves. Many priestess teachings took place in the caves, which initiates would move through into tunnels, into deeper caves to meet with more and more beings… I have written extensively about fae and otherkin magicks and mysteries in the *Oracle of the Dragonfae* and the *Wild Wisdom of the Faery Oracle,* which you may wish to explore further if these beings fascinate you as they do me. They are beautiful beings, and their underworld is full of knowledge, secrets, riches and wonders, and is safe for we humans when we approach knowing that these beings and their dwelling place is ours too, as we share the bloodlines, only in differing proportions.

Then there is ordinary world, where all three combine: It's important to understand that while there are veils between these worlds, they often overlap, and interact, and when Avalon was in her full peak of power, there was often a great deal of blending between all three worlds. Of course, we create our world, and Avalon can be an inspiration for the creation, which will be a direct projection of our interior landscape, our geis coming into this incarnation, and the choices we make in each moment. Avalon as an archetypal energy can help us create a beautiful, enmeshed and meaningful life, in the here and now and in the everyday!

Incarnation after incarnation: The Avalonians believed that wise people, animals, plants and elemental beings all had souls, and that these souls lived lifetime after lifetime, often after a "rest" in the Otherworld, or the Summerlands. In addition to this Universality of the soul, there was no "hierarchy" in these incarnations. Druids believed that in order to be wise, one needed to have experienced many things, understood what it is to be a fish, a hawk, a deer, a man, and this extended to the expression of elements, too. It was considered right to have been a rock, a fire, a drop of sea water and so on… all things have their wisdom, and without having been one with them, 'twas impossible to be wise as a being in whatever form your current incarnation took.

Shapeshifting: As well as moving through incarnations, many Avalonians – not all, but many more so than now – had the ability to move through forms, or transform their "shape." This is an essential part of their training, to this day – that we must know what it is to be "other" and to be able to change. In order to do this, we work closely with the animals and the elements and elementals. Shapeshifting, sometimes called skin-changing, enhances all our abilities, including the ability to shield ourselves and our loved ones, the ability to see what is taking place, the ability to be invisible, and the ability to know the wisdom of the earth and the skies. Shapeshifting is not undertaken lightly, as it is within the nature of things to have their rightful shape, and we do not "play" with that shape. We know we have a natural ability to change form, but we do so with respect and reverence.

This links Avalon directly to Atlantis and to Lemuria, where shapeshifting became such a divisive and hurtful issue for the beings there. Shapeshifting is respected, revered and treated with dignity in Avalonian lore and culture. The beings who are natural shapeshifters of the greatest skill are considered wise. We do not interfere or tamper with the shape without consent and even then it is rare – we would never "operate" or "experiment" on beings. Those that do are ruled by the law of Geis, which means they become outlanders, and are banished to realms where they can do no harm.

WHY LOST LANDERS TRAVEL

I have noticed how much spiritual people, the Lemurians and the Atlanteans and the Avalonians love to travel, or long to travel if they somehow feel they cannot this lifetime.

I wondered what that was about. Could it be in our bloodline? After all, Julius Caesar stated that the Druids would train in many locations, in Ireland, Gaul (modern-day France and Germany) and Britain.

"The idea of training abroad was something that was very strong within the tradition," explained Kylie McDonough, which helped me understand the variety of influences that kept coming through. They also travelled a great deal to keep the energy lines running fully, flowing and singing in tune with the planet. Walking the ley lines is still common today, and we all walk the pilgrim path, and as we do we sing the land into renewed health and vigour, which is returned threefold to ourselves, as our mother the Earth is so generous!"

"We also travelled to absorb local ambient energies and new ideas," Kylie said.

"Training often took place within other island communities. The training for men and women was carried out separately and women would often spend time training in different Avalonian centres such as Brittany. Regarding Brittany, there is a very ancient and strong feminine element there that has been held onto since the Neolithic times, which is one of the reasons why it was a centre for female development. This is where I believe I was trained, as well as on what is now known as the Channel Islands. Many young men who were being trained to become Druids or leaders of some type would spend much of their time abroad also. The path of Druidry was strongly aligned with the priestess path of Avalon. Despite what may have been taking place politically at the time, many young men and Druids spent much of their time training in the Norse Lands and also the Highlands of Scotland… Training was varied and multifaceted but took place in a very traditional way, including elements of witchcraft, shamanism, animism, journey work, meditation, sacred movement, arts and earth magick. Travelling, and liminal experiences were very important phases of gaining Avalonian wisdom. Long walks and pilgrimages to sacred sites were quite common."

"I believe that travel, and particularly travel to United Kingdom is embedded in our genetic structure, because we are so used to it as part of our lives in the past, and also as part of our learning and rites of passage though life in order to grow."

So travellers really are singing the planetary ley lines to health again. And if we consciously travel in healthful and generous ways, we bring the global matrix back to birth. And like Tolkien says, all those who wander are not lost!

Finding Avalon, finding Lemuria, finding Atlantis within are all beautiful – but finding them outside of myself, in a way that was so expansive and hopeful changed me, immeasurably, but maybe none more so than Avalon. I wept for weeks upon returning, but tears of bittersweet happiness – how happy I had been there, how happy I was to have her in my heart, how blessed I was to be able to share her wisdoms with others... If she is in my heart and soul, then indeed we can never be truly apart.

Adopted children sometimes search for years and years for their birth mother, in a similar way, I, the adopted child of my country, needed to find the mother of my blood, in the land that sang a song I too could sing without ever having been taught it.

I found that mother in Avalon.

And she held me, and soothed me, and sent me forward into a new life, her child.

AVALONIAN PANTHEON

The Goddesses and Gods of Avalon number in their hundreds, but some of their names are lost to time, although their energy lives on. Here are some of the most enduring, beloved and magickal of them all.

Grian

Grian is the sister of the moon Goddess (and Dragonfae being) Aine, and is a solar Goddess/Dragonfae Queen. She is of the golden light, and brings warmth and courage, joy and growth wherever her feet fall...she is the force that drives the plant to flower, the fruit to be born from the vine, the seed to spring forth into life. Her hands glow with this life-force, and her Dragonfae and bee and fae and flower companions breathe flames around her as she sleeps to ensure she is warm...she brings warmth and fire to those in wintry climates, and carries with her the coming of spring. She is very spring/summer in her feel, and is very much about the dawn and the new light, and sunset, and "dying light". She is necessary for our continued life, for moving forward in comfort, and she is a being who can also bring forth abundance and luxuries, those that spring naturally from the planet. She is very beautiful, and warm, and comforting. For anyone experiencing cold, fatigue and even joint pains, she breathes ease and joy into us.

To connect with her, grow something! Herbology. Earth magic, solar connections, solar energy, warm-blooded creatures, smiles and reaching out physically to people have a similar quality to that of Grian's love. Solstices, particularly the summer solstice, the time of Beltane, and any sunny warm day are the perfect time to connect with her.

Warm wind, and growth spurts in your life, when energy flows with ease and momentous change happens easefully. Wear reds, golds and yellows to create sunshine energy in your life, even on the greyest of days.

Taliesin

The bard of bards, this Merlin (leader of the Druids) wrote poetry that inspires us to this day, with its examinations of life and afterlife, shapeshifting, and cellular memory.

> "I am the wind upon the sea
> I am the wave upon the ocean
> I am the murmur of the strand of grass in the field
> I am a bull of seven battles
> I am a hawk upon the cliff
> I am a ray from the sun, and I am the fairest of flowers
> I have been a blue salmon

I have been a dog, I have been a deer
I have been a goat on the mountain
I have been a trunk
I have been a beech
I have been an axe in the hands
I was lanterns of light for a year and a half
I was a bridge that stretched over sixty estuaries
I was a path, I was an eagle, I was a coracle in the seas
I was a bubble in beer
I was a drop in a shower of rain
I was a sword in hand
I was a shield in battle
I was a string in a harp, enchanted for nine years
In the water as foam
I was a spark in fire
I was wood in the bonfire
I am not one who does not sing: and I have sung since I was small"
  – Taliesin

The son of the Goddess Cerridwen, Taliesin (which means *radiant brow* – inspired and full of fire in the head!) is a master of finding inspiration to express your spirituality, to create song and poetry, to live well as a being of mixed blood. Call upon him when you need to be a compassionate and creative leader who can express complex ideas on behalf of a group. He will help you find your true purpose, and your own creativity, your own source of Awen, no matter what obstacles there may seem to be!

Arianrhod

Arianrhod is the lunar Goddess, whose name means "silver wheel" and who is the Goddess-bridge between Middle Earth (this world, physically) and the world beyond (oft-called the Summerland.) She rules past lives, karma, and fate during each lifetime. A mother who loves her children, a woman who places strict geis (boundaries, borders, limits) on our behaviours, this beautiful Goddess proclaims that there is a natural law and an innate order to both this world and the next. She shines silver, and is ultimately very much her own being, despite there being tales of Kings wanting to control her, with geis...but as she is the ruler of geis, or law, she cannot be bound by such things, and follows her own course, as it is natural and right to her. Arianrhod is celestial in nature, and her home is Caer Arianrhod, a crown, or cauldron-shaped constellation that can be viewed from the Northern Hemisphere. She connects the earth magicks and the global weavings with the great galactic web of life...a moon-woman and star being both, she is compassionate and transformative, and takes us to the other lives we shall live both on this planet and beyond...

Merlin: The wizard

Merlin is the title for the head Druid, masculine. But the being known as Merlin is ages old, and is considered by many to be an Atlantean wizard who has had many incarnations and is extraordinarily long-lived in each of those incarnations. Merlin was present in Atlantis, Egypt and Avalon, and is guiding us now.

"Merlin was the guardian and the teacher of two children, Arthur Pendragon and Morgan le Fay, the dark Lilith of our island legend, sometimes identified with the Lady of the Lake, and reputed to be the half sister of Arthur. But who was Merlin with his profound science, and these two children whom he taught – the fairy woman, not of mortal birth, and Arthur, whom the magician bred according to some secret science of his own ... ?" So said Dion Fortune, the great 20th century mystic, who lived for a long time in Glastonbury.

This magickal wizard, thought during the middle ages to be devil-born, but who is half-fae, truly built the bridge between the old ways and the new, ensuring that the old traditions were extended forth into the new world. Without Merlin, we may have forgotten many of our songs, our celebrations. Could it be he who ensured that Yule became Christmas so that the birth of the Sun God became the birth of the Son of God? Not to swallow up the old truths but to ensure they were buried treasure, just bright enough so that we would, with just a little digging, find them?

Merlin is a being who can be worked with when you need guidance and wise counsel about how to walk between two worlds. Questions such as: How can I be simultaneously successful and spiritual? How do I remain a true leader, and yet rule with compassion? How do I choose a partner who allows me to be myself, but with whom I can feel the One-ness of true love? Be gentle and powerful?

These important and seemingly paradoxical considerations are the domain of Merlin, who will assist you in reconciling seeming opposites.

Merlin is said to have guided the building of Stonehenge as a resting place for his father, said by some to be the Roman Ambrosius, but said by others to be a faery king, also called Ambrosius, or according to the Church folk of the 1,400s, a demon! (The word Daemon is an ancient one, and was not considered synonymous with evil until it became adopted by the Church. This use of the word took fierce hold in the Burning Times, and has been used most indiscriminately since. Daemon often meant, in the olde worlde, a spirit, an animal totem, or even a faery or elemental being.)

"According to the legends that have come down to us he (Merlin) was conceived in a somewhat unusual manner, having a virgin mother and no discernible father. *The Arthurian Formula* suggests that he may thus have been a Theosophical Manu of some kind, his conception having taken place perhaps between an Atlantean temple priestess and a powerful Fire Elemental or even an angelic Lord of Flame," says Gareth Knight, Arthurian and faery scholar.

"On the other hand, the pious Robert de Boron writing in the early 13th century could not countenance the apparently blasphemous thought of what appeared to be a virgin birth, even if conceived in the womb of a nun. Thus the Otherworldly father had to be cast in the role of an incubus demon, sent by the Devil – whose nefarious plans however were thwarted by the innocent virtue of the pregnant holy maiden under direction of her confessor. Thus the youthful Merlin was diverted from being a false prophet and confirmed his holy credentials."

Merlin is the forebear of Dumbledore and Gandalf, and the archetype of the mage and wizard. He is the doorway between realms and times and epochs, the master-teacher of future generations, the keeper and sustainer through millennia of magick secrets.

He is also the master of the mist – obscuring what is not yet safe to reveal under his cloak of invisibility. He is a master of teaching each of us to use our psychic gifts and our powers of divination – but also he helps us through those times of transition. As we move into a new world, he is with us again, guiding our way.

Merlin can help you with this transition, which can increase your sensitivity. If you feel bombarded or overwhelmed with messages as the veil between the worlds thin, respectfully ask him to make them simpler, clearer and to turn them down a notch! It is hard for those on the etheric plane to work with us unless we are absolutely clear. Also be ready for beautifully clear communications with the plant kingdom after connecting with Merlin.

Connecting to Merlin is as simple as calling him. You can use your own words, simple and straight from the heart, or be more formal. Please feel welcome to work with this invocation! "Honoured Merlin, great sage wizard of Avalon, dissolve all blocks which prevent me from seeing, hearing, smelling, tasting and in all ways experiencing my psychic powers. Allow me to see the signs which are all around me, and to read them with clarity, courage, detachment, compassion and for the highest good of all concerned. Allow me to know that it is now safe to be fully functioning clairvoyantly, clairsentiently, clairaudiently and through my dreams and every aspect of the natural world and the etheric plane. Help me trust the messages when they come, and pass them on without becoming involved in the message itself, and to know that this process is sacred, safe and for the highest good of all concerned."

What is Merlin's own energy like? I find him wise, humorous and very loving – and he is unafraid to point out to me my own "faults"! However, his energy will be unique for each being that experiences him.

The location of a connection can have a powerful impact on our interaction with all sacred beings, but this truism seems even more so with Merlin. I have found it is often best to communicate with Merlin out of doors, in beautiful natural surroundings, or in an energetically soothing place with soft light, peaceful music, and crystals. One of the most powerful geographical locations to call on the great Wizard is in Merlin's Cave, at the base of Tintagel castle, Arthur's birthplace and Morgan's home in Cornwall.

Jo Byrne, a spiritual teacher and crop circle enthusiast, has spent much time in Merlin's Cave.

"As I entered this space I immediately felt the energy of a wise man come to my side and make his presence known. The energy was intense but comforting all at once and I felt as though I could have moved in and stayed there forever!"

"I was fortunate to spend most of my visit there alone so I was able explore this place and enjoy connecting with the energy without any distractions. I'm sure Merlin planned it that way as we had quite a good chat! I really didn't want to leave and felt afraid when I did. Merlin's Cave is located directly under the castle of King Arthur's Birthplace in Tintagel – it is an amazing site but I have to say that there is more than one type of energy going on in that place! As I made my way up the side of the cliff face I began to feel anxious and afraid! It was the strangest sensation I had ever felt! I arrived at the first section and took a few moments to gather my thoughts before I forced myself to continue the journey to the next part. I didn't make it! It was just so overwhelming that I just sat there and cried! I was in a total state of fear and panic and all I could think about was leaving which is what I did as fast as I could. When I got back to the bottom I felt relief and the feeling of fear finally left me. To this day I'm not sure what happened but it was intense and like nothing I had ever experienced before. Perhaps I had tapped into some sort of past life experience?"

I wondered too... could Jo have been flashing back to a past life as a pagan being dragged from the cave, and being punished for her spiritual beliefs? Perhaps Merlin's Cave was a place of safety and sanctuary for her in a land hostile to magickal practitioners? Leaving that space may have brought up a past-life memory of great significance, in order for Jo to clear it, and come fully into her power this lifetime.

Brigid

As the Goddess of childbirth and a female warrior, Brigid helps the Goddess bring forth or birth the Sun God. If you are wishing to conceive in the near future, or need assistance with childbirth or birthing new projects, simply ask for Brigid's assistance.

Light a candle to her on solstice night and she will come to your side to aid you and help you find your inner source of strength. As a female Goddess of the Tuatha de Danaan, she is written about in the ancient Irish text *The Book of Invasions*, and her image has changed little since.

"Brigid was a woman of poetry, and poets worshipped her, for her sway was very great and very noble. And she was a woman of healing along with that, and a woman of smith's work, and it was she who made the whistle for calling one to another through the night. And the meaning of her name is *Breo-Saighit* – a fiery arrow."

To connect with Brigid, light your candles on winter solstice eve, and leave them burning throughout the evening. This little ritual symbolically welcomes the light.

Our ancestors' lit candles and kept fires burning on solstice eve as they felt it assisted the Goddess and gave her strength as she gave birth to the sun. Just as Brigid gained confidence and cheer from the light of the flame, you too will gain strength from your candles' soft light. As you light them, remember you are consciously aligning yourself with the power of gentle change in your own life, soon will come new ideas and fresh starts. When you see swords, swans, flames and wells, you know you are connecting with Brigid. Call on her especially for issues to do with mothering!

The Green Man

The Green Man, a masculine face emerging from forest foliage, at one with nature, represents humanity's coexistence with the things of this earth. The life force is apparent in the buds and leaves bursting from the Green Man's visage, his expression varying from ecstatic to astounded, as is ours when we realize that which we share with all other beings that seek the light. The Green Man is represented heavily in Celtic magical traditions, but is also found in India, and has his counterparts in the Pacific. We are not simply human – we are of the very earth and the things that grow, die and are reborn upon it.

The Green Man is often called upon during Beltane. He is found in Christian churches across Britain, and despite mass defacing, lives on in the hearts of pagans worldwide.

His echoes are found in Pan, the Horned God, Cernnunos, Cerne, Dionysus and even in the devotion displayed to the Shroud of Turin.

We work with him when nature seems to be suffering: he will reignite the flame of life within the root of the tree and the seed, and new green life will spring forth, even through the destruction humankind has wrought. He is the life-force of the green world, and as such, he can re-green those desolate places within our lives, too.

The Lady of the Lake

The Lady of the Lake is known by many names, and is variously regarded as a Priestess, a fae-being, and a Goddess. To me, she is all of those, and more...and as the head of the Priestess Grove of Avalon, she is the Guardian of the doorways between the worlds, she governs all who may enter, part the mists, cross the water, and be taken to Avalon...and all who will be turned away, seeing only an endless mist before them.

She is a being who can move through the elements; shapeshifting and embodying the consciousness of the lake and the land, of fire and of earth. To Avalonians, land, sea and sky were regarded as sacred, and the Lady of the Lake could move between all three.

As the head of the Priestess Grove of Avalon, the Morgens look to her for her wisdom and guidance, allowing them to continue to move through the nine cycles of occult knowledge which they must become adept at...

These tasks include:
- **Earth magicks***:* The knowledge of minerals, stones, going deep inside to work change... earth alchemy, the ogham (the secret language of each tree being), building stone circles, charting the earthly ley lines – most especially the Dragon lines of the planet which run through the British isles, sections of Europe, Australasia, south east Asia, China and Tibet.
- **Starcrafting:** Charting and divining the meaning of the movements of the celestial bodies, communication with the celestial beings, galactic communications. (Priestesses of Arianrhod were particularly skilled in this area.)
- **Healing:** Overseeing medicinal and magickal healing, overseeing the Awen transferred, sensuality as sacred plant medicine/herbology.
- **Elemental communication:** Speaking to the elements, and to the elemental beings. Calling and caring for magical beasts, as well as keeping the communication going between "us" and "them". (There is truly no "us" and "them"! Such are the limits of language!)
- **Brehon law:** The giving of Geis (boundaries and justice).

The Morgens' main role is to embody their priestessing: in dance, sensuality, song, chant, birthing, croning, mothering, ritual, building, growing, harvesting and so forth...

After nine cycles of thirteen moons, the Lady of the Lake initiates the Morgens...and in time, from them, the next Lady is chosen...

She goes out into the political world to represent the interests of the Avalonian community, and consults with the masculine counterparts of the Morgens, the Merlins... druids of the old ways. She sets up healing, engages in battle if and when necessary, raising the mist to enshroud the shores of her land to protect her.

The Avalonian Priestesses were the wellspring of the community, living in solitude, yet in service to society, in the form of a village or township. They were self-sustaining, honoured, and powerful. The Priestesses and their teachings radiated out from Avalon itself, and her communities were spread throughout the Avalonian world...from Ireland, to Skye, throughout what is now called Europe, Spain, France... Many, as Avalon herself was, were inland, yet surrounded by land and water. The mist is the element that combines air and water, and shrouded the locations of the temples, a magickal skill given to the first Lady of the Lake from the Tuatha de Danaan...thus the priestesses are associated strongly with Dana. One Lady of the Lake was Brigid, who is alternately viewed as a Goddess, and as a saint...she was a Lady of the Lake, and her dwelling place can be seen at Bride's Mound in Glastonbury today... she is the coolness of the wells, the sweetness of water, and the heat and fury of fire. She is the Great Mother of the Priestesses, and of women, and of birth, and was one of the Great Ladies of the Lake. When we work with the Lady, we are often being called upon to exercise a teaching role, to step up into authority, and wield power without diminishing that of others... we have reached a place, not of perfection, for there is none, but a place where we will learn by teaching, sharing, bringing through younger beings, mentoring. We may also have an interesting relationship with other women...look at how you respond to older women. Do you have an elder, or a mentor, who is your teacher? If the answer is no, it may be time to open up to the possibility of finding your own feminine guide and mentor – your own Lady of the Lake.

Morgan

The witch-priestess, the one who is of the fae realm and of the earth realm, a being who is sovereign (complete unto herself) and who can teach and wield the priestess arts, which have now been so very diluted of power due to our disconnection from the natural world. She is related to the Morrighan, the Goddess who was accompanied by raven or crow – Morgan is spoken of by the 12th Century historian Geoffrey of Monmouth as having being able to shapeshift into a raven. She is of the law, of the old ways, rebel, sorceress, a woman alone yet mother, lover yet unmarried, the one who comforted and prepared those around her for their transition into the other world, the one who can take us into Avalon. Morgan is of the indigenous blood, of the line of fae and humans, and she is a dark and powerful goddess. She invites you to look at your rage and pain, and to transform these into magick and action, power and love. In the darkness can be found rest and love, honesty and transformation, the bright face and the dark face in one... She works between the worlds and can communicate with those who are in transition or those who are in the Summerland for a time.

The Morrighan

The Morrighan is the ancient shapeshifting Goddess of death and change: she came to me while creating the Oracle of the Dragonfae and told me that she was part woman, part raven, part dragon, part fae! She not only gave warriors premonitions of their passing so they could make preparations, she eased them through their passage to the other side. Thus she rules transitions in our lives: not simply the ones from this life to the next, but the ones that take us into the unknown, through our fear, and into the alchemy of magick, where we are able to show who we truly are. A triple Dragonfae Goddess, she is fierce, fair, and utterly without malice. She is, however, a straightforward and sometimes abrupt teacher and guide. Be strong, and be prepared for deep change when she makes an appearance. Do not go into fear at those words: let your courage feel inspired, and know that destiny has given you an opportunity to be the courageous being of action that you truly are.

She comes to you when you are at a turning point in your life, when that turning point absolutely demands action on your behalf, and backing down or avoidance is not the answer. The Morrighan calls you to take action and to face your fears. This way, your transformation will be one which gives you great strength and wisdom. Feeling frightened, alone, and hesitant will only lead you astray, follow her guidance, know that she will walk forward, and assist you in uncovering strengths you never believed you had, drawing strong boundaries, and claiming your space.

She encourages you to face trouble rather than turning away. Confronting injustice and changing the rules by which you have felt bound. There are many ways in which she can intervene and be of great assistance. Breaking free from stagnating jobs and pursuits, and relationships that offer no life source. Crossing over into a more spiritual path, and learning to work with your strength and your own ability to create deep change. Losing fear of your own power. Invoking natural laws, knowing you have been acting in integrity.

Oenghus

This musical deity is the Celtic God of deep true love, commitment and passion, and of communication between lovers. Oenghus has many parallels with Aphrodite and Cupid, so he is wonderful to call on to assist you in your search for a lover who will ignite your soul, your passion and your deep love. He delights in carrying messages between people who have never met, in this life anyway, so if you have dreamed of a soulmate who has yet to materialise, Oenghus can sing an energetic message between the two of you on the etheric plane, which will draw you closer and closer until meeting is inevitable. You will know when you meet this person, because the recognition will be so strong it cannot be denied by either party. He also protects lovers who are being vilified or separated by people who do not approve of their union. He himself has experienced this with his love, the Goddess Caer, and understands the longing to be one with your soulmate. Thus he stands as a strong guardian of those who are meant to be together.

The best way to connect with him is to sing to him! Try these words, and raise your voice in invocation! "Beloved bard Oenghus, please sing to me through your message of my love. Help me to understand who it is, and to bring us closer to each other. Allow this person to be seeking me, as I seek them. Allow them to know me, as I will know them. Allow us to be together, without strain or impediment, for all the days of our lives."

Dana

Dana is the Celtic Goddess of alchemy and deep change. She can assist you in honouring yourself, considering yourself worthy of assistance and finding helpful, strong and powerful mentors to guide and support you. Call respectfully on Dana to assist you with issues around finances, deserving and prosperity. She can also help and support those of us who experience confusion regarding our purpose in life – what we are meant to be doing with our time and our career. She stops us prevaricating, self-sabotaging or talking ourselves out of following a wonderful idea through to fruition.

Work with Dana to allow yourself to receive the help offered by others. Stop trying to control everything – Dana will help show you who is trustworthy and who is not.

She also works at dissolving ages-old bonds that may in this lifetime be manifesting as vows of poverty... She will assist you in becoming an abundant, beloved child of the Goddess and the God, able to create prosperity and positive change, care for yourself and others and make a contribution to the universe in its material form that makes a strong difference. Allow you to break through conditioned thinking and be enabled to manifest exactly what you need at the perfect time.

Rhiannon

A powerful, compassionate and enchanting Goddess, Rhiannon is a lover, a mother, and a woman who communicates with the animals. She can hear the songbirds call, and because of this association with birds and she has the ability to shapeshift into a calling songbird. She is a woman who is of the horses, running wild and free, untamed and fierce, often underestimated. She can shapeshift into the form of a horse, and can often be seen running wild for the sheer joy of it. Rhiannon pulls us forth, and challenges us to travel outside of our comfort zones, and be unbridled and yet directional, purposeful. She is a beautiful, strong mother as well as a passionate lover, she is one who stands up against injustice and who understands and brings out the truth...the inspirational truth (the Awen) of a situation. She has been unjustly accused of being an unfit mother and, after many great trials, she grew in strength, and proved her innocence. Her name means, in the Welsh, Great Queen...and so you must look to your own sovereignty when you are called by Rhiannon...she can speak with you through nature, and know that she runs within you, as your heartbeat itself.

Guenevere

We have reclaimed Morgan, but what of this Goddess of the land, whose body is Avalon? She is one Goddess who is very close to my path, and my heart. It took meeting with an Ayurvedic master to understand this connection, though! I have met the acclaimed doctor of medicine and master metaphysician Deepak Chopra several times. He excitedly told me over dinner one night in Sydney that my archetype is Guenevere. And that very day I'd been writing and channelling and working with her. A Goddess whose time is returning...and to have that confirmation from him, from the masculine, was such a blessing!

For such a long time, my reaction to the energy of Guenevere was governed by the 16th century Arthurian versions of her tale, which equated her with Eve. However, as a Goddess she pre-existed this re-telling. Her Goddess self in the form of the White Phantom, the Goddess and Sorceress of the land...so here is our chance to begin the work on reclaiming Guenevere. We've worked at reclaiming Morgan...thanks in no small part to Marion Zimmer Bradley...but there's another woman at the heart of Avalon who has been painted as weak, jealous, a traitor, a faithless woman. But she is the woman who delivers the round table to the Court and that is the symbol of the Goddess herself, and her seasonal workship and cycles. The Round Table is circle, the wheel, and the cycle of the seasons, life being cyclic rather than linear... It is, as if by gifting the Round Circle to the court, Guenevere delivered to the King and to the Knights a calendar of worship of the Goddess of Avalon.

Guenevere truly is a woman of the land. Her names means "white phantom" and this white, or shining aspect of her name links her directly to Taliesin's radiant brow, the Shining Ones of the Tuatha De Danaan, fertility and purity.

Llew/Lugh

The Celtic Sun God (known as Lugh in Ireland and Llew in Wales) has very strong, powerful masculine energy. He is kind, vibrant, caring, nurturing and sexually passionate – just what many of us consider extremely desirable masculine traits. He can be invoked to help shift any negative experiences you have had with men, whether as partners or as friends. He assists in healing rifts between lovers and also shows men how to be balanced – how to be both masculine and caring, both strong and kind. With Lugh's help, men can show they care without feeling weak or threatened. He also loves laughter! He is a master of shapeshifting for personal safety too, and one of his many forms was that of an eagle. He can show men how and when to shine, and when to change form in order to make it through lean times. Lugh was done some large injustices by those who wanted to diminish his strength and power and deny his Godliness. He became known as Lugh-chromain, or little stooping Lugh, and was thought of as simply a mischief maker. This name was Anglicised to Leprechaun, and he became a harmless figure of fun rather than the God of strength he really was. To me this symbolizes the loss of strength so many men felt as they were forbidden to reveal their wholeness, just as women have been too. But now Lugh is taking back his former shape, and once again coming into his beautiful, masculine power, as the wounded male energy on our planet heals, unfurls, and stands tall and strong once again.

Blodeuwedd

Blodeuwedd was "made" by the great Wizard Gwydion to be the bride of the Sun-God Llew. She was made of nine flowers – broom, meadowsweet, oak blossom, primrose, cockle – the cockle once grew wild in Britain, their vivid pink adorning cornfields – bean, nettle, chestnut and hawthorn. Over these plants Gwydion meditated, and chanted, until he fell into a great sleep. When he awoke, there stood the maiden of flowers, Blodeuwedd, and she was as soft, alluring, healing, beautiful and fertile as the flowers after whom she was named.

However, Blodeuwedd was no complacent creation. She had a will of her own, great intelligence, and a deep, wild and pure heart that longed for her own true mate. And so she fell in love, even though she was married to a God. Her love was not only for this other man, but for her own true self, and her freedom. And with that love came great magicks, such as the ability to shapeshift. She could go from flower-form to feather-form, in the shape of a white night owl within moments...and at night, she would hunt, and be free. She is both women: the owl and the flower, the huntress and the soft, the dark and the bright, the maiden and the death-bringer...she shows us how we can have many faces and yet we are always the one being. It is knowing when to be flower, when to be feather that is true wisdom.

Cerridwen

Cerridwen is a threefold Goddess, keeper of the triple cauldron. Within these three cauldrons, she brews and bubbles the gifts of intuition, second sight, of shapeshifting, herbcraft, animal communication, hearing and comprehending all things of this earth, and many more wisdoms. Essentially, Cerridwen knows the recipe for Awen (flowing inspiration) which she was given by the fae, and with her help, you can transform your shadows into the flowing bright joy of Awen, too.

She made this brew of Awen for her son, Morfren, whom she felt had nothing but that which she could give him... She positioned him at the foot of the cauldron, ready to receive three magical drops which would give him all these gifts and make him a great Merlin, and thus give her blighted son a place in this world. But Gwion, a young sorcerer apprenticed to Cerridwen to stir the cauldron while she slept, received the three drops instead of her son. Cerridwen cried out in pain, and Gwion ran...and so began a legendary chase, where transformation into other beings led the two to take the forms of the creatures of the earth and the water and the sky and the fire. They travelled through all elements, until Gwion, transformed and hiding as a grain of wheat, was found by Cerridwen, who shapeshifted into a giant black hen, and swallowed him whole. Nine months later she gave birth, to Taliesin, the druid of druids, the great Merlin... and so Gwion became the kernal that became Taliesin, Morfren became a knight of the Round Table, a warrior prized for his valour, and Cerridwen so loved her son that she continued her cauldron work, until all bards were inspired so that she became the protectress of the poets, whose songs were born in her cauldron's bubbles and brew. She is a transformative creator and destroyer, who teaches initiation, death to the old self, and helps birth the new.

SOUL-LOVE IN AVALON

There are some beautiful words in the old language to describe the relationships between people. Firstly, handfasting, a formal public bonding overseen by priestess or druid announced a pair to be bonded for a year and a day. Within this year and day, the pair could see how their teaming was going – and then, if all went well, after a year and a day, these vows to each other were renewed. Many more people today are choosing to be handfasted, or to incorporate the bonding process that takes place during a handfasting into a traditional marriage ceremony. The name comes from the tradition to "tie" the wrists of the couple together, and they stay this way till ... well, they need to come apart.

The bonds however are energetic as well as literal ... indeed the ribbons that bind their wrists are as nothing to the energetic cords that run between lovers when they agree to this blessing. The word honeymoon comes from the post-handfasting Avalonian tradition of the pair going to a perfect and small secluded shelter in a forest, or by the sea, and drinking mead (made from honey) and making love for a full moon cycle ... of course, foods and waters were left by the end of a small pathway near their door ... but this tradition has now evolved into the honeymoon so beloved of modern marriages.

However, the traditional form led to an incredible bonding, which increased the couple's tenderness, passion, connection and teamwork – all perfect ingredients for a loving and lasting union, and which is a wonderful foundation for bringing in children to the relationship.

Loved ones called the other "caread" or dear heart, beloved. Priestesses too could be handfasted in this way, if both lovers were members of the community. Otherwise, a change in circumstance, where Priestesses no longer lived within the Avalonian community took place. This was not to "shun" others, but to extend the bonds and magicks of the community outwards, rather than attempting to draw all, "inwards."

In Avalon, I asked for a soul-love, my own caread at Bride's Mound, and lit a candle in the gently sloping field, made an offering at the spontaneous altar that had been created, and sent out my soul-wish. Who it would be, how it would be, I left up to Bride (Bride is the maiden-form of the triple Goddess Brigid … she is the Goddess of the spring festival of Imbolg, and of fresh, new love). I felt her innocence and her wisdom would bring to me one who would make my heart sing. I simply sent out my wish, lit my candle, and let myself stand in that sacred place, and believe.

The concept of meeting beings in soul groups is not new. In Avalon, it was expected that apart from meeting your true love – your "caread" that you would also encounter several of these friends to your soul, anam-caras along the path of this lifetime, meeting and re-meeting them through incarnations. These loyal and steadfast friendships are many-hued, and involve a close, unbreakable bond that is a kind of soul-kinship. We all have these beings in our lives; being separated from them is very painful energetically, leading sometimes to ill-health.

A LOVE SPELL TO MEET YOUR CAREAD (SOUL MATE)

This is a variation on the ceremonial spell I worked at Glastonbury to meet my own caread. Never ask for a specific person, no matter how firmly you "believe" that person to be the right one for you. It is always best to tell the Goddess of your desire, and let her conspire to bring you both together.

You will need the following magickal ingredients:
– One rose quartz heart
– One pink candle
– Rose petals
– One pink charm pouch

Instructions:
On a Friday, go to your altar, and open your magick circle.

Using your index finger, cast a circle of light around yourself, tracing it in the air, anti-clockwise if you are in the Southern Hemisphere, clockwise if you are in the Northern. See a beautiful circle of white light protecting, balancing, and energising you and your magickal space.

Call in each of the elements.

Say:
I welcome the spirits of the earth, air, fire and water to this circle. Blessed be!

Take your pink candle and carve into it your name, and the word "Love".
Take your candle and hold it to your heart. Feel the love in your heart pour into your candle, activating your love energy, ready to be set alight and sent out into the world.

Say:
By Rhiannon, Guenevere and Maeve
I now create, I now pave
The way forward in loving well
I draw this down
With this bright spell
By all the power of three times three
As I do will, so mote it be

Feel your heart's powerful alluring energy of love, attractiveness, desirability pouring into your pink candle. Place it on the altar, and light it, feeling your attractiveness come even more alive.
Next, take your rose quartz heart, and hold it to your heart.

Say:
By Rhiannon, Blodeuwedd and Guenevere
A loving heart I will now share
By all the power of three times three
As I do will, so mote it be

Place your rose quartz heart on your altar with the pink candle. As you do so, feel the power of your love spell radiating its energy out into the world, an ambassador for your heart.
Take your rose petals in your hand, and hold them to your heart.

Say:
By Rhiannon, Blodeuwedd and Guenevere
A love so sweet I do now dare
To bring into my life divine

With this wish, love will be mine
By all the powers of three times three
As I do will so mote it be

Place your rose petals on your altar along with your rose quartz heart and your candle.

As you do so, understand that whomsoever shall come to you now is for the highest good of all concerned, and that this love will serve your happiness.

Stand with arms outstretched, and feel the energy of the planet's unconditional love for you pouring into you, lighting up your every cell, activating all your potential for true love.

Say out loud in a strong clear voice three times:

I am a beautiful, desirable being.
I am worth loving.
I love. I am loved. I love. I am loved.
The balance is now restored.

When your candle has burnt down, take its wax, your heart, your rose petals, and place all three together in your pink bag.

Tie the cord three times. As you do so, say:

Bound around this spell shall be
By all the powers of three times three
My true love now comes to me
As I do will, so mote it be

Thank and farewell the elements, and close your magick circle by pointing your index finger in the direction you began in, and tracing your circle clockwise, drawing the beautiful energy of the circle back into you.

Ground by eating an apple, the fruit of Avalon, and have plenty of water.

Carry your charm bag on you for the rest of Friday's daylight hours.

On Friday evening, take your rose quartz heart out of its pouch and wear it around your neck for at least one week. You may wear it longer if you wish, but be sure to wear it until the following Friday, at the same time you put it on to fully activate its magick.

About this spell:
This is a simple spell – but there are powerful, and ancient magickal traditions built into it. Here's some insight into its construction.

Your magick circle creates a sacred and safe space in which to work magick – a world between the worlds.

We do this spell on a Friday, as Friday is Freya's's day. Freya is the Nordic Goddess of love, who flew across the skies in a golden chariot, her throat adorned with amber.

Rhiannon is the Welsh Goddess of true love, magick and independence – she will assist you in drawing a love that is true, and who respects you as an individual, and as a magickal being.

Blodeuwedd is the wild-hearted Welsh Goddess of magick, and personal freedom in love: she will help you leave old relationships behind, and find a relationship where you no longer have to play the "nice girl." Your shadows will be loved into health when you call upon her...

Guenevere is the White Goddess of the land: she will help you find the right partner who will ground and protect you, and bring bounty to your family, and to yourself. You will have a sharing, equal relationship, as it was Guenevere who owned and created the round table as a gift for Arthur.

Maeve is the Irish Goddess of love and intoxication, a queen in her own right, she led cattle raids and asked for a man who was fearless enough to be her equal, powerful enough to allow her to be fully herself.

Saying your spell three times binds the spell – and three is the magickal number of manifestation.

Candles ignite your inner flame. Pink represents success.

Rose quartz is a stone that grounds the energy of our heart chakra. It is a wonderful love tool, and is without peer in creating pure love. Thus, the love that you draw to you with this spell will be safe, grounded, and good for you. Rose quartz also disperses our own negative patterns that can inhibit our ability to allow ourselves to be loved through self-sabotage.

The heart shape of the charm assists in opening your own heart to its highest potential.

Rose petals draw love that is true, passionate, and faithful. They also ensure that your love is as fine and strong as the planet itself.

Your pink pouch holds, and alchemizes your success spell.

Tying the cord off three times "binds" or holds the spell.

Finally, your heart transforms into an amulet, to keep your spell activated.

AVALON... THE LAND OF HONEY

"Ask the wild bees what the druids know..."
– Traditional British folklore

While in Glastonbury, I saw so many bees. Bees have been a special part of my life for a long time. I am allergic to them, and when young I would be treated with medicines and cold compresses to bring down the massive swelling. One small sting from this powerful creature in my foot would swell my entire leg to the thigh to three times its size, throbbing with heat, itchy and feverish. If I was bitten near the throat, I knew I would be taken straight to hospital.

A beehive functions in great harmony – it needs to. Each bee is clear on their role and each is vital to the life of the hive. Because of this, bees are brilliantly industrious and productive.

No doubt I needed bee medicine when I was young. No doubt those valiant stings from that brave bee gave me something I needed. I must have needed to be shown that to be small is to be powerful. That fear is of no worth. That if I work hard and well, there will be honey. And that honey is sweet indeed.

Healers today work with bee stings to heal people of asthma and other fear-induced conditions...we are sometimes, when bee-stung, fearful of the environment – and sometimes rightly so! But I feel my bee-stings gave me so much. They gave me the strength to run far, to be brave, to know I was small, and one of so many, but necessary, needed and loved within a community.

In Glastonbury, even though it was chilly and wet, I walked to the Tor. And on my hand perched a small bee. This small bee, gold and a deeper bronze, with its fur and fuzz, stayed on my wrist the entire time. Just before leaving Sydney I had walked the Harbour Bridge, a massive walk across the enormous harbour that divides Sydney into her northern and southern aspects of self. And on that day, a bee had landed on my left hand too, and travelled with me the whole way. When I reached the top of the Tor, this bee sat with me for a while. While I am allergic to bees, I felt very peaceful, as I had on the bridge that day, and simply sat still, speaking to the bee in my head, sending her loving vibes, wishing her well, and sharing my impressions of the landscape with the bee. I looked out over the "neck" that seemed to extend out from the body of the hill, and saw clearly how it became, from a position above, a flying swan stretched out in space... I looked down, and found a white feather, and felt happy. I had been seeing swans all the way to Glastonbury. Bees and swans. I wondered what to make of it all.

We sat quietly, the bee and I, and through my head drifted some words I'd learned:

"Ask the wild bees what the druids know..."

I smiled at my friend the bee, so small and so strong, and so gentle, and whispered to her, "What is it you know of the druids...?" She raised her translucent wings once, twice, and then flew off, in a spiral first, then into the distance, into the mist...

The Druids believed the bees come from the sun, and that the creation of mead is the transference of solar energy into liquid gold...and through that liquid gold we alchemise life, vitality, industry, love and sweetness.

Mead is a drink that can be both alcoholic and non alcoholic, and I made it my mission on my way down the hill to bring mead into my life. To bring liquid gold, amber light, drenching sweetness and at some stage, a honeymoon which I could revel in would be mine. It's also associated not only with Grian, but with Maeve – she who was like firewater in the veins of her lovers – intoxicating and unforgettable!

I wondered if it could be any more coincidental to have had two bees travelling with me weeks apart on my left hand as I walked for more than twenty minutes.

Seemed it could NOT be.

So the druids were talking to me, and I would let the bee tell me all she could, of the druids and of anything else she may know, any time she wished.

I went down the hill, popped into the local general store, and bought some mead.

It seemed fitting

The small size of the bee is overwhelmed by their power and generosity. The bees gift us with the tasty nutrition and geometric beauty of honeycomb, whose antiseptic qualities boost our immune system and heal wounds. Their wax is a powerful sealant and waterproofer, invaluable to ancient peoples, and the bee gave us honey, which sweetens, energises, heals, and provides us with a direct source of healing solar energy.

In Avalon, bees were revered for their wisdom and honey. They fed from sacred healing herb gardens co-created by Priestesses. Their honey had special, powerful properties, much like Manuka honey does today. Beekeeping was a sacred task, and the modern-day attendants of the Goddess Temple in Avalon, and of the Goddess Association in Australia, are called Melissas. The word Melissa comes from the Greek, and means honey bee, or honey. The word may originate from Minoan culture, where Melissa was a nymph who was gifted the secrets of honey by the bees, and who taught other women its magick and its health-giving powers. She fed baby Gods and Goddesses honey, rather than milk. Could the wisdom of Avalon be a form of life and health giving honey, which the modern day Melissa's are feeding us, to return us to the Divine?

I called my friends the bees "she's" because they come from the sun – and the sun in the Avalonian way of understanding was not just masculine, as it was in the Greek and in the Roman...like the Japanese, the sun is feminine and masculine. She brings LIFE. The Sun is both Llew, and Grian. Grian is a being with whom I had shared many powerful conversations, but never before had I made this connection between Grian and the bee.

I suddenly "remembered" that as in one of my Avalonian lives, I had been a beekeeper! When I asked other Avalonians about this connection, they eagerly shared their stories too. "We kept honey bees; in fact beekeeping was an important discipline to us as we would learn of beekeeping practices and ritual use of bees. We used the honey in our food and drinks such as meads and ciders," one told me.

"The latter stages of my training took place in the traditional Avalonian 'hive' of the Tor. So I spent my late childhood and early teens in Brittany and the Islands, and from my twenties onward with the Tor community. The time I spent priestess training would be the equivalent to high school and university now, about nine years. I call the Tor Island the Hive because I consider it to be at the centre energetically (even if not geographically the centre) of the Avalon tradition. All other communities were considered to be sister cells of the main Hive – no less important – but much of the teaching and lore stemmed from the Avalon of the Tor."

The bee-imagery again. As I read more and more of the ancient historians, I learned that druids and later in the early years of Christianity monks had "cells" like hives in the mountains, each "cell" like a portion of the honeycomb. They saw themselves as God's bees! Not only were they of the Goddess, they were of the God. I could hear the Lady Grian's honeytoned voice telling me all this as the bee flew far away…hopefully to somewhere warmer than the breezy chilly Tor!

As the Lady Grian had always been so associated with flowers and warm light that brings life, I found it entirely reasonable that she appeared to me in that form, at that time. Her message deepened, flowering into a beautiful channeling, which made its way into the *Oracle of the Dragonfae* card deck. Here it is, to remind us of the power of opening our heart.

"I am of the earth and of the Sol-star's light. I am the opening of the flower, the love
that lives in the flower of your heart. I love you, and wish for you to draw this love energy
into your being.

I am a power source that you cannot neglect. Because even if you feel you are a being of
winter, that your heart has grown cold and hard in order to ease the pain, I tell you that you
are now ready to reveal your own life source and warmth to another being.

The love you have to share will be appreciated, and returned. More so, this warm and
loving heart energy will be its own reward, as you awaken again to your own feeling nature.
Please open your heart in this moment.

Allow yourself to love. See the beauty in warmth, and smile as often as you can. Bring forth
your joy, and see the opening of others' hearts. Wear yellow, red and gold: all the colours of
my friend, of the sun, and you will feel a great flow of energy awakening throughout your body
and energetic being. Please see that the seeds you planted need warm earth in which to grow.
Yes, they can survive when it is cold, but they cannot thrive. So be warm, extend your energy,

and know that your truly radiant self will create great opportunity and abundance around you. Simply extend some heart energy out, and I will support you, and love you, till you are the radiance of the sun incarnated in your own form. Love. Be loved. Love."

Her Dragonfae beings appear quite tiny in some respects – like beams of light and flame, from the sun...like bees! She is sensuous too in nature, and protected...I see her as almost speaking in a breath like flowers, which of course need the bees for pollination... as she speaks, or walks, or breathes, things spring into life. As she speaks, flowers form in the air before her... her radiance is kind and gentle, but immeasurably powerful. She has the power to change landscapes, climates, and our feelings...

THE SACRED NATURE OF TREES

They teach many things to the noblest of the race in sequestered and remote places during twenty years, whether in a cave or in secluded groves.
– 400 AD, Mela, Roman Historian

To know something of the wisdoms of the trees is to know Avalon, deeply.

Many of the peoples known as the Celts, the Gaels and the Bretons studied tree-lore; certainly, all Avalonian communities worked with groves, healing herbs, and communicated with the spirit of the plants themselves. In Avalon today, there are oaks and ash, apple groves and elders in abundance, as well as the unique sacred thorn tree.

"Avalonians practiced a very early form of what could be described as permaculture. In keeping with their observation of the ecology of nature and how things worked, gardens were spiral designed and companion planting was used thoroughly. Apple trees grew throughout the island in groves and wildly and their fruit was considered sacred. One particular apple tree grew high upon a cliff and contained an entry point to the Underworld, this tree was centuries old, yet still bore magical fruit, which was used to decorate the many natural altars in Avalon," says Kylie McDonough.

The Tree of Life is a universal symbol, found in practically all cultures and magical traditions. In Druidic lore it relates to the worship of trees, in the Asatru or Nordic tradition to the World Tree, and in the Kabalistic tradition, it represents the 22 pathways to wisdom, via the 10 spheres, or numbers, in the Pythagorean tradition. For hermetic magicians, it is a serious, absorbing study for lifetimes. The Yggdrasil is the Norse, or Asatru World Tree, upon which Odin hung, gaining wisdom, and was given the language of the runes...there is too, a Kabbalistic version that closely resembles the Druid Tree of Life, and there is also a Mesopotamian Tree of Life. They too epitomise as above so below, their root structure mirroring their branch structure ... connected to all, they breathe out what we need to breath in, our relationship close, necessary. Without each other, we will not live.

The trees can tell us so much: It is time to begin to communicate with our trees in the Avalonian ways...we have much to learn from our indigenous brothers and sisters, and from our own energetic explorations into this realm of knowledge and beauty....

In Glastonbury there is a sacred tree that is so revered that each year, the British royal family are delivered a snippet of it, for under their Yule table. It is from the sacred thorn at Wearyall Hill that this clipping is taken. It is interesting that the thorn tree is sacred to faeries – are the royal family acknowledging their own magickal past and bloodline when they do this, however unawares they may seem?

The Thorn tree of Wearyall Hill takes time to walk to...she is stooped by the wind, hunched over, protecting herself, and looks a little like a crone...but when you get closer you can see that she is maiden, mother and crone. She flowers twice a year, and only cuttings taken from this mother thorn can grow in Britain. She was said to be planted here when St Joseph of Arimathea returned to Glastonbury to found the Christian church. Exhausted from travelling (oh, how we can relate to that!) he sunk to his knees on Wearyall Hill, thrusting his staff into the ground to keep himself upright. While he sagged, the staff held firm, shooting roots into the good earth, growing the instant it touched the hill. I looked at the tree, its twisted self strong and reaching up and along, drawn to the south, in the direction of warmth and fire in the northern hemisphere. I spent time with the sacred thorn, making peace with my Christian mentors, the nuns, growing up, and making peace with the part of me that was devoted to Mary, the part of me that was healthy heathen, another part that is pure Priestess of the Goddess, and my wildish self, so reckless and fae.

Oak, ash, thorn, birch and reed and willow, and many others, made up the sacred nemetons of Avalon. These blessed trees were often formed into groves, clearings which would open unexpectedly within the dense oak, hawthorn and birch forest that once blanketed Britain, keeping her soil warm and fertile. To come upon the open sky, a ring of trees, and a field of flowers, after walking for days along a dark, narrow and crooked track must have seemed such a miracle!

The Nemeton is both a goddess and grove, and the oak groves were sacred. Nemetona is the Avalonian Goddess of these holy places: these are usually naturally formed groves of trees and within the landscape. Naturally-formed rings and forests of trees are her spaces, and she guards and watches over them. She is of the trees herself, and could be confused or mistaken for a dryad... but she is a Goddess, and her power ranges into every space that is called sacred. I see her as being formed like a tree, and being both above and beneath the grove. Nemetona works with faeries a great deal, helping them to do their energetic working with grass, flowers, trees, roots and leaves.

Avalonian Priestess rites were held outside when possible under the sheltering branches of the sacred trees of the grove.

Particular kinds of healings were created in groves attuned to the healing energy required to work well with the element. So, for example, people suffering from growing older, a sense of being "broken" and literally for broken limbs, bones, ribs and so forth worked in the oak grove. This oaken hall of healing helped bones knit faster, revived people's feelings of stability and made them feel that they could endure their tragedy.

Willow groves were constructed to work with ailments such as headaches, or a sense of the "head" being disconnected from the body. Many Avalonians greatly respected the head, and the head was felt by many to be the repository of the soul. Not at all in the way we westerners have lived in our heads, this sense was of the ancestry and the wisdom and the soul itself having and finding eternal life and expression in the head.

Talking heads were common: heads of ancestors lived long after bodies returned to the earth, and were often venerated, and asked questions. This is strikingly similar to the headhunter tribes of the New Guinea highlands and regions such as Borneo, where communities have lived until as recently as 40 years ago. The willow could repair the soul, as it worked with correcting the flow of fluids and bloods around the entire body, but most especially in the head. Rowans are the sacred tree of protection, and it was to the Rowan groves that the Unicorns fled, to hide amidst the sheltering mists, until Arthur, and Avalon returns.

YOUR OWN SACRED AVALONIAN TREE

Your birth date will fall within a span of time that a tree guards and influences...its energy softly changing and shaping those who are born under each tree's branches...here is a brief rundown of what is oft-called your Celtic tree sign...

Birch: December 24–January 20
Slender, pure, fragile externally, undaunted internally. Lends support. Clarity, determination, integrity. Able to stand up for what they believe in, those born under the branches of the birch are hard on themselves...

Rowan: Jan 21–Feb 17
The Whispering tree...its berry is as a five pointed star, and thus is sacred and magical. This is the tree of magicks and enchantments, of glamour and of power. Intuition, precognisance, channelling... this tree protects those who are "different" from persecution.

Ash: Feb 18–March 17
Empathetic, fast energy, exhausted easily, goes very deep and finds it difficult to make a decision at times. Strongly connected to the elemental realm, highly sensitive to animals and to plants.

Alder: March 18–April 17
So strong and solid, this being can be depended upon when all others and all else fails. However, this dependability also creates a kind of rigidity – it is necessary for those born under this branch to build, not waste, their incredible strength.

Willow: April18–May 12
Shifting and changing, the beings born under her trailing branches soothe others and can change to suit their circumstances, and know exactly how to read the moods of others... they are drawn to emotions and to the psyche, they are conduits of feminine flow.

Hawthorn: May 13–June 9
You can create – and you can destroy – and you can also create borders between your own selves, so that you hide the truth from your heart...however, you are a genius of change when you accept its transformative qualities...be patient...take time...you will change...

Oak: June 10–July 7
Ages old, the oak endures and protects...it can survive a lightning strike, a fire, and devastation...you have strength of character and can lead others...choose wisely, because you are capable of so much....

Holly: July 8–August 4
Holly Wood is not in California! It is a symbol of masculinity and potency... and if you are born under Holly, you have balanced, even, flowing energy. You are able to create respect and admiration, and can be a spokesperson for many people.

Hazel: August 5–Sept 1
You have hidden, inner treasures and gifts. You are a being of deep knowledge to share and gift to others. Your insights and communication gifts mean you can transform the world in an act of magic with words...know you have power...be wise in its use...

Vine: Sept 2– September 29
You are delicious, intoxicating and able to gather people around you with your charm

and laughter...you enhance a mood, guide others into play and dance, and release inhibitions.... you need time alone, sometimes, to draw back your strength, as you give out so much.

Ivy: September 30–October 27
Ivy is a survivor...she can move and grow and travel and find a foothold where no others dare to tread...an explorer and discoverer and adventurer, you lead the way for others to follow, never knowing how amazing you truly are...

Reed: October 28–November 24
You are stronger than anyone knows...and your strength is of the deep, the dark, and the intuitive. You are able to drink very deeply, and sustain yourself from a deep and ancient well of wisdom...you shelter many, and care for others, but stand alone.

Elder: November 25–December 23
You are one who can live lifetimes within one; one who can regrow your own soul after a shattering experience, who can up and move countries, partners, and change, change, change. You are a free spirit, a liberated being and we are excited by your wild heart.

MAGICKAL AVALONIAN BEINGS

Before we move more deeply into the sacred landscapes of Avalon, it may be helpful to meet their inhabitants!

Tylweth Teg (Welsh, meaning the faery folk)
The Welsh term for their indigenous beings who remain with us to this day, particularly in nature. They have merged with the Welsh people, too, and many have Tylweth Teg blood.

Tuatha de Danaan (Irish, means the children of the Goddess Dana)
The original inhabitants of Ireland, who shapeshifted into the land itself, the wells, the fire, and blended their bloodlines with those of the Mil, and thus the world in the present day – many Australians have this bloodline.

Pixies
From the word "Pict", meaning Scottish indigenous, Avalonian. Little and dark, the word, and they, became "pixies".

Sidh

(Pronounced "Shee" thus the ban-sidh became the banshee.) Broadly speaking, fae.

Many humans have fae-blood, like Jessica, or Morrigan. Her whole family carries this line, making her a very powerful individual!

"I was raised in a home with my mother, grandmother and great grandmother... four generations living in the one house. If Mum's car keys went missing, my great grandmother used to say that the fairies had hidden them. If you put clothes on in a rush and they were inside out, the fairies were playing a trick on you....and if you changed, they would do worse...because you ruined their fun! My best friend in school had pool fairies. I prayed when I went to Glastonbury that they would invite me home. My favourite movie was a cartoon called Excalibur!" She is magickal indeed – no wonder I see faerie beings with her!

All faeries are very delightful, and some can play sweet tricks to remind you of their presence. They are not vengeful or tricksy, but playful and cheeky. The fae beings of the Wild Wisdom of the Faery Oracle often play good-natured pranks. Some decks even arrive with a special feather embedded into a card of great significance for the new owner! I love their way of showing us the magick of life, all the time.

Morgens

Priestesses of Avalon, named for Morgan le Fay, a lady of the lake whose name means sea-priestess, or of the sea.

Melissas

Pre-initiate priestesses, named for the honey bees, who were the Goddess-source of the sacred mead.

SACRED SITES

Each Avalonian community has variations upon the following...

The Tor: A high place upon which rests a stone circle sky connection plus earth connection, bringing into relationship the celestial and the terrestrial within which is the underworld.

Upon the Tor is the entrance to the underworld.

The Red Spring: A natural spring, which is mineral rich. The Glastonbury red spring is associated with the bloodline, it having an iron-rich content. It can directly tap into your ancestry and help you understand the cellular memories you may hold within, and be able to sift these from past life memories. It is strengthening, gives you vigour, and is grounding.

The White Spring: A spring which runs clear and sweet and pure, and has a calcium-rich content...it is connected to your incarnations and to your shapeshifting abilities. It is the mother spring, and will nourish and nurture you, support you and comfort you. Drinking from her is like mother's milk for her child: the best protection and nutrition!

Both springs come from the underworld, the womb of the mother. In Glastonbury they are sadly separated by a road...moves are being made to venerate them and to sustain their viability for our future ancestors. Both are sourced from the earth (or the underworld) – the goddess herself, and they are considered sacred, healing, and precious. Their healing properties have been recorded by the thousands upon thousands of pilgrims who have drunk from them for millennia.

The Well: A waterplace with many beautiful purposes. To scry, to call other priestesses, to drink, to work with in order to create potions and healing brews, to drink, to bless, to bathe.

It connects with the underground waterways, so messages can be sent "down" the well, where they are flowed into the waterways and sent to their rightful emotional destination. Brigid's well, in Kildare, Ireland, communicates right through to Bridie's mound, in Glastonbury.

A mound: A place where your physical form was to be put to rest in the earth...there are many mounds behind the sacred places, such as Avebury. Newgrange, in Ireland, is one of the most famous mounds, and is a solar temple of the dead, carved with beautiful spirals and symbols. Deep connections with the Tuatha de Danaan can be made there.

Gog and Magog: The ancient oak trees that remain at present-day Avalon. Each Avalonian community had a procession of healing trees. To be healed, you would walk through the healing groves, and dwell within their energy for a time, before returning to the world whole and well once again. Please see the section on Nemetons for more information.

Stone Circles: The great 20th century mystick, Dion Fortune, is just one of millions of souls who have wondered at the power and purpose of the great standing stone circles found in the Avalonian landscape. "We may dismiss the tales of Avalon," she said "but we cannot dismiss the great stones on the uplands, nor the ancient roots between them." A circle of standing stones is a kind of calendar, clock, and temple, one which connects heaven and earth, creating an energetic portal through which energy can be raised, conducted, and information received through kenning...inner knowing.

Underneath the stones were chambers, the halls of the underworld, where we could enter into the shadowy realms below, and explore what lies beneath safely, and in love.

We did this for thousands of years.

Serene Coneeley feels Stonehenge is absolutely ancient. "The people who constructed this great stone circle – and the hundreds of others that were scattered across the Isles – had the same philosophies, the same worship of nature, the same attunement to the seasons and the skies above. And that was from 3,000 BCE or even earlier," she says.

All stone circles have great power, but with different energies. Avebury is an enormous and gentle circle of great power and healing, others induce trance, past life memories, or can slow and reweave time itself. Those of Ireland feel full of faerie magicks!

Dolmen: Three or four stones, two or three standing, one laid across the top, forming a bridge/arch. Chanting, raising energy within the dolmen healed the being within the arch...often a small pit was dug beneath the dolmen arch, and chanting would take place for some days. At others, an element would fill the small pit.

Coracle: A small boat, sea vessel to cross the lakes or oceans to the Avalonian communities; often made of animal skins, waterproofed. Avalon's were decorated, oft with triskeles, dragonheads (not actual, though if a dragon gifted its body parts to the community of Avalon, they could be used) and knotwork. In later Avalonian times, as in Arthur Pendragon's, they were called sacred barges...referred to in the Merlin Taliesin's poem about life and afterlife...

The Apple Grove: The sacred grove where the apple grew, again, to sustain the community via food, medicines, sacred wood...note the connection between Avalon, where all was at peace and bountiful, and Eden...note too the connections between the telling of the story of Eve, and the telling of the story of Guinevere... When an apple is split, a five-pointed star appears!

THE WEAVING PLACE – THE LABYRINTH OF AVALON

Walking, or moving in a pattern brings about a deep state of trance, in which Awen can be felt, experienced, accessed... Designed to take us deeper into ourselves, walking a labyrinth in a place of power like Avalon can be profoundly spiritual and transformative. The labyrinth is not the same as the maze, which is a puzzle, and thus an activity of logic... the maze, by virtue of its structure, is a problem to be solved by the left brain, rather than a knowing, which the right-brain-stimulating labyrinth gives us. There is a powerful labyrinth that has been walked into the Tor by the feet of the thousands upon thousands of pilgrims who have navigated its winding paths. One minute you are clinging to the bare side of a frosty steep hill, the next plunged into a dark thicket with stinging nettles, in others, a gentle wood brings peace and cheer. Walking the Glastonbury labyrinth is a test of sorts, as to whether you are prepared to go into the heart of yourself.

Each of the labyrinths of the Tor's seven levels corresponds to a chakra, and each is challenging in its own way to walk. This is no simple spiral, no gentle hill … this is a challenge worthy of spiritual athletes!

To walk into the labyrinth and complete that journey to the inside of self can take up to three to four hours, depending upon your level of physical fitness and weather conditions, and what you feel compelled to do! I felt like running through sections. I was so altered, and felt such a rush of pure life force flow through me fiercely, with great delight I knew I was changing while walking! Yes, even the crawling through nettles and scrambling up hills brought a grin to my face – I felt challenged, certainly, pushed, oh yes, but so alive and exhilarated! Besides, isn't that life herself – she sends us challenges and we rise to greet them, stronger and more powerful, more full of love and gratitude than ever before!

I felt just a little overwhelmed by this amazing experience, so I walked out on a different day – the seven hour process can be demanding for even relatively fit people. I also wanted some time to process and farewell what I had left behind. And I knew as well that as I walked in, I could leave something "behind". I made an offering at the beginning, and tied a red ribbon round my wrist to signify my connection to the land and my mother. I collected a swan feather along the way, and a crow feather – the black and the white, the polarities I'd created out of my own self. These would be brought to peace during this walk of the soul. I let go as I walked, feeling lighter and lighter, and yet more connected as I let go and surrendered deeply to the journey. I let go of the heaviness of my marriage not working out the way fairy tales tell us they ought, I let go of not "fitting in" or being normal, I let go of my fear of coming out completely about my magickal path … I walked the path, and as I walked a great light began to shine in my soul – and in my body. Was this something of what it meant to be to be a "shining one?"

I grew "lighter" in other ways too. Amazingly, just those two walks in seemed to release so much on a cellular level – I had let go of three kilos of weight (that's about six pounds) while walking the Glastonbury Labyrinth … I must have been holding on to so much pain in those cells, and I am so grateful to the landscape of Avalon, the Goddess, for freeing me. And I am grateful to myself for letting them go!

As I researched more and more upon my return, I was made very happy by one of those curious pieces of serendipity that so often shows you're on the right – even if it is labyrinth-like track! I learned that the labyrinth of Crete was overseen by women, whether by Goddesses or by Priestesses is lost to the time goddess! One of her roles was to distribute honey to those who completed the labyrinth walk – could this have been a message from the bees who had visited me both as I walked in Sydney, and on my second day when I walked to the top of the Tor, accompanied by a friendly bee?

All I know for sure is that honey and sweetness has been mine since I walked that path carved by the hand of the Goddess into the sacred hill. Maybe I was the bee, drawn to the flower of Avalon, and took home with her all the means of creating honey from her magickal essence.

Hints on walking a labyrinth:
* Drawing labyrinths is a wonderful exercise. There are finger labyrinths that can soothe and calm your mind. These are wonderful exercises to work with before attempting to walk one or to build one!
* Labyrinths create harmonious interaction between the right and left brain, bringing both into peace with the other. This serves us in many powerful ways in our day to day lives.
* As you walk into the labyrinth, whether on paper or in the landscape, focus on a part of your life that you are ready to release. Prepare yourself to let go of this, with every step you take towards the centre, when the process of saying goodbye will be completed.
* When you arrive at the centre, make an offering, and ask a question. See who you are … and know that you have nothing to fear from looking into the shadows of your own soul. See the truth, and know you are whole.
* As you walk out, you will receive a gift … you will know what it is. You may receive a feather, as I did, or hear words, feel soft breezes or be accompanied by a friendly guide or goddess, or an ascended master! A guide, like Mara the Atlantean, or one of the Avalonians may also make an appearance, sending you a message or simply assuring you that you do not walk alone.

I have walked many labyrinths since … on my own, tracing energy patterns in the Earth, swimming them in the oceans, and creating temporary ones at workshops and conferences.

But this labyrinth, the ancient one of Avalon, supported a deep release, and gave me a gift that makes my soul sing to this day.

THE ENDING … THE MIST RISES

"Like the mist, the spirit wants to shift, rise, disappear and return."
–Tom Cowan

"We shall draw from the heart of suffering itself the means of inspiration and survival."
–Winston Churchill

Overwhelmed by cold, mist and indefatigable male and female warriors, the Romans pulled out of Britain in the early years of the new millennia. Having decimated many of the tribes, despite the valiant resistance by women warriors of Avalon, such as Boadicea, Britain was in disarray. Their groves had been cut down, their priestesses slaughtered, the druids in hiding. The sacred isle of Anglesey was decimated, its inhabitants slaughtered, its sacred oak grove immolated. We know this, because the Roman historian Tacitus was there.

"On the opposite shore stood the Britons, close embodied, and prepared for action. Women were seen running through the ranks in wild disorder; their apparel funereal; their hair loose to the wind, in their hands flaming torches, and their whole appearance resembling the frantic rage of the Furies. The Druids were ranged in order, with hands uplifted, invoking the gods, and pouring forth horrible imprecations. The novelty of the fight struck the Romans with awe and terror. They stood in stupid amazement, as if their limbs were benumbed, riveted to one spot, a mark for the enemy. The exhortations of the general diffused new vigour through the ranks, and the men, by mutual reproaches, inflamed each other to deeds of valour. They felt the disgrace of yielding to a troop of women, and a band of fanatic priests; they advanced their standards, and rushed on to the attack with impetuous fury.

The Britons perished in the flames, which they themselves had kindled. The island fell, and a garrison was established to retain it in subjection. The religious groves, dedicated to superstition and barbarous rites, were levelled to the ground."

History has a terrible record of oppression, and we can hear in the voice of Tacitus some of the horror men of compassion felt when witnessing atrocity.

For hundreds of years, the tribes struggled to reform, and were broken again and again by the marauders of the Saxons, who decimated the population. Over time, the invaders became settlers, slowly beginning to merge with the indigenous peoples of the

British Isles, those descendants of Atlantis and Lemuria. The magicks of Britain were poured into the melting pot of Cerridwen's cauldron, and Awen lived, in new forms, shapeshifting again to stay alive. But with the magicks of Wyrd (Anglo-Saxon wizardry) and wand came also the fear of the Church, the hatred of women, the fear of nature, and with these, the greatest threat to Avalon arrived. The pure energy of Avalon was vanishing, and in great danger of disappearing altogether.

And then a momentous decision was made

Caught between the old ways and Christianity, and fearing her destruction, the priestesses raised the mist as a shield behind which Avalon and her love, her energy, her bloodlines and her magickal beings could be preserved.

And so Merlin's vast cloak of invisibility was spread over all of Avalon, and peeking through were echoes, whispers and dreams, clues enough for those who were called by the Goddess to trace their steps home.

Other Avalonians remained in the physical world, and went westward to Ireland, through the mists of the Irish Sea. Some ventured into another dimension, to hold the energy and protect Avalon, and the King, till he was called home. Others shapeshifted into great birds: ravens, owls and hawks. Others still became otter, fish and dolphin.

More still went out into the world as teachers, midwives, nuns, healers, village wisewomen and witches, volunteering to keep the wisdom alive and available.

The druids hid the groves deeper and deeper in the forest, and told the Romans they were cursed and full of horrors, told them tales of sacrifice and pain, to keep the invaders full of fear, and away from the last of their sacred places.

Past life memories of this time can be most painful, but very revealing.

"During the period when I lived, there was a great deal of civil unrest taking place outside of Avalon, and oftentimes warriors would seek the blessings of the Priestesses of Avalon for success in battle," says Jessica, who as Morrigan, was named for battle.

"I think after 900 BCE, the physical Avalon started to go into hiding. There were still hidden remnants of it in a smaller scale even during the Norman times. I think the landscape has a way of swallowing up the physical evidence that the community ever existed there. After a while the idea of Avalon as a physical place gets relegated to the realm of pure myth as that becomes what the majority of people think. And as long as people believe that, Avalon remains hidden," says Kylie.

Jesssica also shared with me her memories of the end-times. "I remember not only spending time in Avalon but also in Anglesey. I, unlike many of my sisters, used to take part in hunts and so would often move around the area. I was not involved in Avalon's separation from the world … I believed it went against all that I was taught, but after what happened in Anglesey my sisters feared the worst and unlike me they were uncomfortable with warfare. I was, after all, named after the goddess of War, the Morrighan. I left to continue to spread the word and hoped one day to be able to return, the day did not come... I did my duty," Jessica said. She, a being of lightness and beauty, was in that moment a true warrior, grave, solemn and purposeful.

CERRIDWEN'S CAULDRON RELEASEMENT MEDITATION

To release the memories of the ancient past, as well as the times we would prefer to be healed from this lifetime, I would like to take you through this Avalonian meditation, where we will connect with the Goddess energy of Cerridwen...

As a Priestess of Avalon, as a Druid of her Old Ways, you are able now to drink fully and fearlessly from the cauldron of life.

You may be one of the Merlins...the wise ones who radiate wisdom...they are attracted to crystals and to staffs, they can shapeshift and blend into almost any environment... you may be a crystal healer, a gardener, a wise one who cooks and brews the herbs of our Mother the Earth...

Perhaps you are of the fae...flirtatious and lively, but with a great and serious attachment to nature...wayward, some call you, but I know that you are free...you may be an artist, a writer, a storyteller who tells great truths and keeps wisdom alive...

Or of the Dragonfae, both dragon and fairy, and Goddess too...feeling like you can fly, that sometimes you need armour, frightened sometimes of your own temper...

Or a Lady of the Lake...Nimue, Morgan and Viviane...gentle wise ones and priestesses who are their society's healers...you may be a nurse, a therapist, an energy healer, or simply one whom others turn to for advice...there are many other Avalonians...among them the knights and the ladies of the court...

Whatever Avalonian you feel kinship with; all the sacred things of this earth are your treasures...

For you have been star and stone, and sea and sky...and now, it is time to become whole again, with the healing energy of Cerridwen's cauldron...and of Avalon.

Are you ready? Know you are very safe...that I will be with you every step of the way... you are very loved, and very protected...

Let us begin...

Cerridwen's cauldron is that of inspiration....is that of transformation...is that of rebirth...

This meditational yet very real magickal ceremony is a genuine ritual of rebirth...just as the Celtic warriors were reborn of old, so too are you being reborn in every moment... with every breath...when we meet with Cerridwen, the patron Goddess of poets and creativity, of mothers and fathers, of children and of magicks, we take firm steps forward into a future full of love and wisdom...

See before you now a sacred grove...in a ring of ancient trees you see Cerridwen, the threefold Celtic Goddess and keeper of the cauldron...She has with her three great cauldrons...

Are you ready to speak with her?

Yes?

Then let us continue....

Cerridwen now speaks, telling you that within the cauldron closest to her she has placed magickal herbs from the slopes of Avalon's sacred Tor...she asked for the blessed waters of the red waters and white waters from the sacred springs of Avalon to come to her, and be poured into this cauldron...under this silver cauldron lined with pearls she lit her holy hollyoak fire of transformation, and she stirred it with an apple branch for a year and a day...

Cerridwen continues speaking with you, telling you that a year and a day is the usual length of initial study for a being studying Avalon craft...in this span of time we can celebrate each of the great festivals of the wheel of the year, work with the lady Arianrhod and her 13 moons...and within that year and one day, we can make a commitment, every day, to be true to who we are...

She shares that within her cauldron are the gifts of intuition, second sight...herbcraft, shapeshifting, hearing and comprehending all the beings of this earth, of stone and sky and sea and star, communicating with the animals, forging bonds with the God and the Goddess, and the key to reawakening to who we truly are... all are Cerridwen's domain... for you are earth, and water, and fire, and air, and spirit, and the great truths of our being are that we have already incarnated as each of these elements...and you are now ready to learn more...

But before you can drink from this cauldron, there is something that must be declared, and released.

Allow what you wish to release to form etherically before you now...See it, without anger and pain, but knowing that you now are ready to release the pain, but you will always retain the lessons.

Take this energetic representation of what it is you wish to release forward, and Cerridwen gestures to a cauldron next to her...within are the nine sacred woods, softly burning, with blue and violet light, waiting to clear for you all that you wish to leave behind...Speak in the vast space of your mind and energy self that which you wish to

let go of...name it...say it...know it...own it...and now with love, see it enter the blue and violet flame of the cauldron of transformation.

It vanishes, with no pain, no hurt, consumed by the violet and blue flames that cleanse all such things...You may feel lighter...joyful...more free, or simply soft and open...

you look into Cerridwen's eyes, and you know she understands.

She says:

You are now free. You have no further need of that. Allow us to take this burden from you ... now, and at any time you may have need of this in the future...at the end of each hard day, come to me, and let us transform the hurts of the world together, into your lessons and strengths, and know that they need not be repeated...

You nod, and accept her kind offer.

Cerridwen now hands to you a Grail, a sacred cup, which is brimming with all the blessings of Avalon, which she has taken from the cauldron of rebirth ... you take it, and you drink from it, and you feel around you the increase in your perception ... feel the language of the land and of the birds, and know that you now have the energy to study and to learn, and that each time you connect with Cerridwen, you will learn a little more ... for this is just the beginning of a beautiful journey ... you can taste the delights of the world, her sweetness and mysteries...you are bathed in golden light and you know that in every day, there will be blessings from this cauldron of knowledge, and that the cauldron of transformation has helped you to shed your burden today... and that the cauldron of rebirth has helped you remember the gifts you may have forgotten... In the third cauldron, there is a deeper mystery that you will learn in time ... but for now, know that who you are is a gift, and that you are loved, innocent, and of wild and pure heart.

You know now it is time to return, to your world. But before you go, Cerridwen smiles, and wants to know if you have a question to ask of her...

She waits, as you taste your new knowledge, and feel your new freedom...

Your question forms...

Ask your question, now...

She considers, and she begins to speak with you, telepathically...hear her words echo within you, now...

She finishes, and you give her your thanks, and farewell her for this time. Know that you will see each other soon and that each time this healing will be safe, and beautiful, and complete...and each time, you will learn something new, and true, and beautiful about yourself.

Turn and walk down the path that opens up before you through the forest...until you reach your own self, your own time, in the room where you are now...refreshed, revived, and full of the love and lessons of Avalon...

May the magick of Avalon accompany you on every step ... and may you listen and know her wisdom and love, all day, and all night long...

For you are beloved of the God and the Goddess ... and you are a child of Avalon.

And Blessed You Be.

TALISMANS OF AVALON

Now, as the earth undergoes another transformation, the misty cloak of Merlin's is lifting, making visible all that was once unseen. As Avalon's energy rises again, coming to us when we work in circle, when we feel the heartbeat of the planet, when we acknowledge the turning of the wheel, when we raise our arms to the sun and dance by the light of the moon, we begin to notice the language of the world again. And when we notice Avalon's energy, we begin to heal inside, and the mist between this world and the next disperses just a little. She is returning, and can be found within, as well as in the landscape, wherever you may be on this beautiful blue and green planet. Wherever there is a spring with clear healing water, a mound where ancient burials took place, a hill that soars to the sky, a gathering of trees grouped in circle, women who help, heal and nurture and strong men with spiritual gifts, there is Avalon. Here are her sacred talismans.

The Staff: Associated with the wand, this is a tree-being transformed into a talismanic tool which directs energy, giving the energy the flavour of the trees magick and healing powers... Oft-seen with Merlin, the Arthurian leader of the Druids. What tree would you wish to be gifted a branch to create a staff? What would you use your staff for?

The Stone: The being of the earth, and worked with in the forms of the standing stones, crystal therapy and talismanic jewelry via gemstones. The rightful leaders of the place known now as Ireland had a sacred stone...a throne, which would call out if the rightful king sat upon it. The stone was the guardian of the sword Excalibur, until the rightful king of the land could draw it forth... What would you use the stones to ground? What would you wish to connect with? Where do you need this righteous recognition in your life?

The Sword: Swords are about power and how it is used!...Within swords are great lessons to help us deal with our own power and be able to walk through this world without giving up our power or being overwhelmed by someone else's. Swords are shaped, forged, and tempered by forces that are external meeting their own unique blend of ore....

Swords can give you strength, and skill. They can be used to defend, not only to attack. And they can cut you free from the past... They are a sign that Brigid is with you, helping you to cut the cords to draining energies, and fight the good fight.

Every sword gives you the opportunity to change your life. Allow them to help you, and watch the divine magic that occurs as a result of action.

Swords are very powerful for women to connect with. Here Jessica shares her dream of being gifted a sword... "I was presented with a sword in a dream...I was with others and we were in caves that seemed to be circling round and round. Almost like an underground labyrinth. The air was extremely cold and damp; it felt strange in my lungs. I could feel cold earth beneath my feet. It was extremely dark and we became separated. Suddenly the space around me grew larger and I found I had left the tunnels I was in and entered an open space; it was scary as I couldn't see or feel ahead of me. I closed my eyes and crouched down to touch the earth and reconnect, to calm myself. I took a few deep breaths and felt the air grow warmer. When I opened my eyes there was a shining sword in front of me, suspended in the air. It was a silvery white colour and about three quarters of the length of my body. It had a large, transparent green crystal similar to an emerald at the hilt. I reached out my hand and grabbed the hilt. It wasn't until I pulled it towards me that I felt its weight. It was heavy but not unbearable. I began to move with it as if I had trained with it my whole life. I focused on it for a while, and wondered if my friends had a similar experience. I closed my eyes and thought of them...where they were, if they were ok? Suddenly I felt them near me and when I opened my eyes I was with them again at the entrance of the caves...we began to move back towards the daylight, the sword was still in my hand. That was when I woke up...

I got up and took the stance I remembered from my dream, and when I focused I could still feel the weight of that sword in my hands. I call on it anytime I feel threatened or frightened." Like Jessica, you too can be gifted with a protective, magickal sword in visions, which can be worked with to strengthen you in everyday situations that are unnerving, threatening or unjust. If you have been robbed of your power, connect with the sword.

The Cauldron: What is boiling within...? Is it the cauldron of rebirth, into which the heroes of Avalon were entered, even if cast apart, and brought together whole again? Is it the cauldron of plenty, that will feed us when we bemoan our lacks, proving to us that we are indeed rich beyond measure? Is it the cauldron of wisdom and inspiration, which Cerridwen brews and bubbles and boils, creating a magical potion of such power that was directed to Cerridwen's son, the Merlin Taliesin? Your cauldron is your passion, your desire, your energy...and when it bubbles and brews inside of you...feel it. Hear it. Drink fearlessly from it. It is your deep sustenance and will help you recreate yourself, die to the old, and bring in the rebirth you are longing for.

SYMBOLS OF AVALON

"We have this language of the omens, the language of the signs. It is an alphabet that is directed to us. If we do not fear to commit mistakes, and if we take the language as a help to cross that particular day, then we start to get deeper and deeper into the soul of the world..."
–Paulo Coelho

They come to you in meditation, trance, and dreams...when they cannot reach you that way, you will pass a billboard or sign that coincidentally speaks to you. Avalon and her symbols are powerful, and will appear within the landscape herself, in the form of mountains, rivers, groves and crop circles. They are powerful energetic gateways into deeper states of consciousness, where truth, direction and purpose can be revealed simply through the appearance of the appropriate symbol.

Powerful, magical and infinite, sacred symbols and signs empower all our magical rites...they also have a personality and an energy that has power. So when we see an Avalonian symbol, we can feel her. When we consciously work with her, we can infuse our meditations and pathworkings with these symbols to enrich all of our life.

Some of her most powerful symbols include:

The Circle: Magickal when cast, always profound, the circle represents the Infinite, a world between worlds, akin to zero – the place or space of infinite possibility, protection, magic, the womb, the egg, and sacred magic. Wheel of the year – showing the eight great Sabbats... they have a symbolic reflection on the other side of the planet in the Lakota Medicine wheel – showing the four great directions which we honour in circle.

Vesica Pisces: The overlapping of the three worlds demonstrated via two circles overlapping. This ancient symbol has been adopted by Christianity, but her origins and deeper meaning are to be found in the Goddess worship of Avalon.

This beautiful symbol is featured over and over in sacred landscapes, like that of Chalice Well in Glastonbury, England.

The Sigil of Ameth: Ameth is Hebrew for truth, and this is technically "not" an Avalonian symbol. But as a Wizard of Britain brought this symbol through, I felt it worth including. This highly complex sigil was used widely by the Elizabethan wizard, John Dee (who also recognised Glastonbury as a place of healing, and its well as abundant with healing

waters). Within this complex symbol are the names domains and directions of angels, secret names of God, and codes for the secret language of angels. It is a living symbol, a visual laboratory and textbook of Enochian magicks.

This complex symbol was channelled by the great magician of Elizabethan England, John Dee, and his partner in Mysteries, the medium Edward Kelley. It is a complex sigil which speaks of the truth of the way the Invisible world is constructed.

Spiral: The spiral is an ancient symbol of evolving consciousness, and the search for wisdom. It is symbolic for many of the circular path, rather than linear, of women's knowledge, and of the Goddess. Spiral labyrinths are walked across cultures as diverse as the Tibetan, and the neo-Celtic, as in the spiral labyrinth of Glastonbury Tor. The spiral is a fundamental shape in all things of this world – and of others! From the nautilus to the Pleiades, the spiral forms the basis of the shape of life. When used ritually, it can also represent the journey inwards, followed by the journey out...followed again by a journey within, in an infinite dance. The spiral appears on many Avalonian monuments, including the great Underworld temple of Newgrange in Ireland.

The spiral seems so simple, but it is a beautiful illustration of going within, letting go, discovery, and then returning to the "outside" again. Spirals are found carved into sacred stones outside Avalonian sites such as Newgrange in Ireland. They are shamanic in nature, representing the journey into the Underworld, the gathering of wisdom, and the return to the Upperworld. They are the shape of galaxies, of DNA, and of the nautilus.

Galaxy: Our home in the galactic web of life. Galaxies are often spiral in shape, reflecting the shapes found here on earth. Again, the alchemical maxim, As Above, So Below, is shown to be true.

© Amber Moon

Awen: The three rays represent the breath of inspiration from the Divine...the dots over the strokes signify the "halo" or fire in the head, or the three drops which flew from Cerridwen's cauldron, and the triple worlds, and triple Goddess.

Awen is a symbol worked with in Druidic and Celtic paths: it symbolising divine breath, light and truth. This Awen talisman was created by Blessed Branches.

Celtic Cross: The four directions...an implied circle...pre-dates the Christian cross.

The Celtic Cross may have preceded the Christian Cross as a kind of marker of the four sacred directions. In time the qualities of the Celtic cross became intertwined with those of celtic Christianity, which saw the Cross go from having "arms" of equal length, to resembling the Sword, another great Avalonian symbol.

Thor's Hammer: This Asatru symbol of protection was linked to Avalon via the pollination of ideas from the Norse lands (via the "Lachlan's" – people from over the lochs).

The Solar Cross: Acknowledgment of the rays of the sun...often created in crop circles near Silbury hill.

The Solar Cross too is most often represented by a cross with arms of equal length. It is said to represent the rays of the sun, falling on all without exception.

Brigid's Cross: The solar cross of the Irish Goddess of Fire, Sword and Sacred Places, Brigid, is woven from straw, representing also the witches besom, or broom, joined together as we fly to all four corners, yet linked in the centre by spirit, or Goddess. From her we all spring; to her, we return.

This great Avalonian Symbol is often made at Imbolg to venerate the Goddess Brigid. There are many interpretations of the cross: I often muse on how it resembles four besoms, or witches brooms, travelling in all four directions, spreading the love and wisdom of the Goddess Brigid to every place on this planet.

Triquetra: This symbol is of three in one, and has many meanings. It is often used to represent the triad of maiden, mother and crone, birth, death and rebirth, the simultaneous triple world of the Avalonians, and was popularized by the television show

Charmed, to symbolise the power of three, the three sister-witches or Charmed Ones of the title...

The triquetra symbolises the three phases of the Goddess: Maiden, Mother, Crone, and the blessed nature of the Number three. It is often worked with and used practically in spellwork and witchcraft. Many wear this, as shown in this beautiful image by Druidic Witch Amber Moon, as it is beautiful to gaze upon, and as a symbol of Faith.

Triskele: This beautiful symbol represents divine groups of three. Birth, death, rebirth; earth, sea, sky; maiden, mother, crone; hunter, father, sage are all examples of the Trinity.

Again, the Number Three is shown in symbol: but this time, the three lines, curved and in their own spiralling movement, represent movement, the simultaneous existence of the three worlds, and the movement that exists, eternally – all is energy, moving, vibrating. This symbol also is a beautiful symbol to draw and meditate upon when we are initiating, evolving and completing a stage of our lives... All is interwoven.

Triple Goddess: The maiden aspect, mother aspect, and crone aspect of the Goddess is most often represented by this symbol, which also embraces the threefold aspect of lunar phases.

Ogham Alphabet: The 25-letter Celtic "alphabet" of trees, reconstructed by Robert Graves in the White Goddess, and found in many Pictish and Celtic stones. Often assumed to be runes, each Ogham or letter consists of a stroke or groups of strokes that represent a tree, and its secret magic, healing powers and sacred usage. Each of these tree-names, or symbols also corresponds with a letter of our modern-day alphabet.

Featuring stark, linear strokes branching off a vertical or horizontal line, it is entirely possible to write letters, or even your Book of Shadows and Light, in Ogham.

The Ogham is an ancient Celtic system of communication, divination and tree lore: each simple symbol connects deeply to the magick of a sacred tree.

Runes: Nordic symbolic divination wisdom system consisting of strikingly bare, pictorial graphics – some runes continue their life in popular culture today, as in the rune Tyr, used as the basis of the peace sign, and again symbolising Odin's getting of wisdom by hanging upside down on the World Tree. Through gaining wisdom, therefore, peace may come. There are various forms, or interpretations, of Runes. Some are Anglicised, and date from around 900 AD, and others are Nordic, and even older. Be aware that some rune books and teachers have freely adapted the I-Ching, a Chinese divination system, and melded it with traditional rune seership. If you wish to study the Avalonian ways of working with runes as authentically as possible, please do investigate your sources.

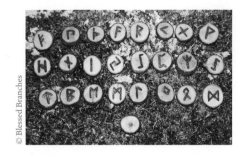

Runes are symbols that have endured for thousands of years: their origins are the Nordic magickal system known as Asatru. These runes are hand crafted by Blessed Branches team Natasha and Michael Heard.

LANGUAGE IN THE LAND: THE MAGICK OF CROP CIRCLES

Silbury Hill sits just outside the two great outer circles of Avebury, the formation that sits at the very heart of England. Underneath her intricate and still-mysterious geometry is the very centre of the Dragon line (sometimes called the "Michael" line.) She lies beneath the shadow of the hill, protected, watched over.

Silbury Hill is a strange place: it is essentially a man-made hill, a pyramid if you like, and theories about her purpose abound. To some archeologists, she must be a burial mound, though no bodies have been found there. The inner life of the hill is said to be teeming with faeries, tunnels, intelligent beings from other galaxies and dimensions, and well, good honest earth. Some of the tales stretch the very borders of belief. But what is undeniable is that Silbury Hill plays host to other symbolic activity throughout the brief English summers.

In the fields of Avebury and Silbury Hill, each year appear symbols. Crop Circles. Messages. A language that we are learning to read.

To many people these complex and geometric masterpieces are pointless hoaxes made by students with flat boards pushing down the crops after too many meads … But to many others, they are the symbols that there is an intelligence that speaks to us at a symbolic level, which we need to understand to become fully ourselves.

And while these circles appear all over the world, they appear mostly in the fields around Avebury, East Field, Wiltshire.

I wanted to talk to someone who has devoted themselves to understanding and experiencing the messages of the circles, so I turned to my friend Joanne Byrne, who has spent summers following and recording the signs as they appear across Britain.

Why would so many circles be appearing in this area, the very heart of England?

"The reason I think that so many of the crop formations are happening there is because of the ancient lands and the ley lines that are present in this area. England is the heart chakra of our mother Earth and I see the ley lines as the veins, if you will, that feed that heart and in turn that heart pumps out the vibrations of the formations to the rest of the planet as a heart would pump the vital blood in a human body. I think that this process is in some way healing the earth and transmuting negative energy that has been created through our lack of understanding that we, as humans, have towards our beautiful and delicate planet," she explained.

Now, Jo is a very down-to-earth person, with a great sense of humour and wonderful family. She tends to make light of her knowledge – but once she gets on to her subject, her passion is obvious, and powerful! I was fascinated by Silbury Hill, and I wanted to know what made this hill a magnet for crop circles, mysticks and magicks.

"I have ideas that this hill could be a gateway to other dimensions. Much unexplained activity has been linked to Silbury Hill and many Crop Circles have formed beneath it. Balls of light are commonly witnessed here and there is an energy that is alluring and mysterious to say the least..."

Silbury Hill's finds include an abundance of hazel twigs – one of the sacred druid woods, and one particularly sacred to Irish druids! The lawn-like exterior of today is excellent camouflage for seven concentric rings, made of white chalk. It once shone white and bright across the fields, as do Rhiannon's chalk horses of Wiltshire today.

Near Silbury Hill is a smaller man-made pyramid, known as Merlin's Mount, complete with a spiral path winding to its tip, which is now difficult to access, being as it is in the grounds of Marlborough College.

Crop Circles have been appearing in the shadow of Silbury Hill and Merlin's Mount for a very long time. Jo told me the first report of a formation was recorded in 1678, when it was called "the mowing devil."

(All through Britain are ancient structures that have been dubbed "the devil's" this or that! There are devil-stones, devil's dykes, and devil's chairs! These are, clearly, not their rightful names!)

Jo told me that since the "mowing devil" and witches circles of the 17th centuries, crop circles appear all over the planet but unfortunately most go unreported. "In 2008 there were 56 reported Crop Circles in countries other than England. These countries include Germany, Italy, Canada, Netherlands, Poland, Czech Republic, USA, Switzerland, France, Brazil and a very interesting one in South Korea," says Jo.

"I found that each and every formation contained its own unique energy. I experienced mostly love and total bliss while being inside the formations but I also witnessed my husband struggle with some of the intense energy that was contained within them."

"It seemed evident that not every formation resonates with every person, so I would say to anyone visiting them that if it doesn't feel good then don't go in. Sometimes upon leaving a formation we would be on such a high and then suddenly we would be so completely drained of energy that we would have to pull off to the side of the road in our motor home and sleep!"

"This happened on several occasions but it would only take about 20 – 30 minutes sleep and we would be completely recharged and ready to visit the next formation."

"In the early 80's the media became interested when they reported on a group of circles that appeared in a field below the white horse in Westbury, Wiltshire. This was the beginning of the many thousands that have now been reported over the last few decades. I think that they have been happening far longer than that and perhaps even many thousands of years! If you look at ancient cave paintings and art you will see what could be evidence of their existence for as long as we have been here."

That made sense. I had seen the symbol of a circle, with the cross within it, on aboriginal sacred sites north of Sydney, and in underwater caves off Mexico. These symbols seemed to connect with us at a cellular level, at a DNA level – in other words, they were beyond time, and space, and gender, and even culture. They are telling us who we are, and where we originate from …

I wondered what Jo would think about this common "parent" for symbols and crop circles … were they connected to the Lost Lands of Lemuria, Atlantis and Avalon?

"There has to be some connection to these places as there have been so many formations with symbology from these times. What the connection is I am unsure. Perhaps they are telling us to look at times past to find wisdom or maybe they are just letting us know that they have been with us and watching us since these times. I think the people of these times were far more aware of the universe that they lived in than we are. They knew exactly how to work with the earth, its seasons and energies to have the resources they needed without damaging her structure. Maybe the circle makers are letting us know that it's time for us to become more in touch with the world in which we live, and find new ways to satisfy our needs."

It is also possible that crop circles are creating waves, or pulses of energy, perhaps linking up different "regions" of the planet … In 1969, a dowser from Avon in England, Guy Underwood, suggested in his book *The Pattern of the Past* that the sites of stone circles, burial mounds, and of course the churches (often built OVER these sacred sites) were places where subtle earth currents converged, and could "bubble" to the surface, making these great points of power in the landscape.

His geodetic survey of Silbury Hill captures the intricate flows of energy on complex and beautiful maps of energy he created. He felt that our ancestors had interacted with these energy flows, such as the Dragon line running from Cornwall to Norfolk, with their ancient science. Do different crop circles in different regions link up, forming an energy grid that is protecting or enhancing the energy of sacred sites? It seems undeniable that they are interacting with them in some way!

"I'm not sure if they do or not," said Jo honestly, "but I am convinced that they are connected to the earth's own energy grid lines which connect and pulse this energy around the entire planet."

I thought about the waves, and the whales, the whirlpools and the oceanic "circles" I had seen moving in the water while staring out to sea. These rings were formed from deep below, or perhaps from above, and seemed to me to be functioning in a liquid way that was akin to the earthways of the crop circles. I wondered what Jo made of that?

"As water is fluid it is a bit difficult for patterns to form there but there have been reports of circles forming in snow and on frozen lakes and rivers. There have been reports of crop circles forming in clouds as well! Some people believe that they are connected to underground streams."

I wondered too about the ancient dictum that had informed so much of this journey through the Lost Lands … were the circles signposts, somehow elaborating on the dictum of As Above, So Below? Are the circles literally coming down from above, or perhaps rising up from below?

Jo feels it is a combination of both. "There is definite evidence showing that there is some form of an energy column coming from the crop circles. Planes that fly directly over them sometimes experience difficulties with their instruments and even loss of power and cameras often fail when directly above or within them. There has been footage taken of birds flying towards a crop circle only to split into two groups to avoid flying directly over the formation and then regrouping once they have passed by the formation. Animals seem to have a sense that we have somehow masked. I have been questioning the involvement of the earth itself...has there been a blueprint put down upon the earth that is lying dormant until the circle makers are ready? It is a very real possibility. Again I am sure that the energy grid of the earth is a major player in the crop circles forming."

But who are the creators of these beautiful symbols written into the land itself? Galactic beings from other planets? Our future selves? Our own consciousness? Beings from within the earth? The earth herself? Lemurians? Atlanteans? Avalonians? Opinions vary as much as one person does from the next.

"I believe that they are being formed by an intelligent form of light that is working together with the earth's energy. Many people have witnessed and filmed balls of light just before and after the forming of many crop circles. Scientists have found that a plasma vortex in the higher atmosphere forms a kind of cylinder of swirling energy similar to that of microwave energy. This energy comes rushing towards the earth and on impact somehow forms the crop formation."

One of the most fascinating aspects of circle lore is that more and more of the circles are said to be unambiguously referencing Quetzalcoatl, the Mayan God who is said to be returning at the end of the fifth world. His signature, a symbolic version of a feathered or plumed serpent, appears at the end of many of these circles being formed. It seems strange – here's the Mayan plumed serpent appearing in the midst of the English countryside! Why are there so many Quetzalcoatl symbols? Is the Mayan feathered serpent akin to the Dragonfae beings that I had so long associated with Avalon and the galactic energies?

"The Mayans believed that Quetzalcoatl would return and as we are now approaching the end of the Mayan calendar there seem to be more and more formations dedicated to this theme. There are many theories about what will come about in this time and I guess only time will tell," says Jo.

There are also many formations with Avalonian symbology. "While I was in England I had the privilege of experiencing two stand-out formations, the first being the Vesica Pisces and the second one being without a doubt the Goddess. Both of these formations had a positive effect on me and left me feeling elated. I'm not sure there is any one function. I think they are here doing many things and on many levels both for human consciousness as well as to our planet," says Jo.

These powerful signs in the landscape, those made by man, and those made by mysterious means, are all showing us we are here for a reason: we are beings of light and intelligence, too – and we must start respecting each other, this planet, and living in love.

At least that's what the signs told me!

AVALON RISING

"She has come back to us, piercing us all with her sweetness and beauty…
she has come back to us…"
–Homeric Hymn to the Goddess Aphrodite

How can we bring through even more peaceful, harmonious, strong and purposeful healing Avalonian energy, returning to us the sweetness and beauty of the Goddess? In some of the most ancient ways, it would seem.

To this day, there are four galactic entry points on this planet, days through which the galactic energies pour in, flowing down from above, filtered constantly by the ebbing and flowing of lunar light. There are four Gaian entry points every thirteen moons on this planet, when energy rises from below and is filtered and cared for by the trees, flowing to the surface through the veins of the leylines and the songlines of the sea, and sent into the heavens like a prayer from the earth for the cosmos.

When we all work at the same time, with our intention set, we create powerful magicks that restore this planet – and ourselves, to health, wellbeing and beauty.

As above, so below. As within, so without.

Litha: Summer solstice – falls between December 20-23 Southern Hemisphere, June 21-23 Northern Hemisphere. This is sometimes called the festival of the faeries! It brings slow, warm and fun days, joy, laughter and revelling. It is a galactic portal when the light rays change from full force, to diminishing solar light, in preparation for the going below. The last great flood of life force to the surface, a feast of all that is before the force begins to go back to the Underworld.

This brings lifeforce flowing through the area of the earth it is affecting, allowing regeneration, a second flowering, long warm sultry days and a sense of wellbeing, healing and love to permeate the land, her people and her creatures.

Lughnasad: February 1-2, Southern Hemisphere, August 1-2 Northern Hemisphere. The first harvest. This Gaian portal brings through the energies from below to above – bringing through foods, harvest of grains and goods, the reaping and fulfillment of the intention set. The life force flows still, but the energy sent to us reminds us to harvest and care for the gifts the Earth our mother the goddess has given us.

The Avalonians celebrated this time with two massive all-day parties, from sunrise to sunset. These festivals were held to mark the grain harvest. Communities worked very hard, very long days bringing in the grain, the stuff of life itself. It was a wonderful day when the communities would converge and gather, taking their mind off the necessary work, to the celebrating of their bounty, but also marked with serious notes. Competitions were often held – Olympic-Games-style, athletes would compete, in a rapturous display of physical prowess and celebration of the body. Livestock was displayed and sold, and tussie-mussies – circular bouquets of herbs in which a message was constructed – were given out as favours and to beloveds. This is a romantic time of year – almost sad, but very much a time when we know that long days of separation cannot shake our love if it is true, and we have heart and faith.

These festivities were huge – akin to massive music festivals held at the edge of summer. They were not, however, for a segment of the community – they were for all.

There was then a second festival, to celebrate the harvest of the vegetables and fruits.

Communities from over the land would come together at sacred places – in Ireland at places like Tailltin, named for the Goddess Tailltu, the foster mother of the God Lugh, for whom the first of the festivals heralding the shadowlands is named at Lughnasad – as an aside, in modern Irish language, the month of August is named Lunasa, after this festival, which is held in August in the Northern Hemisphere. Never feel or fear that our sacred times have disappeared – for here they are, all around us, in language and in custom. Awareness is the key.

In Britain, in its Avalonian communities from Cornwall to Skye, we feasted on the harvest, and gave thanks to the mother. Huge corn dollies were created and gathered on altars, surrounded by the bounty of harvest.

Druids would hold their Brehon Law Justice Times, where community and neighbourly disputes – cattle, property, and marriage and friendship conflicts and disagreements were all heard in the open air before the druid Justice Makers. There was no written book of Law, no sheafs of parchment to leaf through to arrive at a judgement. Druids learned their law by principle, example, and were trained to recall The Law, and Justice. Peace was a precondition of the gathering – anyone breaking that peace was treated with severe consequences – usually by being outcast from the community for a time. Community really was a strong undercurrent at this time – naturally, as in winter, when weather is harsher and resources are scarcer, we rely more on each other. We also dwell in closer quarters, inside – thus it is important on a practical level to resolve disputes before we are all in close quarters with each other. Ask yourself how you could personally resolve disputes at this time, particularly with people with whom you have close contact. Peace, remember, is the prerequisite for resolution.

The day was also celebrated by the bards, with singing, dancing, and again, epics were sung out, tales of the Tuatha De Danaan, the Tylweth Teg, accompanied by harps and dancing, joy and laughter, warmth and a feeling of closeness and family within community.

Autumn is the time for us to re-establish this, too...whether we do this personally, at homes, or develop a sense of wider family with a magical community, it is essential to our nature, as we prepare to go within, to have that external support and love of others.

It is a very different feeling and emotional quality that this season has, you can see, when compared to the blissful eroticism and pleasure of summer!

Autumn Equinox: March 20-23 Southern Hemisphere, September 20-23 Northern Hemisphere. (Often called Mabon.) A galactic portal of delicate balance, when the masculine and the feminine energies are beamed to the earth in perfect balance, and where we are at a doorway for communication between the earthly realm and the galactic realm.

This is the "last" harvest, and is a time to make ready for the going within. Energy beaming down helps us ready for that truth.

Fractal geometry in the form of frost sends us messages.

It is therefore a time of assessment, and of discernment, of integrating what we wish to take below with us during the cold dark months, and what we wish to let go of – to *sacrifice.*

When white magical practitioners notice the first turnings of the season from the sun-time to the shadow-time, we acknowledge, welcome and make a place for the time of harvest. Something we have nurtured and grown, cared for and raised, has reached its time, and it is in the time of leaf-fall that we raise our sickles and take what is needed for the harshness and cold times of winter, ahead.

Samhain: April 30-May 1 Southern Hemisphere, October 31-November 1 Northern Hemisphere. Ancestor time, when the spirits of the world below (the fae) and the otherworld rise again and communicate fully with us, so our cellular memory is reawakened to its wisdom. Past life memories come up, as do literally memories encoded in our DNA.

This Gaian portal is about the richness of all that has gone before, and how we can be at peace and attuned with what has past. We have the ability to learn a great deal about earth history at this time.

Yule: Winter solstice June 20-23 Southern Hemisphere, December 21-23 Northern Hemisphere. Significant for the Yule is the celebration rebirth of the Sun God, and of the Sun Queen, Grian, and solar energy flows into the Earth energy grid, reprogramming us for the coming warmer times. At this time what we set up, what we put our thought and our bodies and our energies behind will manifest. This galactic portal brings the life force of the stars to us once again in the beautiful dance of the galactic web.

Using mistletoe, a pagan symbol of regeneration and eternal life, is also a beautiful way of connecting with the fertile energy of this time of the year, but please do not ingest any, in any form, as it's a poisonous plant. Using it as a garland or to decorate your Yule log is safe however, and it will draw passion and potency to you. There's a reason we kiss under the mistletoe in ancient times, it was a fertility ritual. Mistletoe was considered a sacred plant by the druids and priestesses, and has long been associated with healing.

The Romans also valued the plant as a symbol of peace, hence its current associations with Christmas.

Imbolc: August 1-2 Southern Hemisphere, February1-2 Northern hemisphere. The lifeforce delivered down at the solstice of winter comes up from the Earth herself in the form of new life at this Gaian portal! Named for the maiden aspect of the Goddess

Brigid (known as Bridie, or Bride – yes the same word we use when a woman is getting married!), this festival sees baby lambs, and the slight warming of the earth herself to the kiss of the sun she shared at Yule ... like sleeping beauty, her life force awakens, and life in her beauty begins to spring forth. Tender vulnerable and new, it is to be revered, blessed and rejoiced!

Welcome in Bride (Goddess Brigid's maiden form) by lighting a candle. Wish upon it to show the energy where it is most needed ...

Ostara: Spring equinox, September 20-23 Southern Hemisphere, March 20-23 Northern Hemisphere. This is the time to plant your seeds and allow them to be bathed in the energy of the balancing rays of the sun … and ask for balance when wishes are granted to you! Help baby animals, and rid yourself of any toxins in your cleaning products or cosmetics you may still be using at this time – because what happens on this beautiful blue and green planet affects other realms too. As a galactic portal, you are able to bathe in blessed cosmos energies, and be rebalanced and healed at this time of growth, so all growth takes place in a purposeful and positive way.

I adore the spring … that it is still cold, and frosty, and yet all about us we can see the signs of new life. Buds on trees, the slight warmth of the earth, and the sharp, sweet smell of jasmine – my own spring is heralded by personal natural signs. First, my magnolia tree buds after the winter solstice, then blooms as winter loosens her icy grip … by winter's departure, her pale grey branches will bend earthwards with the weight of her beautiful, scarlet flowers, and I know that soon, the jasmine will follow.

I always know true spring has arrived when my jasmine bower comes magically into flower … That first fragrant rush of her aphrodisiac scent sends my senses spinning, and I know the time has come when the sap and our blood runs warmly again. I notice people falling in love, the sexual energy returning, the laughter and sweetness coming back, and the new fruits. The time of the maiden returns, and for a while, there is innocence, hope, and a return to our younger selves, who are wiser for having experienced the harsh crone energies of winter.

Ostara is named for the beautiful Goddess of fertility, Ostara – and is a time of balance and love. Day and night are of equal length, and all is in harmony. It is a truly sacred time, which signifies the coming of the light, of warmth, of the return of life itself. The myths of the Celts, Romans, Greeks, Norse and Egyptians all recognize the spring equinox as the new beginning. In old times it marked the festival of the fertility Goddess Ostara who, with her hare, brought fertility to the land and its people.

Beltane: October 31-November 1 Southern Hemisphere, April 30-May 1 Northern Hemisphere. Watch for the Faery Kings and Queens choosing consorts, falling in love, and being swept away with joy! (Gaia portal)

When white magical practitioners raise the summer fires throughout the Land, we initiate, inspire and rekindle the spark of life, the life force itself. The sacred fires were lit by wise women and wizards from Lemuria to Ys, from Egypt to Avalon, from Troy to Atlantis, and always to coax the sun closer to the earth, for us to be warm again, to be in the light again, to be in love again... across the land, the night lived with fire, the life force of the sun, returning to bless us with the summer time, with full bloom, with ripe fruits and fully grown grains. For our own internal blossoming as men and women, for falling in love with ourselves, and with partners, and for the creation of children... this is the time of summer, and in this, we inheritors of the state of mind and sacred space that is white magic rejoice as we light our candles and raise them to the sky!

When Beltane comes, we are on the cusp of summer – how joyous and wonderful and laden with ripening energy is this time of the year under our southern skies. I love its whirling, giddy, sensual energy, which brings people together for feasting, love making, and love-sharing, laughter and comfort and delight. During summer, the elements conspire to help us to truly become aware of the sacred nature of our bodies, thus it is a time when we can heal, grow and strengthen our connection to our physical selves – healthy, strong, and full of life!

You may wish to celebrate the coming of summer at a wild ceremony complete with an indoor Maypole, a yoni and lingum to represent the great marriage of female and male energies, and at dawn, before day truly breaks, you may wish to create your own dawn ceremony and greeting of the sun. When our first light is met with blessings and ceremonies, when we delight in our summer's birth, we are inspired, reborn and exhilarated.

Summer inspires me to embrace my own womanliness, sensuality, and gritty earthiness. It encourages me to appreciate vital masculinity, strong men, and to accept their love, their energy and their support into my life. With each Beltane, I ask to attract loving, supportive, loyal and strong, true and good men into my life – men who honour me as an articulation of the Goddess, and who innately understand themselves to be an articulation of the God-force.

Beltane can bring you in touch with all that makes you strong in your desire and sensual appetites, allowing you to fully experience yourself as a sacred physical being. The material world, the natural world, and our very bodies are sacred – and summer brings this home to us, directly through its urge that we connect with the sensual world.

For each of this, this connection to summer and the Summerlands (the magical lands where we go and dwell and feast and learn between lifetimes) are very personal and intimate: for me, it is a constant learning process where I am in training with the Goddesses and the Gods, the priestesses and druids, in its own spiralling kind of order. Finding our paths is exactly like walking the labyrinth...

At times, this learning is chaotic, random, intuitive and instinctual. It is sensual, and knowing, and wild at times. At others it is quiet and ordered and studious and has a kind of grandeur to it. At others times it is deliciously light hearted and good natured.

We stay focused, and we stay on the path, but it widens, narrows, becomes difficult and diverges...we learn to trust in placing one foot in front of the other, and to trust in the unique nature of what we have to share, what we have to learn.

A BELTANE DEW SPELL

To deepen your Beltane blessings, increase your natural beauty and truly connect with the new energies of the season, you may wish to work with this beautiful spell.

Say:
By the goddesses
Rhiannon, Bride, Cerridwen, Arianrhod and Branwen
I bless this water...

Immerse your hands in the water, and say three times:
By the Goddesses of Avalon
And their sacred land and lake
I charge this water with your love

Feel their healing energy and great love run through you, and pour forth from your hands, streaming into the water.

Anoint yourself on your chakras with this water, or intuitively where it feels best.

Bottle this water, charge it with crystals either at each quarter around the bottle, or with crystals within the water itself.

Use when you feel guided to.

So important were these sorts of spells, rites and ancient festivals that pre-history's great architects were inspired to design and build powerful, magical astronomical observatories and sites of worship to mark them. Stonehenge, the powerful standing stone temple on Salisbury Plain in England, and Newgrange, an even more ancient site in Ireland, are just two examples of these ancient temples hewn from the earth to mark the winter solstice. On the morning of the sabbat, the first rays of the newborn sun hit the secret inner chambers of Newgrange, thus making these sacred sites not only a calendar to mark the turning of the year, but a repository of ancient wisdom. The resonance there, where such things have been observed and cherished with sacred intent for 5,000, years creates an energetic ambiance that we are all attuned to. Our blood speaks to us at that time.

Above all, these Gaian and galactic portals heal us by giving precious time to our shadow, that part of ourselves we least are likely to observe. We live in a spiritual culture obsessed with proving ourselves good, as children of the light.

But solstice, equinox, and acknowledging the seasonal realities and her energies proves we are also children of the dark, and when we go back into that earth-womb, we can be reborn into genuine happiness, and genuine sources of light and of the Universe.

YOUR OWN PERSONAL JOURNEY TO AVALON...

Finally, it is time for you to part the mists, meet the Lady of the lake, and walk the shores of Avalon. You may wish to find a very quiet, private sacred space in nature, where you can read this to yourself. Or, you may wish to read this journey to a friend, who can do the same to you in return. Alternately, both this journey and Cerridwen's Cauldron that appeared earlier are available on the CD Return to Avalon. However you work with these words, take notes afterwards, ground once you have completed the journey with food, and connecting with the body, and be sure travel there often... for she is your home.

Welcome to the world between worlds, the wisdom of the blessed magickal isle that is Avalon...

Avalon is no myth. She resides in real time and space, and in your heart. There is indeed a Lady of the Lake, the wisdom of Merlin is yours to be guided by, and the blessings of Morgan are your birthright...In this meditation, we will take you to meet the priestesses, to the Tor, and to the cave of Merlin, where you will be given great gifts...

For Avalon is already within your heart, your blood, and even your ancestry. Now it is time to re-learn and reactivate her magick in this beautiful adventure into the soul and heart of Avalon, her sacred sites and her mysteries...

Avalon is the sacred island of the druids and priestesses...and she is also connected to the wisdom and teachings of Atlantis, of Egypt, of Lemuria, Mu, Ys and the Babylonians... her energy is unique, and her lessons are deep and ancient... and you are her child.

Now you will be offered the gifts and lessons of the healing staff, the sacred stone, the sword of truth, and you will drink from the chalice, the grail of the lady...

This wisdom can assist you in very practical ways: your work, your love relationships, family issues and self-image can all be worked with in very beautiful and positive ways with the power of Avalon. Simply ask for her help, and it is yours. Honour her, and you in turn will be blessed.

Each time you take this Immrama, its energy will become more attuned to you, and you will learn more and more about who you truly are... each time you do this work with me, you will be refreshed, recharged, and reconnected to the wisdom that is Avalon...

Together now we will journey to Avalon...

Are you ready to begin?

Come... take my hand. You are very safe... and very loved.

First, let us close our eyes gently, and take three deep breaths...

One (breathe in... then out)

Two (breathe in... then out)

Three (breathe in... and out)

See with your inner vision a dark screen, which very gradually now comes to life, swirling with mist … there are curls of silvery greys and soft violets, pale blues and greens moving around you … the Dragonfae of the mist welcome you, and long for you to come home to Avalon with them … Do not be afraid … you are very safe …

Look down … See how the mist wraps herself about your bare feet, obscuring what lies before you … what lies behind you. What lies beyond you. There is only NOW, and the space you are in at the present moment. Open your senses to this world... See the colours before you, the golden light shining through the mist, and feel the cool delicacy of the misty air, smell the sweet faint perfume of apple blossom … you walk a few steps further and find that your feet are now being lapped by silvery water … you are at the edge of the lake of Avalon …

Before you the mist disperses slightly, and you see coming towards you a coracle, a small wooden boat, elaborately carved, and moving without sail, without oars … It has a gilded dragon's head at its prow, and it is gliding towards you through the silken waters.

At the prow of this coracle stands a tall, pale woman with long red hair that falls to her hips … her blue robe swirls about her, and her eyes look at you with infinite welcome, and with infinite love … She gestures for you to come on board, and you find yourself effortlessly standing with her, as the barge turns and glides into the mist, and all around you is the gentle kiss of the veil between worlds, and the comfort and companionship of this woman. It feels like you know her, but you do not know from when … or where … just that she is friend, and mother, and sister …

You gaze out, and the shimmering surface of the lake lies before you, a great mirror above which the mist floats, a mirror in which you can see the past, the present the future in the now … this is the great lake of Avalon, and your guide is the Lady of the Lake...

The Lady of the Lake raises her arms, and lowers them in a simple movement, and before you the mist evaporates … you see a beautiful island rising from the waters … this island is covered in lush green grass, and wildflowers grow freely … there are tangled stretches of ancient forest, and a procession of tall and ancient oak trees, whose roots stretch back to the beginnings of time, winding all the way to the top of a very tall and sacred hill...The Tor.

As the silver shore meets the green land you can see that along the sides of the hill are ridges, pathways … a path carved into the hill by the footsteps of the many pilgrims, priestesses, druids, seekers, healers and wise ones who have walked there before you … on its summit is a tower … a church tower that seems ancient, but which feels somehow wrong in the landscape.

As you wonder at its presence, you catch fleeting glances of the magickal beings of this place...they are shy, yet they bid you warm welcome.

You step out onto the ancient earth, and you turn to thank the Lady of the Lake for bringing you here … but she is gone.

You walk forward…the green grass is cool and soft underfoot… You begin to climb the hill and as you do, your eyes search for the Church, but it is growing fainter…and fainter…until it fades completely from view...from within the ground you see a mighty stone circle rising…until in place of the tower stands a circle of stones…nine tall monoliths, each different…perfect… unique… Slowly you walk through the procession of oaks to the top of the hill…as you pass each oak, they bend in greeting to you, and you smile in wonder as you hear their ancient voices speak words of welcome to you… these are in another language, but there is perfect understanding between you. When you reach the final oak, a branch is extended towards you, and you are gifted a long, oaken staff, winding and smooth under your hand, and so full of power you can feel its song.

You bow and thank the tree and you journey on to the top of the Tor.

You are drawn to the stone circle, and as you reach the summit, you walk around it once, feeling the energy of the place…you walk forward, and you place your hands on one stone…your hands vibrate and shimmer with the energy that emanates from this stone, and a corresponding murmur of voices is heard all around you…and within you…outside of you these are the voices of the ages being awakened and you know that the stones too speak, that they have a language, and that they are now communicating with you…

The voices soften and fade, and at your feet you now see a crystal, created by the sounds and the voices you have heard…a sister stone to the great stone circle...You reach down and hold it, and slide it into place on the staff the oaks gifted you with…

You now see before you an entrance on the side of the Tor…between two trees, there is a darkening opening into the hill itself…you reach this place, and the earth herself parts, and invites you to enter and experience her mysteries…

In front of you, as you move forward, you notice a golden glow, growing brighter and brighter… You step through an entrance and into a deep, large cave…filled with sparkling crystals…the softest violets in tone…they shine so bright, yet you do not look away… and they give off the most beautiful sound…you notice the crystal at the end of the staff glowing brightly, humming to the others, and you know you are hearing the same sacred sound you heard when you met with the circle of stones.

At the center of this cave, directly under that stone circle, stands a circle of nine beautiful women…they are the Priestesses of Avalon, known as the Morgens…they send out so much love, acceptance, and compassion that you can feel your body, your chakras and your aura vibrating with this energy…they gesture for you to come closer, and as you do, you are embraced by each priestess…who says to you as she kisses your cheek...

Thou art blessed...

As you receive each kiss, each priestess transfers to you a part of her gift…the gift of power, the gift of sensuality, the gift of knowledge, the gift of love, the gift of beauty, the gift of expression, the gift of divination, the gift of wisdom, the gift of truth...

They are the Priestesses of Avalon, known as the Morgens, and they love you very much...you are a child of Avalon...and they welcome home...

You gently but firmly feel a hand taking yours, and you know you must surrender... and trust...and you find yourself moving forward into another tunnel, even deeper and darker than before...

You notice that you are in the center of another cave...deep amethyst and obsidian glow all around you...in front of a silver cauldron, over a blue fire stand three beings... one is The Lady of the Lake...

One is an ancient man, with long silver beard and twinkling blue eyes...he is Merlin...

The final is a beautiful woman, with long waving hair the colour of ravens' feathers...

She is Morgan.

From the cauldron pours a healing smoke...it is clearing all that is no longer needed from all of your systems, and all three stand back, and allowing the black-haired woman to stir this silver cauldron with a silver apple branch... The beautiful, healing smoke continues its clearing work...

As the smoke clears, you see at your feet a large stone...within it is embedded a sword, shining like it is made of light...Merlin, the Lady of the Lake and Morgan all gesture for you to take it...and you feel full of wonder...

You place your hand upon it, and you draw forth the sword from the stone...

This is the sword of your own Truth, and sovereignty. You are now free. You are strong.

You are home.

Merlin, the Lady and Morgan smile, and gesture for you to come forward. You sheathe your sword at your side, and the lady hands you a grail...a shining chalice from which you drink the waters of the red and the white springs, refreshing you so deeply, you finally understand how deep your thirst has been.

BREATHE...

Refreshed and free, with your oak staff and your crystal stone, with the water of the grail and the sword of truth, you thank and farewell The Lady, Merlin, Morgan and the Priestesses...and you gently close your eyes...

And when you open them you are back on the Tor...where you began this journey within.

You slowly walk down the procession of the trees, knowing it is time for you to return to your world, with the knowledge of this world now firmly at one with your every cell.

As you approach the shore, the mists once again swirl about you... The Lady of the Lake joins you once again, and you embrace, as she ushers you onto the sacred barge... as you step on board, you know you have been initiated into the mysteries and the magicks of Avalon, and that you have received some of her deep wisdom on this day...

You glide over the water, and reach the shore of your home, and you are farewelled by the Lady...you know you have passed a test, and that you are forever changed, and have been given great gifts.

Know wherever you walk this day that you are a child of Avalon. And you are most beloved of this Holy Isle, and of all who dwell there...

You are home...

Afterword:
Travelling well when on your Immrama

Now that you have travelled so far and so wide, you may be contemplating planning your own Immrama to a Lost Land. Perhaps you will travel to glorious Hawaii, searching out the remnants of Lemuria, or to gentle blue-green Thailand with her healing waters. Lemuria may pull you in the direction of the islands of the Pacific, or to south-east Asia, or even to the shores of wild Madagascar.

Perhaps you are drawn to explore Greece and her magickal islands, vibrating with the power of sleeping Atlantean energetic centres right to the heart of Egypt and the Sphinx, that symbol of the shapeshifters. Or perhaps it is the Ancient Avalonian lands that are calling you, with their stone circles, their gentle hills, their faery mounds.

Regardless of which land, or which part of this beautiful blue and green planet is asking you to come home, there are ways to travel that will make your Immrama truly magickal.

I truly understand how challenging it can be to leave home, family and what we call our "responsibilities."

It can be hard to get me out of the kitchen, where I do much of my writing and cooking and spellcasting. But I know at heart I am also a wanderer. I am a nomadic soul, and I have a passion for finding my own spiritual homes, the energetic locations which have unique blueprints, the parts of the planet that sing to my soul. And I know of the healing that can take place when our soul meets the part of ourselves that once dwelt in a sacred place. My wish is that you give yourself permission to find your own. For they are out there.

The Immrama calls all of us Lost Landers: to take the wonder voyage and reclaim those lost parts of our souls and selves. I walk a great deal, singing the lines of the land, and I swim, and I surf, and they are wanderings and they are meditations… I avoid, where I can, the experience of traffic and build-up and tension that can be part of the modern experience of movement. One place that I cannot avoid when I wish to travel to those miraculous far flung places, my Celtic homelands or the mountains of Tibet, or the low lying sacred lands of Cambodia's ancient Temples, are aeroplanes. And I do not love the energetic and physiological impact of being in an aircraft cabin for up to 24 hours at a time… but it must be done! So here are ways to make the arduous flight a part of the sacred Imramma!

You see, it once discombobulated me to fly, to be taken from one place to another so quickly. While I adored flying in meditation or soul work, actual physical flying in a plane seemed so...impractical and unlikely. I would suffer from nervousness afterwards, and sleep did not come easily. I travel so much now for my teaching work, it soon became necessary to create safe ways of moving my entire self around – my physical and auric bodies, and my chakra systems needed to be moved as one. And I felt that flying somehow had these three systems, which of course are the Trinity, out of sync with each other...

Thankfully, several years ago when I spent that very fulfilling and enchanted time in Glastonbury, I met a wonderful woman there at the vegetarian cafe in Magdalena street who told me about her cure for jet lag.

"When we fly," she told me, "our energetic body can literally get lost. We are still connected to the earth of where we were...and yet there we are, our cord stretched thin, and sometimes it takes days to find ourselves again, and to nurture our cord back to health..." I recalled my own times astral travelling and knew that I had often seen the cord that extends from my energetic body to my physical body, between me and Mara, my Atlantean guide, for example. And it made sense that there were cords of light connecting me to the earthly places where I spent most of my time. "So pull your cord into yourself, and let it down when you land..." she instructed gently.

Now, I have sometimes been hit hard by jetlag... It's in a class apart from the fatigue that can take you over when you have travelled an enormous distance in an extraordinarily short amount of time. Jetlag is the syndrome of having your own body's cycle disrupted: its balanced rhythm of light turning to dark suddenly undone, and you find yourself unravelled, either flooded with the longest day, and longing for the rest of the shadow, or the longest night, and starving for colour and brightness. Both outlooks can result in long term feelings of dizziness, disorientation, even nausea, as well as the raging desire to wake up sometime around 2am!

This is the syndrome known as desynchronosis – literally, being out of your own body's time...thus your physical and energetic bodies are lost...while you in fact have arrived elsewhere. The results can be tearfulness, depression, lack of appetite and lack of sleep.

The energetic symptoms can be finding yourself ultra-sensitised to an environment, picking up spears and arrows in our light body, being easily triggered in our pre-existing woundings, being vulnerable to lower energy forms, deactivated chakras and heightened sensitivity and susceptibility to entities who may wish to feed off our energy. Really.

You see, our lightbody, or auric field, when on an aircraft, actually contracts tightly around our physical body, pulled in by our retracting chakras – this does not only take place on aircraft. It can take place in massive crowds or in environments that feel hostile.

On a plane, however, there is little chance of movement, which accentuates the impact.

Also, we are taken out of our light/dark rhythm, again accentuating the impact. Now, if there are nervous folks about, and if the passengers are tense or if there is any delay (as there so often is) these auric fields become very tight and constricted, meaning not only does your blood have trouble flowing as freely around your physical body, your auric body closes in tightly, and your energy too can "pool" in certain areas...resulting in restlessness, headaches, and a sense of being trapped. Not a healthy environment for we beings of heaven and earth! There is no point longing to go to the Lost Lands if we do not make it there healthy and well and ready to receive the energies!

Thus the trigger points in our light body (the woundings which can sit there, benign until triggered) are more easily stimulated as result of this inward pulling effect. They can be felt very easily by sensitive people. And yes, there are spirits on planes. I have seen them often, and I have also found that many flight attendants are very sensitive... they are often wonderfully compassionate beings, but as they are also in energetic stress most of the time, they too benefit greatly from meditation, healthful eating and exercise.

This light body goes to the extent of our outstretched arms, with a narrow tube running down the centre, which directly connects to our spinal cord and to our chakras... in nature it is luminous and radiant and expansive. In a city it retracts and becomes very uncomfortable, akin to wearing a too-tight energetic suit around your physical body. And restrictive energy fields create dilemmas not only in our energetic fields, but emotionally, mentally and   physically. When we are outside, in nature, our energetic selves have room to breathe and expand. Our expansive energetic imprints, memories, past live codings and so on co-exist easily with our physical bodies. In the packed hold of an aircraft, we shrink, and our energy becomes tight, and we can sense the energies of others around us. Thus, we are triggered more profoundly.

When I energetically gaze around a plane, I see so much that is between the world of energy and matter – there are many ghosts on planes, and we are with others and their "stuff". The luminous energy field becomes toxic when we cannot cleanse or be in a natural environment...in planes, I can see pools of sludge as the flight continues, the flow slows, we become lethargic, unconscious...numb.

How to decrease the impact, and arrive sound in body, soul and chakras?

Before flying, please take time out each morning and night to listen to a CD or particular piece of music. By doing so, you are programming your whole self – giving your mind, body and spirit triggers to which it will react. It will know it is morning when you play your morning piece, it will know it is time to relax and go into the sleep state and dream when you play the evening music...

I often ask powerful beings, such as the Dragonfae, to "clean up" this sludge...which they lovingly do (Dragonfae have also always got me to the airport on time: or rather, they have stretched time so I can get to airports with plenty of time to spare. Angels and the Goddess also help me find the plane with the most healthful energy, and sometimes the most miraculous things happen on the flight, and I sit next to exactly the right person. Mostly, though, I am happy to chill!)

Interestingly, women are generally more susceptible to jetlag than our brothers, as our estrogen is vulnerable to conditions such as depression and tearfulness. In other words, our hormones and our own cycle can be affected by flying.

HOW TO HAVE A SOULAR-POWERED FLIGHT

Tips for energetically healthy travel to the Lost Lands:

*Before flying: In the days up to the flying, rest as much as possible, and feed your energetic body with soothing music, and exercise your chakras and illuminate your auric field. Flush out and de-sensitise your own woundings and triggers prior to flying.

*Again, prior to boarding, find a moment in which you can draw up the golden threads or roots that connect you to this part of Gaia. Draw them into your root or base chakra, which is the area from which they extend. Place them there for "safekeeping" during your flight if you wish.

*See your auric, chakra and physical systems as interconnected (as they are.) Exercise, eat healthfully in the lead up to flying, with the aim to be very well when boarding. Be well-hydrated, and call upon the four directions prior to boarding the plane. Creating sacred space creates safe space, and this counters the potential hazards of flying – and takes the edge off the nerves! This sacred space becomes the container for your auric, chakra and physical bodies.

*Check in with your chakras, and send each of them love, appropriately recognising them for their domain. Clear and release woundings or areas of darkness, any barbed wire and thorns and sludge and so forth from those areas again prior to boarding. Preferably in the weeks leading up to air travel, have daily releasements and clearings (keep it simple!) so you are free of areas which can be easily triggered during flight.

*Once on board work with each chakra once every four hours. Drink water, and for people who suffer sore throats, send love and soothing energy to your throat chakra (throats are very susceptible to the dryness of the cabin).

*When you walk about the cabin, stretching your body, gently flex and stretch and extend your auric field too, before drawing it back in.

*Use essential oils of lavender to soothe and relax you. A few drops in mineral water can be used as a hydrator for the face and to re-energise the air around you. On arrival, use essential oil of lime or sweet orange to uplift you and help you focus on the trip through customs.

*When you arrive, find another moment to unfurl those golden connective strands of energy, and allow them to find a nurturing place on the new land where your trinity (our physical, auric and chakra bodies) finds itself.

*Stay well-hydrated. Work with the day and the night of the area you are now in. Rest, and receive as much daylight, moonlight and starlight as possible to nurture you in this new energetic place.

*Know your body is one, that you are one, and that you are well-loved and able to continue your adventures in peace, love, excitement and discovery!

MAGICKAL THERAPIES

Homeopathic remedies for jetlag include arnica, which is made from the mountain plant leopard's bane. It works very well when you feel weak and aching because of severe fatigue. (Works very well for me on the long night of the soul that is the flight from Australia to the UK!) Cocculus is also used widely, and works well for nausea and decreased appetite (never one of my issues).

Acupuncture can also heal and rebalance the energetic disorientation that is jetlag. It can leave you feeling energised and whole again. (Have it as soon as possible after arrival).

Massage, too has a healing effect. En route to London from Sydney, you may stop at Bangkok. I always check in for a reflexology session to ease the physical and energetic stress of the flight.

Aromatherapy, which works on your physical and energetic body, will assist your blood and lymphatic systems. It can also lift energy – not-so-coincidentally many airlines now offer products with essential oils in their business class gift kits. I recommend them for their almost instant calming impact: for people who find being confined with other people's energies brushing up against theirs a challenging experience (definitely one of my issues)!

Bush flower remedies work wonders, too. Ian White's Bush Flower Essences do a marvellous remedy for jetlag, and bottlebrush is highly recommended. Other people swear by their rescue remedy. Bottlebrush will help you to release fears prior to flying, and balance and centre you.

Place your bare feet on the earth of the place you land....

And finally, I also have either a salt-water swim in the ocean, or a salt-water bath on arrival. Salt cleanses our auric body of energetic debris that may have become attached to us, making us feel somewhat grubby.

And then, adventurous soul, you can enjoy your experience and revel in the energies to your – and their – highest potential!

IMRAMMA MAGICK

This simple, sweet spell will keep you safe, positive and energetically in tune while you cross the world on the journey of the soul!

Open circle...

Take a few moments to clear yourself, then breathe in blue light. Take a silver ribbon, and, on a map, pin the ribbon along the route you are taking, from departure to arrival and back again.

In a blue pouch, place a silver coin, one seashell, leaves from a lemon tree and earth from your home, keep this in a safe place, and know that you will travel, explore, and return safely...

Close circle...

Happy wonder voyaging to all you Lost Landers, wherever your soul calls you! May your every Immrama be blessed, safe, and full of peace and joy.

The Priestesses of Atlantis

When I was writing *The Lost Lands*, I had a series of clear visions in which I was shown a disturbing side of Atlantis. I had other visions, too, of an earlier time, a golden time, a time teeming with potential and shining with beauty, but my overwhelming impression was one of corruption, greed and hubris. I was left with a great sadness, and felt wary and cautious about Atlantis. I know for some readers this brought great relief; for example, those who had memories of being operated on, enslaved or oppressed felt that their experiences had finally been validated after so many years of people assuming that all experiences in Atlantis were serene, wise and "advanced". However, for others, who remembered exactly those positive aspects of Atlantis, the visions and experiences I shared brought up confusion and in some cases, a sense that I was not being balanced in my appraisal.

That observation is certainly true in many ways. You see, I was recalling my own experience, my own memories, very powerful and distressing memories, and these recollections did flavour much of the work in *The Lost Lands*. It was, I feel, part of the purpose of *The Lost Lands* to tell the saddening side of the tale of Atlantis.

Since that book was completed and brought out by Blue Angel Publishing in 2009, I have taught many more workshops on Lemuria, Atlantis and Avalon and have shared what was taught to me in seminars and at many gatherings. It has been of great comfort to me to have feedback, over and over again, that validated the memories I shared in the first version of the book.

Still, as I continued to speak with many people about their memories, there were some who felt I had done Atlantis a kind of injustice. Some folk felt offended at what I had written and how I presented the side of the story of the so-called slaves and Things who had rarely been heard from before in Atlantean works. I can understand. I was challenging – and in some ways changing – some of the most precious memories and perceptions they had. I did not feel any resentment in return – I understand it is not easy to discover there are many sides to all stories, and it takes time to integrate diverse, and sometimes contradictory experiences and memories. It is a mark of someone who has done a great deal of deep, honest work – on themselves – and research into the nature of Life Herself to be able to hold almost paradoxical beliefs simultaneously, and we can rarely do this unless we have spent time in discussion with those who have a different viewpoint and experience to share and then spending time in personal contemplation, making peace with the contradictions.

But there came something of a turning point for me in 2011. In September of that year I travelled to Adelaide to present a two-day workshop on *The Lost Lands*. During this workshop, which was attended by a group of extraordinarily gifted and aware people, some very interesting things began to happen for me personally. I began to have very strong visions of healing temples in Atlantis. This was quite unexpected for me, as I had not experienced these before. They would occur while speaking to the extraordinary men and women within that class on another, loosely related topic, my third eye region simultaneously playing out a past-life film of "fresh" memories.

This continued, again over several days, and has occurred intermittently since, so the information and memories have become a little more 'well-rounded" and I've had the time and space to explore them in a deeper way. When I have these breakthrough moments, where so much information is screened and offered, I usually spend a fair amount of time integrating the information, emotions, thoughts and visions. I guess this happens in some way because I am doing a lot of work, continually clearing and cleansing on a cyclic basis. I had done so much to help me integrate and come to terms with the lifetime as a slave caste diver from Lemuria who was harmed, oppressed and ultimately operated on in Atlantis. I had thought about this very carefully and with as open a heart as I could muster. I had then had my very special experience with my occasional guide, Mara, teaching me for three days and three nights, where she let me see the arc of the Story of Atlantis – both the beautiful beginnings, the Golden Age, and then the tragic and disturbing underbelly that developed, which led to the fall.

Perhaps because of this work I had done, by this time, I was ready to start to see and experience some of the Beauty of Atlantis, including some of her magical secrets of her Healing Temples and Sacred Priestesses.

Such beauty. Such mysteries. Such secrets. On the screen of my mind's eye, I saw the interior of a large circular structure, its ceiling a series of perfectly proportioned geometric panels that slid into intricate shapes – they followed the arc of the sun, the travels of the stars. These openings could be shaped to make certain symbols, and pure sunlight would be focused and poured down through the ceiling in very concentrated ways. Like straight beams of liquid amber, rays of honey coloured light, pure and healing and so sweet. Within this vision, the first, I was simply observing the healing taking place. I saw a woman lying on a structure of crystal that was quite difficult to recognise and to describe. It was like crystals I had seen before, yet its energy and appearance were unique.

These visions led to some more work with Mara, who had promised me she would connect with me again. (I was very happy to see her again!) The time frame was very much the same – three nights, three am, and again, not much warning, just straight into it. It's just the way this sort of intense work seems to take place with me. I had always wanted to revise sections of *The Lost Lands* as I spoke with more people, and my own experience extended and deepened, and so this additional chapter for the new edition feels like the right way to introduce this new part of Atlantean experiences that have become a huge part of my own recent healing. So much of my own mistrust of, and caution around those who are more "Atlantean" in their energy has now transformed. I am glad to be evolving, and integrating new experiences. Change is life.

VISIONS OF AN ATLANTEAN HEALING TEMPLE

The Atlantean Healing Temple I saw in my visions appeared to be in a very isolated location. It was very close to the ocean, in a forested yet quite clear area – one which had been cleared in a very sensitive and organised, sophisticated way to maximise the healing potential of all the trees, minerals, caves and groves within this location. The air seemed suspended, moving slowly and time seemed stiller in this place of beauty and, as I was to discover, great healing energy. The Temple was of a shining, pure white, quartz, at a guess, and circular in shape, a dome. There was, by some technological, or magickal, intertwining of intuition, light and mechanics, a way in which the ceiling could be changed, and it slid and shifted into patterns above us all. There was a central room, massive, with very quiet acoustics for a place where noise should really be echoing, bouncing. Everyone was very, very quiet. I could barely hear a footfall in this place, although I could hear the sensuous rise and fall, very slow, of the breathing of the women in the room, including one woman lying on the bed who was utterly relaxed, open and vulnerable. There was so much to take in, and so much taking place – yet all was happening within a space held by a full and gloriously rich silence, a silence which held EVERYTHING – all potential. This was no tense silence such as we find in our modern world, the anxious suspenseful pause, the impatiently held breath. This was a rich and living silence. Perfect. Healing. There is a sense of holiness to this place.

The woman on the healing bed is lying on her back, and she is dressed in a very simple garment, undyed, transparent. It is so light, so diaphanous is has no "weight" at all. It is like pure woven energy in the form of a garment.

The ceiling above smoothly, glassily moves, and shapes pour in – glorious shapes shine down upon her, very, very fast, strobe-like. The smallest movements in the ceiling adjust to her. The women around her move back and extend their hands towards each other. They wear no jewellery. This is not a place of theatre or adornment. It is simple, and very strong, as the forms are complex and jewel-like.

They do not touch, and the energy is held within the circle, channelled back to the radiant woman on the bed in the centre...the light is now glowing brighter and brighter, gleaming in very exact and quite complex shapes over the floor, the walls, the woman, the Priestesses. We are within this dance of light symbols. These symbols are fractals

– and they become more and more complex by the moment. The light is shining like a gleaming knife or fine laser in one part of the woman's body, each Priestess focusing on it with her mind. Their minds, no, more than their minds, this is beyond intellect – their essence, their souls, their energies and their strengths are linked and focused with a purity and intent that could be described as fierce, yet feels gentle. It is very powerful and needs expert and well-trained Priestesses or Adepts to be sensitive enough at once to perceive the shifts within each Priestess, and anticipate the energy and shapes and symbols that are coming. They must be powerful and strong enough to channel and direct this light energy cleanly, without breaking focus, which could see a kind of short-circuiting take place. The energy, if not within its correct and proper form, or if leaked, could become harmful.

The light is doing its work; it is very fierce and strong, like a light of laser-like intensity, running right through this woman's body, and aura... I can see her energy field lit up and there is some work taking place there, but the bulk of the work is taking place within her chest area. It is being operated on. It is beautiful and awe-inspiring to behold.

Unlike the visions I have seen previously, I have no sense of there being any danger or malintent. All feels right, and wholesome, and good, and fiercely authentic. There is no hiding what is inside in this place. These women are Priestesses, and they are in some way, at least while in this space and while doing this work, perfect. They are doctors, nurses and they are utterly focused, committed and on purpose. They are singular and undisturbed and they have no questions about what they are doing, and how they are doing what they do. But they are not robotic. They are so harmonious.

The scene fades from my view. I am left with the feeling that the Priestesses doing this work are in a form of High Optimum Health – they are energetic athletes, they do not compete, but they are at very high levels of fitness in terms of energy work. They are all exceptionally well.

I do not know how long this has taken place for. But it is no longer day. There is a cool light entering now. It is silver. It is dark. It is night.

The healing has been taking place for hours. Yet there has been barely a sense of time passing at all.

The women stand apart. One moves to the centre, and assists the woman in the centre off the bed. It is glowing in the darkness, a kind of gold glow, and the light is silver.

She is gently led to a corridor. I find myself following them, and they walk outside. There is a room formed of entwined trees, oaks, and there is a bed. She empties her bladder into a small pool outside, then showers in a natural running waterfall. She drinks from a jug that a young priestess brings her, and eats some fruits. The temperature is perfection: there is low humidity, and it is very warm and caressing. It is not dry like a desert, where the heat stings and dries the delicate membranes of nose, ears, eyes.

It's not the swimming, drenching heat of tropical climates. It is clean, soft heat, so balanced. So beautiful. It feels...like it is being filtered from the sun. I look above, and I see that there is a crystal "generator" on top of the building. It seems to be somehow mirroring or modifying slightly the light of the sun. It is most definitely throwing a refined environment in the surrounds of the temple, this isolated, not so much secret, but very protected and pristine place. It is sophisticated and natural. It is intelligent and harmonious. There is a sense of everything being in perfect balance. It may not last.

It is very quiet. But the forest has far more breath and life and natural sound than inside the temple. Mara shows me that there is much sound healing taking place and I realise that while it is a temple, and sacred, the only kind of church that seems to be recognised here is that of healing.

There are other rooms, with paths, where people and beings go each day for their sessions in the temple. I do not know where the priestesses, the female healers I saw, live.

There are caves, crystalline with animals within them, and they are speaking with their priestess, their healer in soft voices. All is very still, all is very good, all is as it feels it should be. There are pools of healing for each being. It is a sublime place. The energy of the people and beings treated does not feel sick... not toxic or harmful. I don't feel anger or hurt. I do feel pain, but there is a kind of nobility to these beings. They are stoic, and yet seeking healing. It is most beautiful and soothing viewing all this. Seeing this, feeling this in this mild way, I am inspired to create greater levels of healthy energy in my own life by pure training, practice and clean, powerful focus.

And this is part of Atlantis I had not seen before, and it is good to see this, to feel this. Because I am healing as I witness this other side.

It does not mean that some of these priestesses will not eventually use similar technology to operate on beings, the animals and the Lemurians, and try to graft a new form of creature from them. For now, at this time, it is in balance, at least in this silent, good, place.

Everything is beautiful.

CORRESPONDING VISIONS

After experiencing these visions, I asked a cross-section of healers, trance channelers, lightworkers, shamanic practitioners and other aware, awake souls to share their experiences. I was interested to see where the crossover points occurred:

Many practitioners reported the following:

- *Temples were located in lush, remote settings of natural beauty and wonder*

- *Dome shaped ceilings*

- *Altars, of crystal, upon which those being treated would lie. Many reported these crystal beds were suspended, seeming to levitate.*

- *Surgical instruments of crystal to help pinpoint the areas needing clearing and healing, removal of cords and activation of dormant energy centres. (In my own visions I later saw I had a whole "surgical set" of crystalline knives and tools to work with. Very fine and strong, but they had to be used with great care and expertise. Could do great harm in clumsy or ill-intentioned hands.)*

- *Priestesses working in silent unison*

- *Absolute and utterly willing dedication*

- *Diaphanous clothing, lighter than...air*

- *A perfectly attuned energetic environment adjusted for individual needs*

- *The intelligent interaction and manipulation of light sources*

- *Fabrics, stones and forms of matter that are akin to our own, but which are quite different*

- *Light and sound were utilised in very disciplined, intricate ways.*

- *There was, in the beginning, no hierarchy but divisions of roles depending on talents, and general service to the energetic, physical, mental and emotional health of the community. There were temples where men worked with women, where men worked solely with their brothers, where animals created and held space, temples that focused on galactic communication. It was an intelligent system and it interacted intelligently with earth, her seasons and elements and beings, and it also interacted with star people and energies from the cosmos.*

- *Many creatures were treated: Galactic beings who were ill from time travelling and had a kind of dimensional sickness, who needed assistance in adjusting to Gaian energy.*

- *At later times, I feel this temple became central in terms of its energy practices being misused and appropriated and utilised in ways that were not intended. This mis-use of the pure energy I witnessed eventually would become the theatres, the beautiful healing crystal beds the operating beds, the shapes and forms instead of healing, altered without consent, and with the intent of power, not the intent of loving healing and high good health.*

In particular, the contents of my visions were echoed in the words of two practitioners I have a great deal of respect for, Gypsy Maggie Rose, a strong woman from Western Australia, and Petta Mussolino, a gentle, sensitive artist, healer and teacher from South Australia. The similarities were stunning in some cases.

Maggie's visions included a temple with a dome-ceiling, with a roof that rolled back to allow light to shine on altars within the temple. Maggie also saw a crystal altar, but the crystal was not quite identifiable. The Temple was for Priestesses and was in an oceanic location.

In Petta's visions, she saw a Temple of the Sun. "The Temple of the Sun was strictly a priestess temple. The temple itself was constructed of 12 tall crystal columns holding a roof that was open at the central/top section above the central altar. The central altar was a large crystal held, or rather more suspended in air, upon/above a stone altar. There were no walls. Here the priestesses would take shifts in standing at the columns and working with the central crystal. It was maintaining a balance for the area while also powering up light and energy. There was magic used to shield the location of the temple and Mother Nature surrounded it. The sun shone through the open section of the roof, directly overhead at precisely midday. I have no fear-based feelings attached to this lifetime. To me, it was one of the rare lovely lives with only warmth and wisdom to offer."

WAYS TO WORK LIKE AN ATLANTEAN PRIESTESS

- Become attuned to the movement of Light – experiment with light on bodies, auras, emotions and observe its impact. Learn more about the effect of kinds of light on humans and animals, and the benefits exposure in disciplined ways can have.
- Avoid light sources that are artificial.
- Study the use of coloured light and its healing wavelengths.
- Work with crystals to "remove", dissolve or cut out energies within your aura you may no longer wish to connect with. Use crystals like selenite, laboradite and clear quartz to cut energetic cords. Work with naturally formed knives of obsidian to protect, bless and strengthen energetic areas. Blue and Green Kyanite knives are wonderful tools to begin surgical work with. They do not require cleansing in the traditional ways most crystals need in order to stay clear and operating on a pure frequency. Work with crystals under moonlight, and at specific times (for example, on astrologically significant dates, throughout the lunar cycle, at seasonal festivals). Experiment!
- Discover the power of silence, of focusing, moving and healing with intention and energy, with no "talk" at all.
- Experiment with sound healing: chanting, singing and toning which disperse energetic debris which may be caught in your energy field. This work literally sings out – dislodges – shards, spurs and hooks of energy, broken fragments that may be creating energetic infection, swellings and blockages.

- Take regular energetic baths in moonlight, eclipse light, rainbow light, twilight, dawn's light. See sunrise and sunset.

- Wear light, undyed, simple clothing. Remove jewellery and makeup and do not use artificial perfumes, deodorants, food additives, hair dyes. Allow your hair to be free from chemicals, bleaches, dyes and sprays.

- Charge up the energy in one area of your home or surrounds by using falling water, ferns, light wells, crystals.

Recommended Reading, Listening and well, Anything List

Many inspirations, many moments of conversation, memory and the natural epiphanies that occur when contemplating mysteries became my guides during the writing of this book. The simple flash of memory became a beacon that would lead me to a new discovery, and so I am thankful indeed for these small moments. Of course, I read many, many books on Atlantis and Lemuria, and there remain even now many more I have not read. For this book, my most valuable companions in some ways were the "original" sources: the mythologies of the world's indigenous peoples, and the mystics and voyagers who ventured into unknown lands for the first time.

The original texts hold so much wisdom. While they can be dense and challenging to read at times, they are very worthwhile for the gems you will unearth, and the insights into other times they will share with you. They include:

* Madame Blavatsky *The Secret Doctrine* Theosophical University Press
* Plato *Dialogues*
* Homer *The Odyssey and the Iliad*
* *The Irish Book of Invasions*
* *The Song of Amergin*
* *The Mabinogion* (Welsh mythos, tales of the goddess and god)
* Geoffrey of Monmouth *A History of Britain, Life of Merlin*

I must also credit the many people I interviewed extensively. I thank all of these many present-day Lost Landers for their generosity and their courage.

I spent a year in North Dakota when I was seventeen – it changed me forever. Thankyou to the Lakota people for keeping their stories alive. I have to thank, too, many sources for the myths and legends of ancient peoples being kept alive. Keep telling the stories. We are listening!

* James Churchward, Ignatius Donnelly and Edgar Cayce are must-reads.
* Serene Coneeley *Seven Sacred Sites,* Blessed Bee Publishing, 2008
    Gorgeously produced adventure through seven sacred sites on the planet, complete with personal magicks, historical and energetic perspectives.
    www.sevensacredsites.com.au
* Nevill Drury *Magic and Witchcraft*, Thames and Hudson Ltd London 2003 particularly for its brilliant chapters on shamanism, but the entire book is wonderful and gorgeously illustrated.

* *Mists of Avalon* by Marion Zimmer Bradley
* *The Mahabharata* and the Vedas... for background and understanding of Hinduism.
* *Song of Gilgamesh* for background and understanding of the Persian and Mesopotamian cultures
* *Hymm to Aphrodite* Homeric Hymns (not written by Homer, but during his era.)
* *Spheres* magazine: Beautiful, energetically uplifting spiritual information.
* *Spellcraft* magazine: Scholarly, beautiful to look at and very Goddess-flavoured.
* I highly recommend the gorgeous work of Irish American shamans Tom Cowan and Frank MacEowen. Their books are beautiful; poetic and deep, they are steeped in the sensibility of the Druidic mind and heart set. Similarly, I adore Caitlin and John Matthews' scholarly, serious approach and graceful wordsmithing. All their work is wonderful.
* Phillip Carr Gomm's work on Druidry is always an inspiration.
* Dion Fortune's *Glastonbury: Avalon of the heart*, Aquarian Press 1934 A former resident of Glastonbury, this early 20th century mystic was so ahead of her time!
* Robert Graves *The White Goddess*, Faber and Faber 1948 A brilliant and endlessly lovely work: too often dismissed, it is inspirational and full of parallels that have been fascinating me for years...
* Everything by William Butler Yeats.
* The Greek myths. The Roman appropriations.
* J G Frazer *The Golden Bough*: *A Study in Magic and Religion*, Macmillan 1922 for its scholarly outlining of pre-Christian mythos and world views. First published in 1922, it's a must in any Lost Landers diary as a reference. It's practically an ancient library in itself. Every time I put it on the shelf I get up hours later to get it back off the shelf and refer to it. So I guess that means I should just keep it out!

CONTACTS AND WEBSITES

* Scott Alexander King: www.animaldreaming.com
* Allyson Tanner creates incredible jewellery and energy infused healing salt baths at Mermaid's Garden
* Kylie McDonough: www.kyliemcdonough.com
* Toni Carmine Salerno: www.tonicarminesalerno.com
* Jo and Troy Byrne have a website, www.reconnecting.com.au which has brilliant photographs and information about crop circles... Jo makes her own essences, and is working on an oracle deck featuring the symbols of the crop circles. Hurry up, Jo!

* The Goddess Association in Australia links women and men to Goddess sites and celebrations internationally – they are an inspirational group of women...
www.gaia.com.au

And thankyou to Lisa Gerrard, for her incredible music, which kept me voyaging, when I had long lost sight of the shore...and to the sound-spells of sonic witch Wendy Rule for helping me cross the nine waves...and to the songbird Julie Walton for her album *Pagan Fire*...
www.lisagerrard.com
www.wendyrule.com

And to my family, and my wonderful friends. I thank you so much for the support, the encouragement, and the understanding – even when you didn't quite understand! Thankyou to Khumara and to Mara, and to the other beautiful guides and beings who stepped through the veil and showed me the way, so many times. But most of all, thankyou to my daughter Thomasina. Mummy is back, darling. And next time, you're coming too!

Lucy Cavendish is a natural witch who works with the elemental and celestial realms. She works magic every single day of her life, embracing it as a creed for personal fulfilment and happiness, and as a belief system that sees us as part of nature, and thus gives us all the motivation to respect and revere and delight in our unique experience here on Planet Earth.

Lucy is the author of *Oracle of the Mermaids*, *Oracle of Shadows & Light*, *Oracle of the Shapeshifters*, *Wild Wisdom of the Faery Oracle*, *The Oracle of the Dragonfae*, *As Above, So Below*, *The Oracle Tarot*, *Magical Spell Cards* and *White Magic*. Her work has been enjoyed and recommended by beings as diverse as Deepak Chopra, Louise L. Hay and Fiona Horne.

Lucy Cavendish created Witchcraft magazine in 1992, the first magazine of its kind in the world. She is a feature writer for *Spellcraft Magazine*, *Spheres*, and has appeared in anthologies like Disinformation's *Pop Goes The Witch!* She appears regularly on mainstream and alternative television and radio, explaining the Craft and demonstrating magicks and the power of intuition. She is a classic book witch and adores writing and reading, listening to and playing music, connecting with the wild and creating enchanted workshop experiences. She is a founding member of the Goddess Association in Australia.

Lucy Cavendish lives in Sydney, Australia, with her pixie-like daughter, and their menagerie of plants, animal companions, spirit beings and beloved elementals.

Visit Lucy's website at: www.lucycavendish.com

Wild Wisdom of the Faery Oracle
by Lucy Cavendish

You are invited to enter the realm of Faery!

Wild Wisdom of the Faery Oracle is your doorway into the magickal realm of the Faery. Each gloriously illustrated card is brimming with secrets, messages, insights and guidance directly from the most helpful and wise of nature's guardians, delivering clear messages and direct and loving guidance. Easy to read, yet deep, mystical and rich, *Wild Wisdom of the Faery Oracle* includes an in-depth guidebook revealing the secret lore of the Faery realm as well as clear lessons on how to connect, create and nurture deep relationships with your own Faery guardians and allies. The included card layouts allow you to give powerful, insightful and accurate readings for yourself and others.

When you connect with the Fae, their powerful natural magicks can assist with healing and enhancing your health, activating vivid psychic abilities, gaining insight and direction within your relationships and awakening your innate connection to abundance. Your life then becomes an inspirational experience, full of meaning and joy. Your own ability to see, sense and feel the Fae accurately will grow stronger and clearer each time you work with this enchanted, inspiring deck, steeped in authentic, deep Faery magicks.

Artwork by Selina Fenech
Deluxe large-format set
Features 47 cards and 188 page guidebook

Oracle of the Dragonfae
by Lucy Cavendish

New revised edition!

In the not so faraway past, we were Gods and Goddesses...we dwelt in dimensional lands... Eden, Avalon, Ys, Atlantis and Mu...we were fully alive and fully magickal. We worked, loved and lived with all the elemental beings...but as time wore on, we were torn away from our strongest, most protective kin, the Dragonfae. Now they are returning to help us heal ourselves and save this sacred planet. This deck is a dimensional portal to allow them to re-enter our realm and deliver their powerful messages of love, healing and protection for a new generation of magickal beings...

Welcome to this journey through a world that has for too long been hidden from all but the most courageous of searchers and mystics. Within these pages, and on each of these magickal cards, you will be introduced to and given messages and wisdom from the boundless world of the Dragonfae, a world which is now ready to be seen by your eyes and experienced by your heart.

When we connect with the Dragonfae, we reconnect with the lost parts of ourselves, allowing us to fully explore the gift of life on this beautiful planet. They help us to access knowledge from deep within and reconnect us with the knowingness that we are all one.

This new, revised edition features 12 new artworks by Jimmy Manton.

Features 43 cards and 164 page guidebook, packaged in a hard-cover box set

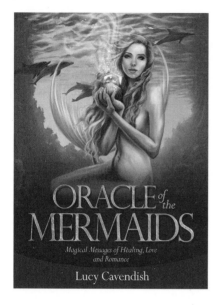

Oracle of the Mermaids
by Lucy Cavendish

Magical Messages of Healing, Love and Romance

Open your Heart... Hear their Song...
Heal your Love Life...

Mermaids have long been the luscious messengers between the world of the Ocean and the world of Humans. Loving, adventurous, kind and daring, Mermaids can teach you ways to heal your past, love yourself more deeply, live authentically, embrace your creativity, and find your life purpose.

When you connect with your Mermaids, you tap into the vast reservoir of the Feminine Divine, which in turn enhances your ability to draw love into your life, raise your self-esteem, create sensual bliss and glow with health and attractive vitality.

Overflowing with mermaid magic, legends and lore, the 168-page guidebook features in-depth messages and clear, accurate card spreads to help you to find answers for yourself, your loved ones, or your clients.

Artwork by Selina Fenech
Features 45 cards and guidebook, packaged in a hard-cover box set

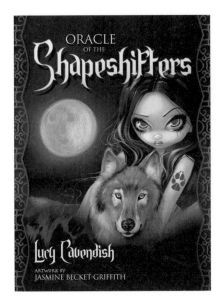

Oracle of the Shapeshifters
by Lucy Cavendish

Are you ready to change?

You now hold in your hands a book of great secrets, one that has been shut a long time. Within its pages are messages from magickal familiars, once the companions of shamans, witches, wizards and wise ones – and now, they are here for you. These mystical allies possess the hidden knowledge of shapeshifting, camouflage, change, invisibility and metamorphosis. They are ready to share their very honest, truly instinctual guidance for personal and planetary times of transition. These trustworthy companions will lend you their courage, point out new paths, help you make fresh discoveries, spark your creativity, inspire you with encouragement and teach you to develop abilities to adapt and change not only for survival – but in order to thrive and find peace, joy, accomplishment and satisfaction in a changing world.

With a 164-page guidebook by Lucy Cavendish revealing the history, legends, lore and magick of the Shapeshifters, including practical spreads for accurate readings, and stunning art by Jasmine Becket-Griffith, *Oracle of the Shapeshifters* is truly a unique and empowering deck.

Artwork by Jasmine Becket-Griffith
Features 45 cards and guidebook, packaged in a hard-cover box set

For more information on this
or any Blue Angel Publishing release,
please visit our website at:

www.blueangelonline.com